OXFORD CLASSICAL MONOGRAPHS

*Published under the supervision of a Committee of the
Faculty of Literae Humaniores in the University of Oxford*

OXFORD CLASSICAL MONOGRAPHS

The aim of the Oxford Classical Monographs series (which replaces the Oxford Classical and Philosophical Monographs) is to publish outstanding revised theses on Greek and Latin literature, ancient history, and ancient philosophy examined by the faculty board of Literae Humaniores.

Jerome, Greek Scholarship, and the Hebrew Bible

A Study of the
Quaestiones Hebraicae in Genesim

◆   ◆   ◆

ADAM KAMESAR

CLARENDON PRESS · OXFORD

1993

Oxford University Press, Walton Street, Oxford OX2 6DP
Oxford New York Toronto
Delhi Bombay Calcutta Madras Karachi
Kuala Lumpur Singapore Hong Kong Tokyo
Nairobi Dar es Salaam Cape Town
Melbourne Auckland Madrid
and associated companies in
Berlin Ibadan

Oxford is a trade mark of Oxford University Press

Published in the United States
by Oxford University Press, New York

British Library Cataloguing in Publication Data
Data available

Library of Congress Cataloging in Publication Data
Jerome, Greek scholarship, and the Hebrew Bible : a study of the Quaestiones hebraicae
in Genesim / Adam Kamesar.
(Oxford classical monographs)
Includes bibliographical references and index.
1. Jerome, Saint, d. 419 or 420. Quaestiones hebraicae in Genesim. 2. Jerome, Saint,
d. 419 or 420—Knowledge—Greek philology. 3. Greek philology. 4. Bible. Latin—
Versions—Vulgate. I. Title. II. Series.
BR65.J473Q665 1993 220.4'7—dc20 92-28444
ISBN 0-19-814727-9

Typeset by The Charlesworth Group, Huddersfield, UK, 0484 517077
Printed in Great Britain
on acid-free paper by
Biddles Ltd., Guildford and King's Lynn

In memoriam Daniel I. Kamesar

1955–1990

Ego te, frater, non requiram?

Ambrose

Preface

◆ ◆ ◆

THE present book constitutes a revised version of my D.Phil. thesis, 'Studies in Jerome's *Quaestiones Hebraicae in Genesim*: The Work as seen in the Context of Greek Scholarship'. The thesis was submitted to the sub-faculty of Greek and Latin Literature in the University of Oxford in Trinity Term of 1987. The revisions, however, have been very extensive, and I have referred to the D.Phil. thesis as a separate work in the footnotes. The interim period has also allowed me to take into account recent scholarship in the area. Of particular importance are two excellent works which reached me in the one case when the thesis was nearly complete, and in the second case after it had been submitted, namely, P. Jay, *L'exégèse de saint Jérôme d'après son 'Commentaire sur Isaïe'*, Paris 1985, and B. Neuschäfer, *Origenes als Philologe*, Basle 1987.

I have learned much from all previous scholarship, but it is probably appropriate to single out the writings of D. Barthélemy. Although I have often disagreed with his views, I believe he has contributed as much as anyone this century to the field of Greek and Latin biblical philology.

It is a pleasant task to thank all of the people who have assisted me in the preparation of this book. These include first of all my supervisors at Oxford, Michael Winterbottom and Sebastian Brock, my 'unofficial' supervisors, Nigel Wilson and Geza Vermes, and my examiners, Nicholas de Lange and Andrew Louth. I would also like to thank Dr Alfred Gottschalk and all of my colleagues at the Hebrew Union College, Cincinnati—in particular Alan Cooper, Werner Weinberg, and Richard Sarason. The following librarians have been of great help to me: David Gilner and his staff at HUC, Mary Sheldon-Williams at the Bodleian, and Jean Wellington and Mike Braunlin at the Classics Library of the University of Cincinnati. I gratefully acknowledge the assistance of J.-P. Mahé, Paris, and Mark Vessey, Vancouver, with regard to various requests I made of them. Tim Saleska, Curtis Giese, and David Nixon helped me with proofreading and the verification of references. I have also come to appreciate the patience and dedication of Hilary O'Shea and the editorial staff of the Oxford University Press. For any errors which remain in the book, however, I alone am responsible.

Finally, I offer my thanks to my teachers in Jerusalem and in Milan, to my parents, and to my wife, Laura Banon.

A. K.

HUC, Cincinnati
August 1991

Contents

◆　◆　◆

Abbreviations, Editions, and References

◆ ◆ ◆

ABBREVIATIONS

PATRISTIC SOURCES

Greek and Latin patristic works are abbreviated according to: G. W. H. Lampe (ed.), *A Patristic Greek Lexicon*, Oxford 1961–8; A. Blaise and H. Chirat, *Dictionnaire latin-français des auteurs chrétiens*, Turnhout 1954.

In abbreviating commentaries on biblical books, both Lampe and Blaise often give only the abbreviation of the biblical book itself. For the sake of clarity, I have added the designation '*Comm.*(*entarii*) *in*' in these cases. Commentaries and related works are cited either according to book and section of the commentary itself, or according to the biblical lemma on which the author is commenting. If the latter is the case, a colon rather than a full stop is used to separate the numbers given, e.g. Jerome, *Comm. in Mal.* 1: 2–5. Sometimes both systems are used together.

Additional departures from and additions to the systems of Lampe and Blaise are as follows:

C. Cois.	*Catenae Graecae in Genesim et in Exodum*, ii. *Collectio Coisliniana in Genesim* (= Corpus Christianorum, Series Graeca 15), ed. F. Petit, Turnhout 1986
CS	*Catenae Graecae in Genesim et in Exodum*, i. *Catena Sinaitica* (= Corpus Christianorum, Series Graeca 2), ed. F. Petit, Turnhout 1977
Didymus, Comm. in Gen.	Didyme l'Aveugle, *Sur la Genèse* (= Sources chrétiennes 233, 244), ed. P. Nautin, Paris 1976–8
Jerome, IH	the translation of the Bible *iuxta Hebraeos*
Jerome, QHG	*Quaestiones Hebraicae in Genesim* (a departure from the system of Blaise for the sake of brevity)

OGM   *Onomastica Graeca minora*, edited by P. de
                     Lagarde, in his *Onomastica sacra²*, Göttingen
                     1887. This text is cited according to the page
                     numbers of the first edition (Göttingen 1870),
                     which appear in the margins of the second.

OTHER SOURCES

Other sources cited in abbreviated form are the Septuagint (=
LXX) and the *Vetus Latina* (= *VL*), biblical and extra-canonical
books, the works of Philo and Josephus, and rabbinic texts. The
abbreviations used are those of S. Schwertner, *Abkürzungsverzeichnis, Theologische Realenzyklopädie*, Berlin 1976, pp. xi, xiii,
xiv–xvii. With regard to the abbreviations of biblical and extra-
canonical books, I have sometimes employed minor Angliciza-
tions/Latinizations, e.g. 'Job' for 'Hiob'.

MODERN WORKS

Modern works, such as encyclopaedias, periodicals, series, etc.,
are abbreviated according to Schwertner, *Abkürzungsverzeichnis*
(mentioned directly above).

EDITIONS

PATRISTIC TEXTS

Modern critical editions are generally assumed in cases where
these are available. The following works are of great assistance in
locating such editions: M. Geerard, *Clavis patrum Graecorum*, 5
vols., Turnhout 1974–87 (ii-iv, 1974–80; i, 1983; v, 1987);
E. Dekkers, *Clavis patrum Latinorum²* (= *Sacris erudiri* 3 (1961));
J. Allenbach *et al.*, *Biblia patristica*, i-v, Paris 1975–91; A. di
Berardino (ed.), *Patrologia*, iii, [Turin] 1978. It is necessary, however, to specify the following:

Jerome

The *Quaestiones Hebraicae in Genesim* is generally cited according
to the edition of P. de Lagarde (Leipzig 1868). This edition is

reprinted in Corpus Christianorum, Series Latina 72. The edition of D. Vallarsi is cited according to *Patrologia Latina* 23.

The column numbers of *Patrologia Latina* 23 and 29 are given according to the editions of 1883 and 1865 respectively.

When line numbers are given in citations of Jerome's prefaces to his translations of biblical books, these follow, for the sake of convenience, the *editio minor* of the Vulgate by R. Weber *et al.* (Stuttgart 1983³).

De nominibus Hebraicis (= *Nom. Hebr.*) is cited according to the edition of P. de Lagarde as given in his *Onomastica sacra²*, Göttingen 1887. This text, in a manner similar to *OGM* (see above under Abbreviations), is cited according to page and line numbers of the first edition (Göttingen 1870), which appear in the margins of the second. De Lagarde's edition of *Nom. Hebr.* is reprinted in Corpus Christianorum, Series Latina 72.

De situ et nominibus locorum Hebraicorum (= *Sit.*) is cited according to page and line number of the edition of E. Klostermann, which is found in his edition of Eusebius, *Onomasticon* (Leipzig 1904 = Die griechischen christlichen Schriftsteller der ersten drei Jahrhunderte 11. 1).

Other Fathers

Eusebius, *Onomasticon*, is cited according to page and line number of Klostermann's edition (see above).

Theodoret, *Quaestiones in Octateuchum*, is cited according to the edition of N. Fernández Marcos and A. Sáenz-Badillos (Madrid 1979 = Textos y estudios 'Cardenal Cisneros' 17). The numbering of the *quaestiones* is in some cases different from that in *Patrologia Graeca* 80.

BIBLE

The following editions of biblical texts are cited by the name of the editor:

Field   F. Field (ed.), *Origenis Hexapla*, i-ii, Oxford 1875

Fischer   B. Fischer (ed.), *Vetus Latina: Die Reste der altlateinischen Bibel*, ii. *Genesis*, Freiburg (im Breisgau), 1951–4

Wevers   J. W. Wevers (ed.), *Septuaginta: Vetus Testamentum Graecum auctoritate academiae scientiarum Gottingensis editum*, i. *Genesis*, Göttingen 1974

Quotations from the Bible in English are given according to the Revised Standard Version.

RABBINIC TEXTS

For information on editions of rabbinic texts, as well as introductory material on rabbinic literature, see H. L. Strack and G. Stemberger, *Introduction to the Talmud and Midrash* (revised English edition), Edinburgh 1991.

Quotations from the Babylonian Talmud, when given in translation, follow I. Epstein (ed.), *The Babylonian Talmud*, i–xxxv, London 1935–52.

REFERENCES IN FOOTNOTES

In the footnotes, the only works cited by name of editor/author alone are the editions of the Greek and Latin biblical texts listed directly above. Other works cited frequently are given by name of author and short title. These works are listed in the Select Bibliography. Full bibliographical details of all frequently cited works are also given in the note where they are cited for the first time.

Introduction

◆ ◆ ◆

Jerome, one of the greatest biblical scholars of antiquity, was born probably sometime in the 340s in the town of Stridon, which seems to have been located in what was until recently western Yugoslavia.[1] He was sent to Rome for his secondary education, where he studied under the grammarian Aelius Donatus. After spending some time in Trier and Aquileia, he set out for the East in the early 370s. He had developed an interest in ascetic living at Aquileia, and sought to pursue this form of life in the great centres of eastern monasticism. He lived for a few years as a hermit in the desert of Chalcis in Syria, but spent much of this period at Antioch, where he deepened his knowledge of Greek and was also ordained as a priest. He was in Constantinople during the years 380–1, and at this time published Latin translations of some works of Eusebius and Origen. He returned to Rome in 382, where he served for about three years as a sort of unofficial assistant to Pope Damasus. He left Rome for good in 385, and after a period of travel in the East, settled in Bethlehem in 386. He founded a monastic community there, and lived out his life as its director. He died in 420.

It was at Bethlehem that Jerome produced the most important of his works. Among these was his famous translation of the Bible *iuxta Hebraeos* (= *IH*), that is, 'according to the Hebrew'. The underlying motive for the project was his belief in the superior authority of the original Hebrew text over against the Greek version of the LXX, the time-hallowed Bible of the Church. He began the new translation around 391. At about the same time, however, he published a trilogy of technical works concerned with biblical subjects: *De nominibus Hebraicis*, *De situ et nominibus locorum Hebraicorum*, and the *Quaestiones Hebraicae in Genesim*. The first two compositions, an etymological and a topographical

---

[1] The exact year of Jerome's birth and the precise location of Stridon are both subjects of considerable discussion. For recent bibliography, see H. Hagendahl and J. H. Waszink, 'Hieronymus', *RAC* 15. 113 (1989), col. 118.

dictionary respectively, are essentially translations of Greek works. The *Quaestiones Hebraicae in Genesim* (= *QHG*), on the other hand, a textual and philological commentary on selected passages in Genesis, was put forward as an original work. In the preface to *De nominibus Hebraicis*, published immediately before *QHG*, Jerome announces the latter composition as an 'opus novum et tam Graecis quam Latinis usque ad id locorum inauditum'.

It is *QHG*, and this description of it, that constitute the primary focus of the present investigation. For such a description raises the issue of Jerome's relationship to earlier scholarship. Already in antiquity Julian of Eclanum claimed that his commentaries were basically derivative works, and modern scholars have often voiced similar views.[2] In fact, the object of much of the research on Jerome's writings based on comparison with Greek works has been to identify his sources.[3] Jerome himself, however, did not deny his reliance on Greek exegetical writings. In the tradition of many Latin writers, he was quite conscious of his position as a transmitter of Greek literature and scholarship to the West, and was in fact very proud of that role.[4] For this reason, when he characterizes *QHG* as an original work, his claim should be taken seriously. Indeed, it induces us to consider the question of his relationship to Greek scholarship from a different angle: what are Jerome's own contributions, and what did he himself mean by describing *QHG* as an 'opus novum'? In fine, it will be the primary purpose of this study to identify what E. Fraenkel would have called 'elementi geronimiani in Girolamo'.

---

[2] Julian, *Tractatus prophetarum Osee, Johel et Amos* prol. (CChr.SL 88, p. 116); G. Grützmacher, *Hieronymus: Eine biographische Studie zur alten Kirchenge-schichte*, ii (SGTK 10[. 1]), Berlin 1906, p. 114; P. Nautin, 'Hieronymus', *TRE* 15. 1–2 (1986), p. 311. Cf. G. Bardy, 'Saint Jérôme et ses maîtres hébreux', *RBen* 46 (1934), pp. 145–64.

[3] Cf. P. Jay, *L'exégèse de saint Jérôme d'après son 'Commentaire sur Isaïe'*, Paris 1985, p. 13, who comments on the tendency in scholarship on Jerome 'à réduire une œuvre à la somme de ses sources'. Jay's own work represents a move away from such an approach, although as H. Savon, *REL* 65 (1987), p. 398, has pointed out, it is actually more of an attempt to explain Jerome 'par lui-même' than a comprehensive analysis of Jerome's relationship to earlier exegetical tradition. Nevertheless, in general, Jay's introduction, pp. 11–14, constitutes an excellent summary of modern scholarship on Jerome's exegetical works. It is therefore unnecessary to provide a similar survey in the present context.

[4] See *Comm. in Jer.* 3. 1. 2, and Y.-M. Duval's remarks on this passage in the introduction to his edition of Jerome's *Comm. in Jon.* (Paris 1985 = SC 323), pp. 74–5 n. 227. Cf. P. Courcelle, *Les lettres grecques en Occident de Macrobe à Cassiodore*[2] (BEFAR 159), Paris 1948, pp. 112–13.

In addition, since Jerome's primary concern in *QHG* is with textual and philological matters, and since the work was written at around the time when the first volumes of *IH* began to appear, the two works seem to have been closely linked. Consequently, the question of Hieronymian contributions in *QHG* is not of isolated significance, but must be considered within the context of the same issue as it relates to the origins of *IH*. That is, how is Jerome's belief in the superior authority of the Hebrew text, which culminated in the new translation, to be understood in the context of Greek scholarship? Does the view represent an innovation of major importance, or is Jerome simply carrying out principles already established by Origen and others? It is to this question that we shall turn first.

I

The Problem of the Text of the Old Testament Before Jerome

❖   ❖   ❖

ORIGEN

I

As far as we know, the first Christian scholar to concern himself in a serious fashion with the text of the Old Testament was Origen. His major achievement in this respect was the so-called *Hexapla*, a multi-columned Bible which included the Hebrew text (according to the traditional view in both Hebrew letters and in Greek transcription), the version of the LXX, the newer translations of Aquila, Symmachus, and Theodotion (= the *recentiores*), and certain lesser known versions of some biblical books.[1] He also put together what appears to have been a critical edition of the LXX, which included critical signs in use among Alexandrian grammarians such as the obelus and the asterisk. This edition is generally designated as the Hexaplaric (recension of the) LXX, although whether it constituted the LXX column of the *Hexapla* or a separate work is not certain.[2]

These work(s) became famous throughout the Christian world. Nevertheless, what Origen was actually trying to accomplish in composing them was and is a subject of debate. The question is especially acute with regard to the Hexaplaric LXX, which more than (the other parts of) the *Hexapla* was Origen's own creation. Already his own statements concerning this work lend themselves to different interpretations. In his *Commentarii in Matthaeum* he

[1] For a recent treatment of the problems concerning the *Hexapla*, see O. Munnich, in G. Dorival, M. Harl, and O. Munnich, *La Bible grecque des Septante*, Paris 1988, pp. 162–8.

[2] For recent discussion and bibliography regarding this problem, see P. Nautin, *Origène*, i. *Sa vie et son œuvre* (Christianisme antique 1), Paris 1977, pp. 455–8; B. Neuschäfer, *Origenes als Philologe* (SBA 18. 1–2), Basle 1987, pp. 96–8. Cf. Munnich, *La Bible grecque*, p. 165.

describes the procedure which he followed in composing the Hexaplaric LXX in the following manner:

τὴν μὲν οὖν ἐν τοῖς ἀντιγράφοις τῆς παλαιᾶς διαθήκης διαφωνίαν θεοῦ διδόντος εὕρομεν ἰάσασθαι, κριτηρίῳ χρησάμενοι ταῖς λοιπαῖς ἐκδόσεσιν· τῶν γὰρ ἀμφιβαλλομένων παρὰ τοῖς Ἑβδομήκοντα διὰ τὴν τῶν ἀντιγράφων διαφωνίαν τὴν κρίσιν ποιησάμενοι ἀπὸ τῶν λοιπῶν ἐκδόσεων τὸ συνᾷδον ἐκείναις ἐφυλάξαμεν, καὶ τινὰ μὲν ὠβελίσαμεν ⟨ὡς⟩ ἐν τῷ Ἑβραϊκῷ μὴ κείμενα (οὐ τολμήσαντες αὐτὰ πάντη περιελεῖν), τινὰ δὲ μετ᾽ ἀστερίσκων προσεθήκαμεν, ἵνα δῆλον ᾖ ὅτι μὴ κείμενα παρὰ τοῖς Ἑβδομήκοντα ἐκ τῶν λοιπῶν ἐκδόσεων συμφώνως τῷ Ἑβραϊκῷ προσεθήκαμεν.[3]

It would appear from this description that Origen was attempting to re-establish the correct text of the LXX by bringing it into accord with the Hebrew text. So much is clear at least from the first part of the passage. For he claims to have 'healed' the διαφωνία of the manuscripts of the LXX by employing the *recentiores* as the criterion in judging between the variants, and these versions were known to be much closer to the Hebrew text than the LXX. However, it is not quite certain from this passage whether Origen favoured a LXX 'corrected' according to the Hebrew Bible with regard to 'pluses' and 'minuses', i.e. whether he regarded the use of the critical signs as part of the 'healing' of the manuscript tradition of the LXX. The structure of the passage would imply that he did, since corresponding to the first μέν there follows further on a δέ clause in which Origen acknowledges that he has been unable to apply a similar method (sc. of 'healing'?) with regard to the manuscripts of the New Testament.[4] The use of the obelus points in the same direction, since this sign had generally been used to mark passages of doubtful authenticity, ἀθετούμενα in the technical language of Greek exegesis.[5] Indeed, Basil

---

[3] *Comm. in Mt.* 15. 14 (GCS 40, p. 388). For a full discussion of the passage, see now Neuschäfer, *Origenes*, pp. 87–94.

[4] The original δέ clause is visible in the Latin translation, where we read the words, 'in exemplariis *autem* Novi Testamenti . . . etc.' (GCS 40, pp. 388–9).

[5] Cf. H. B. Swete, *An Introduction to the Old Testament in Greek*², Cambridge 1914, p. 70; N. R. M. de Lange, *StPatr* 16 (1985 = TU 129), pp. 245–6; and now Neuschäfer, *Origenes*, pp. 124–5. The asterisk, on the other hand, had been used for different purposes and its meaning was consequently not so straightforward. See F. Field's introduction to his edition of the *Hexapla* (Oxford 1875), i, pp. lii–liii, and the sources cited by A. Gudeman, *PRE* i. 11. 2 (1922), cols. 1921–3. Neuschäfer, *Origenes*, p. 125, would connect Origen's use of the asterisk with the usage whereby *versus iterati* are indicated, but the suggestion has little to recommend it.

describes the obelus as it appears in the Greek Bible with the
words ἀθετήσεως σύμβολον (*Hex.* 4. 5). Finally, scholars have questioned why Origen should mention the fact that he has not 'dared'
to omit the passages under obelus, if his method did not carry the
implication that this would be a logical course of action.[6]

On the other hand, in his *Epistula ad Africanum* (= *Ep.* 1) 9(5)
(cf. 7(4)), speaking in general terms about his textual activities,
Origen implies that the critical signs are merely informative and
are designed to save Christians from being charged with ignorance
of the original text in disputes with the Jews. In *Ep.* 1. 8(4), he
makes clear his overall view that Christians are not to 'athetize'
(ἀθετεῖν) the copies of the Bible in their possession and substitute
them with those of the Jews (also an intimation that the obelus
was not to be understood in the traditional sense?).[7] They should
follow the textual tradition sanctified by the Church and safe-
guarded by Providence. The clear implication of this latter passage
is that Christians need not assimilate the LXX to the Hebrew
text.

The problem then, is clear. As far as his textual position is
concerned, there is a tension between the support of a LXX
'corrected' according to the Hebrew on the one hand, and of a
'pure' LXX on the other.[8] Origen's successors understood his
work in both senses. Jerome believed that Origen favoured a
'corrected' text, whereas Epiphanius and Rufinus were of the view
that he remained firmly on the side of the traditional LXX text.[9]
The debate has continued into modern times. P. Wendland and
P. Kahle, for example, have taken basically the same position as
Jerome, and the view of S. P. Brock is in effect not very far
removed from that of Rufinus.[10] However, the formulation of the

---

[6] See most recently de Lange, loc. cit.; Neuschäfer, *Origenes*, p. 102.

[7] Neuschäfer, *Origenes*, pp. 387–8 n. 172, may be correct in thinking that in
this passage ἀθετεῖν must be rendered, 'völlig verwerfen', but Origen is capable of
using technical terms in more than one sense at the same time, as is acknowledged
by Neuschäfer himself, p. 137.

[8] This point has been stressed by I. Soisalon-Soininen, *Der Charakter der
asterisierten Zusätze in der Septuaginta* (*AASF* B-114), Helsinki 1959, pp. 12–13.

[9] Jerome, *Praef. in Par.* (*IH*) 12–16; *Praef. in Pent.* 8–11; *Praef. in Job* (*IH*)
5–7; cf. *Ep.* 112. 19, and below, pp. 59–63; Epiphanius, *Mens.* 2–3, 17; Rufinus,
Apol. adv. Hier. 2. 40, and cf. the interpolation in his translation of Eusebius, *HE*
6. 31. 1.

[10] Wendland, 'Zur ältesten Geschichte der Bibel in der Kirche', *ZNW* 1 (1900),
pp. 272–3; Kahle, *The Cairo Geniza²*, Oxford 1959, p. 240. Wendland attempts to
explain away Origen's remarks in *Ep.* 1 by attributing them to an earlier date. For

problem in this way carries the implication that Origen's approach was essentially 'LXX-centred'. For even if he recognized the importance of the Hebrew original, his formal position concerning the biblical text will not have gone beyond the support of a LXX 'corrected' according to the Hebrew.

A possible exception to this statement lies in the fact that Origen seems to have been willing to put the version of Theodotion at least on a par with that of the LXX with regard to the book of Daniel. In Origen's time it seems that both versions were used in the Church. He calls both versions 'ours' in *Ep.* 1. 4(2). By the time of Jerome, however, the version of Theodotion had replaced that of the LXX in ecclesiastical usage. S. Jellicoe has suggested that Origen was responsible for this transition. He supports the suggestion by citing the fact that all of Origen's citations of Daniel agree with Theodotion and Origen's statement (preserved by Jerome, *Comm. in Dan.* 1 (4: 5a)) that he would follow that version in his commentary on Daniel from chapter 4.[11] If Origen was in favour of replacing the LXX version with that of Theodotion, it is likely that his grounds for this were the fact that the former version contained too many deviations from the Hebrew.[12] If this is the case, we must regard as all the more deliberate his textual position with regard to the other books as we have described it in the last phrase of the previous paragraph. For we will have confirmation that in the case of all books except Daniel he was unwilling to carry the principle of 'conformity with the original' further than the support of a 'corrected' LXX.

More recently, however, some scholars have felt a certain discomfort with the fact that the problem has been posed in the manner stated in the preceding paragraphs. For if Origen was attempting to restore the original form of the text of the LXX, by correcting it according to the Hebrew text current in his own day he will have corrupted it further rather than 'healed' it. The Hebrew text in general was not the proper criterion by which to judge the reliability of the manuscript tradition of the LXX, because the translators did not always strive for a literal rendering, and the one current in the time of Origen was even less suited for

Brock's view, see *StPatr* 10 (1970 = TU 107), pp. 215–18, and cf. now M. Müller, *Scandinavian Journal of the Old Testament* 1989. 1, pp. 112–13.

[11] *The Septuagint and Modern Study*, Oxford 1968, pp. 86–7.
[12] Cf. Swete, *An Introduction*, pp. 46–7.

this role, for it was probably significantly different from the text used by the LXX.[13] On the other hand, however, if Origen was merely attempting to create a tool for apologetics, his project loses some of its value as a 'scientific' achievement.

Consequently, new views concerning this problem have emerged. One such view has been put forward by P. Nautin. In his opinion, Origen's main concern in the composition of the *Hexapla* (which in his view included the Hexaplaric text of the LXX) was not the Greek, but the Hebrew text. And Nautin claims not only that Origen was primarily interested in the Hebrew, but that he composed the *Hexapla* with the intention of arriving at the original Hebrew text of the Bible.[14] This theory is somewhat audacious, since it is corroborated by neither of the passages where Origen discusses his textual work, nor by the *Hexapla* itself. In *Ep.* 1. 9(5), Origen says explicitly that he has concentrated his efforts on the text of the LXX. In *Comm. in Mt.* 15. 14, where he discusses his efforts in connection with ἡ ἐν τοῖς ἀντιγράφοις τῆς παλαιᾶς διαθήκης διαφωνία, we have seen that he mentions only work concerned with the Greek, not the Hebrew Bible. These statements are borne out by the *Hexapla* itself and the Hexaplaric LXX, since it is in the latter text that Origen made corrections and placed critical signs, not in the column(s) containing the Hebrew.[15] In short, none of these sources provides any indication that in the *Hexapla* Origen was concerned with the Hebrew text, let alone its original form.

Accordingly, Nautin has based his theory on the proposition that for Origen the *Hexapla* (and the Hexaplaric LXX) did not constitute an end in itself but a means to an end. It was a personal tool or large apparatus criticus from which one could arrive at the original Hebrew text of the Bible. We must look to Origen's homilies and commentaries to discover the real purpose of the *Hexapla* and the Hexaplaric LXX.[16] Such a proposition, however, seems difficult to accept. First of all, it must be said that Origen's

[13] See S. R. Driver, *Notes on the Hebrew Text and the Topography of the Books of Samuel²*, Oxford 1913, pp. xliii–xliv; Swete, *An Introduction*, p. 68. Cf. (J.-)D. Barthélemy, 'Origène et le texte de l'Ancien Testament', *Epektasis* (*FS* J. Daniélou), [Paris] 1972, p. 252.

[14] *Origène*, pp. 344–53, 359–61. His position has been accepted by T. D. Barnes, *Constantine and Eusebius*, Cambridge, Mass. 1981, pp. 92, 102.

[15] Cf. now Neuschäfer, *Origenes*, pp. 102–3.

[16] Nautin, *Origène*, pp. 344, 351, 354, 360.

commentaries have an exegetical purpose, not a textual one. As we shall see below in section III, he normally uses the various versions and variants not to work 'backwards' towards the text, but to work 'forwards' towards the sense.

In the second place, while there is no problem with the idea that the *Hexapla* itself was a preparatory, private dossier, this is not the case with regard to the Hexaplaric LXX, even if it was not a separate work. The idea that Origen did not regard this text as a finished product, and as a public document, cannot be reconciled with his own statements. That he saw the text as a completed work seems clear from the following words in *Comm. in Mt.* 15. 14: τὴν . . . ἐν τοῖς ἀντιγράφοις τῆς παλαιᾶς διαθήκης διαφωνίαν θεοῦ διδόντος εὕρομεν ἰάσασθαι. By the expression εὕρομεν ἰάσασθαι Origen can only mean that he has 'healed' the manuscript tradition of the LXX already, since it is generally acknowledged that in the immediately following sentence he is describing what he actually did in his Hexaplaric LXX. If the text has been healed, it must constitute a finished product, not a means to an end. An objection to the idea that the Hexaplaric LXX was a private document may be derived from the use of the critical signs. Origen's masters, the Alexandrian grammarians, employed the signs for the purpose of communicating textual information to readers in published texts.[17] It is of course quite possible that the signs were also used in private dossiers, but it is highly unlikely that this was the primary purpose for which Origen employs them in the Hexaplaric LXX, since he explicitly refers to prospective readers in his description of the signs:

καὶ τινὰ μὲν ὠβελίσαμεν ⟨ὡς⟩ ἐν τῷ Ἑβραϊκῷ μὴ κείμενα . . . τινὰ δὲ μετ' ἀστερίσκων προσεθήκαμεν, ἵνα δῆλον ᾖ ὅτι μὴ κείμενα παρὰ τοῖς Ἑβδομήκοντα ἐκ τῶν λοιπῶν ἐκδόσεων συμφώνως τῷ Ἑβραϊκῷ προσεθήκαμεν, καὶ ὁ μὲν βουλόμενος προ⟨σ⟩ῆται αὐτά, ᾧ δὲ προσκόπτει τὸ τοιοῦτον, ὃ βούλεται περὶ τῆς παραδοχῆς αὐτῶν ἢ μὴ ποιήσῃ. (*Comm. in Mt.* 15. 14)

In this passage, the pronoun αὐτά clearly refers to the passages added under asterisk in the Hexaplaric LXX, and τὸ τοιοῦτον to Origen's method of inserting them in the text. It is hardly natural to understand these words as indicating Origen's use of such

---

[17] See R. Pfeiffer, *History of Classical Scholarship: From the Beginnings to the End of the Hellenistic Age*, Oxford 1968, pp. 115, 178. Cf. L. D. Reynolds and N. G. Wilson, *Scribes and Scholars³*, Oxford 1991, pp. 10–11.

added passages in homilies and commentaries, as Nautin does.[18]
In view of these considerations, it seems unlikely that Pamphilus,
Eusebius, and Jerome misunderstood Origen's intentions in treat-
ing the Hexaplaric LXX as a finished, public document. If the
Hexaplaric LXX is to be regarded as such, and if the rest of the
Hexapla served as a preparatory dossier, it is more logical to
conclude that it was used not for the purpose of arriving at the
original Hebrew text, but for the preparation of the Hexaplaric
LXX. And it is within the context of the latter project that one
must attempt to understand Origen's position with regard to the
text of the Old Testament.

II

Of course it cannot be denied that Origen's exegetical writings
should also be examined in an attempt to further clarify his views.
What do we learn from these writings? First of all, we do find
confirmation in the homilies and commentaries of the views which
emerge from both *Comm. in Mt.* 15. 14 and *Ep.* 1, namely, the
support of both a 'corrected LXX' and of a 'pure' LXX. Secondly,
we also find confirmation of the view that Origen's position was
essentially 'LXX-centred'.

The exegetical works corroborate the fact that Origen believed
that it was possible to 'heal' the textual errors in the LXX by
reference to the Hebrew. For he often discusses variants within
the manuscript tradition of the LXX, and in such cases, which
have been collected by G. Sgherri, he follows the principle outlined in *Comm. in Mt.*, and generally regards as correct the reading
which is in accord with the Hebrew.[19] Indeed, with the phrase τὰ
ἀκριβέστατα [sc. ἀντίγραφα] καὶ συμφωνοῦντα τοῖς Ἑβραϊκοῖς (*Hom.
in Jer.* 14. 3), he seems almost to define more accurate codices as
those which agree with the Hebrew.

It has also been established that in his Hexaplaric LXX Origen
corrected proper names to accord with the Hebrew and followed
the order of the Hebrew.[20] From reading the exegetical works we

---

[18] *Origène*, p. 354.
[19] 'Sulla valutazione origeniana dei LXX', *Bib* 58 (1977), pp. 8–9. Cf. Nautin,
Origène, p. 350.
[20] See Field, i, pp. lx–lxi; Munnich, *La Bible grecque*, p. 165. On the correction
of proper names, see further, Barthélemy, 'Origène', p. 260 n. 92.

get the impression that in these cases he determined that corruption had taken place in the LXX by criteria other than the presence of variants in the manuscript tradition. With regard to the transmission of proper names, Origen states that there are often errors in the LXX. He claims to have ascertained this fact through consultation with Jewish informants and inspection of Hebrew MSS, and to have verified it by means of the *recentiores* (*Comm. in Jo.* 6. 212–15). In this case, he seems to have concluded that the LXX was corrupt primarily on the basis of divergences from the Hebrew.[21]

With regard to word order, it has sometimes been thought that Origen followed the Hebrew for practical reasons. Since the *Hexapla* was arranged in parallel columns and each column contained only a word or two, a uniform word order in the various columns will have been necessary or at least highly desirable, in order to allow the user to compare the various texts without difficulty.[22] However, an exegetical fragment would appear to indicate that Origen seems to have thought, for whatever reason, that the divergent word order of the LXX was often the result of textual corruption. In a comment on Gen. 47: 4–5 preserved in the *catenae* under Origen's name and recently re-edited by F. Petit, we read the following words:

ἐπειδὴ ἐν τοῖς *Τετραπλοῖς*, ἐξ ὧν καὶ τὸ ἀντίγραφον μετελήφθη, πρὸς τὸν εἱρμὸν τὸν ἐν τῷ Ἑβραϊκῷ καὶ ταῖς ἄλλαις ἐκδόσεσιν δείκνυται καὶ ἡ τῶν Ἑβδομήκοντα [sc. ἔκδοσις] ἔν τισι τόποις μετατεθεῖσα, ὡς τὰ πρῶτα ὕστερα καὶ τὰ ὕστερα πρῶτα γενέσθαι, ὅπερ καὶ ἐνταῦθα εὑρέθη παθοῦσα, τούτου χάριν καὶ τὴν ἐν τοῖς κοινοῖς ἀντιγράφοις τῶν Ἑβδομήκοντα παρεθήκαμεν ἀκολουθίαν. ἔστι δὲ αὕτη . . . κτλ.[23]

The authenticity of this fragment has been questioned by (J.-)D. Barthélemy on the grounds that it contains a reference to a

---

[21] According to Sgherri, 'Sulla valutazione', p. 9 n. 22, Origen may have thought, quite naturally, that proper names were more susceptible to corruption when transmitted in a foreign language. Cf. also Neuschäfer, *Origenes*, p. 121, who suggests that Origen's familiarity with the geography of Palestine may have led him to make corrections in place-names in the New Testament, even when the manuscript tradition was unanimous.

[22] See A. Rahlfs in the introduction to his manual edition of the LXX (Stuttgart 1935), section 6.

[23] 'Le dossier origénien de la chaîne de Moscou sur la Genèse', *Muséon* 92 (1979), p. 99 (no. 1586 = *PG* 15. 319–20, *PG* 12. 141c). I have made minor changes in punctuation.

manuscript copied from the *Tetrapla*.[24] However, even if such a reference precludes Origen's direct authorship, the substance of the note nevertheless probably goes back to him. For the easiest way to make sense of the attribution and the reference to a manuscript copied from the *Tetrapla* is to ascribe the transcription and possible rewording of the fragment to Eusebius, who is known to have reproduced scholia by Origen from a manuscript of the *Tetrapla*.[25] If such a hypothesis is accepted, the most probable translation of the key words of the fragment is as follows: 'Since it is clear in [i.e. from] the *Tetrapla* . . . that the [order of the] edition of the LXX has been transposed in some places in relationship to the order of the Hebrew and the other versions . . . which [transposition] it [the edition of the LXX] has been found to have suffered here, . . .' In other words, the implication of the passive participle μετατεθεῖσα and the passive notion inherent in the participle παθοῦσα is that the text preserved in the LXX has been corrupted in the course of transmission.[26] Accordingly, restoring the order of the Hebrew in the Hexaplaric LXX will have been Origen's way of 'healing' the text.

Finally, in additional support of the view that Origen favoured a LXX 'corrected' according to the Hebrew, there is the fact that

---

[24] 'Origène', p. 255 n. 48. The objection is valid only if the reference is taken to imply that the fragment was transcribed *after the time* of Origen. The word *Tetrapla* by itself cannot serve as a touchstone and exclude authenticity, for Origenian authorship of some kind of *Tetrapla*, despite the doubts of Barthélemy and others, remains a possibility. See Nautin, *Origène*, pp. 314–16, 342–3, 457–8; Neuschäfer, *Origenes*, p. 377 n. 64.

[25] This is clear from a note in the *Codex Marchalianus* (Q). It is conveniently printed in Nautin, *Origène*, p. 323. This particular note also proves, against Barthélemy, 'Origène', pp. 256–7, that the term *Tetrapla* was used by Eusebius in a technical sense to indicate what in all likelihood was some form of multi-columned Bible.

[26] It would therefore appear that contrary to the view of Swete, *An Introduction*, pp. 480–1 (where this fragment is cited as a comment on Jeremiah rather than on Genesis), Origen does distinguish textual error here. On the other hand, the main clause of the sentence (τούτου χάριν . . .) might give the impression that the fragment could be understood in the following sense: 'Since it is clear that in the *Tetrapla* . . . the [order of the] edition of the LXX has been transposed in some places [sc. by Origen] in order that it should correspond to the order of the Hebrew . . . etc., we have given [i.e. shall give] the order in the *textus receptus* . . . etc.' However, the use of the expressions δείκνυται . . . μετατεθεῖσα and εὑρέθη παθοῦσα would seem to indicate that a logical inference is being made, and a later author objecting to Origen's transpositions would have probably said μετετέθη and ἔπαθε. In addition, for the note to have this sense one would require proof that the fragment should not be attributed directly or indirectly to Origen.

he generally does comment on passages under asterisk, i.e. passages added from the *recentiores* which expose 'minuses' in the standard text of the LXX.[27]

On the other hand, we have seen that in his *Ep.* 1. 8(4) Origen gives the impression that he advocates the text of the LXX which has been hallowed by ecclesiastical tradition, i.e. a 'pure' LXX. Some scholars, however, do not accept Origen's statements in *Ep.* 1 as sincere. According to this view, in *Ep.* 1. 8(4), Origen is merely repeating arguments which were used by his opponents who saw in his textual efforts a threat to the traditional text.[28] But such a position is difficult to sustain, since in Origen's exegetical works we do find confirmation of the view which emerges from *Ep.* 1. 8(4).

First of all, it has often been pointed out that despite some exceptions, Origen usually takes full account of those passages of the LXX which represent pluses over against the Hebrew, that is, the passages marked with an obelus in the Hexaplaric LXX.[29] Most instructive in this context is Origen's comment on Job 42: 17a, where the LXX and Theodotion add a statement about Job's resurrection: καὶ ταῦτα δὲ ῥήματα δεχόμεθα, εἰ καὶ μὴ ὡς τοῦ παντὸς ὕφους ὄντα, ἀλλά γε ὡς τινος τῶν ἁγίων αὐτὰ συνυφήναντος τῇ βίβλῳ· πλὴν ὅμως πάντα δεχόμεθα, οὕτως ἐκ τῶν πατέρων τὸ βιβλίον παρειληφότες.[30] The respect which he reveals for ecclesiastical tradition corresponds fully to the position which he takes in *Ep.* 1. 8(4).

In the second place, there are a number of passages in Origen's exegetical work which are probably best understood in the context of his affirmation in *Ep.* 1. 8(4) of a connection between the Bible of the Church and Providence. Origen says in this passage, in effect, that Providence has made it unnecessary for the Christians to substitute the Bible in use in the Church, i.e. the LXX, with the Bible of the Jews. It would seem therefore that the reliability of the LXX has been guaranteed by Providence. Origen employs

---

[27] See Barthélemy, 'Origène', p. 260. Cf. Sgherri, 'Sulla valutazione', p. 28.

[28] See Nautin, *Origène*, p. 346. De Lange, *StPatr* 16 (1985 = TU 129), pp. 243–7, takes a similar view, although he focuses attention primarily on *Ep.* 1. 9(5).

[29] See Barthélemy, 'Origène', p. 260; cf. Sgherri, 'Sulla valutazione', p. 28. An additional exception is *Comm. in Jo.* 28. 137.

[30] This fragment has been edited by J. B. Pitra, *Analecta sacra*, ii, Frascati 1884, p. 390. Cf. *Comm. ser. in Mt.* 61 (GCS 38, p. 140).

similar concepts in his exegetical writings, and a term which often appears in this context is οἰκονομία. The general impression is that this 'economy' constitutes some form of providential or divine guiding spirit present in the translation.[31] Indeed, this view may be confirmed by the fact that in one passage the expression employed is 'dispensatio providentiae', the underlying Greek of which is probably οἰκονομία προνοίας.[32] However, Origen does not always emphasize the divine aspect of 'economy', but seems to allow for the fact that it has been fostered by a human element as well.

We notice two directions in which the concept is employed. On the one hand, as scholars have often pointed out, Origen sometimes sees some kind of divine or providential intervention as the cause of deviations from the original in the LXX.[33] For example, he notes that the LXX have the habit of putting prophecies relating to Christ in the past rather than in the future tense. He explains, οἰόμεθα δὲ αὐτούς [sc. the LXX], τῷ τὸν θεὸν εἰδέναι τὰ πάντα πρὶν γενέσεως αὐτῶν, καὶ τὸν Χριστὸν αὐτοῦ, καὶ τὰ ἐν τῇ ἐνανθρωπήσει συμβησόμενα αὐτῷ, λέγειν, τῷ λελογίσθαι αὐτὰ ἤδη γεγονέναι.[34] Similarly, he attributes a theological motive to the fact that in Lev. 21: 13 the words ἐκ τοῦ γένους αὐτοῦ are present in the LXX but absent from the original: 'recte illi [sc. Hebraei] non habent scriptum. ablata est enim ab illis propinquitas Dei, ablata est adoptio filiorum et translata est ad ecclesiam Christi' (*Hom. in Lev.* 12. 5). In other instances where Origen notes a difference in the text of the LXX with respect to the Hebrew, as an alternative to assuming an error on the part of scribes, he sometimes considers the possibility that the LXX themselves have made a change 'by

---

[31] Cf. Barthélemy, 'Origène', p. 259; R. P. C. Hanson, *Allegory and Event*, London 1959, p. 164.

[32] This passage is *Hom. in Jer.* (Latin) 2. 4. It is quoted directly below.

[33] Hanson, *Allegory*, pp. 163–4; Barthélemy, 'Origène', pp. 258–9.

[34] *Sel. in Ps.* 2: 1–2 (*PG* 12. 1104c–d). It is difficult to see how Sgherri, 'Sulla valutazione', p. 22 n. 73, can regard Origen's comment in *Sel. in Ps.* 42: 3 (*PG* 12. 1420d) as a criticism of the LXX. Origen points out in this passage that the LXX have rendered a prophecy relating to Christ in the past tense, whereas the *recentiores* have rendered the passage σαφέστερον (i.e. by employing the future). In view of the present passage, however, it is clear that Origen did not consider this feature of the translation technique of the LXX as negative. Cf. Barthélemy, 'Origène', p. 259 with n. 80. Origen did not regard clarity as the criterion for determining the better text. See *Comm. in Os.* 12: 5 (= *Philoc.* 8. 1); *Comm. in Cant.* 1 (1: 2 = GCS 33, pp. 100–1); Rufinus, *Apol. adv. Hier.* 2. 40.

employing economy' *(οἰκονομήσαντες)* or 'according to economy' *(κατ' οἰκονομίαν)*.[35]

On the other hand, it is the accuracy, even if non-literal, with which the original is reflected in the Greek translation that has been fostered by οἰκονομία. Origen expresses this idea most clearly in one of his homilies on Jeremiah which survives in a Latin version by Jerome. After setting out how accurate the translation of the LXX is with respect to subtle distinctions in the connotations of words (under discussion are the verbs 'proici' and 'abici'), he explains as follows, 'dispensatio providentiae, etiamsi non magnopere curavit, ut disertitudinem, quae in Graeco sermone laudatur, Graece interpretando sequeretur, curavit tamen ea quae significantia sunt exhibere et differentiam eorum explanare dilucide his qui scripturas diligentissime perscrutantur' (*Hom. in Jer.* (Latin) 2. 4). In *Ep.* 1. 18(12), Origen maintains that it is possible for the translators to 'employ economy' and render Hebrew etymologies into Greek by using equivalent or analogous concepts. He goes on to say that one finds many examples of such 'economic' renderings in the Bible.

In view of these two passages, it seems that some of Origen's remarks concerning the translation technique of the LXX may be interpreted in a similar sense. For example, with reference to Dtn. 1: 31, Origen says that the LXX have invented the word τροπο-φορέω, since they did not find an existing word in Greek which was appropriate.[36] On other occasions as well Origen comments on the propensity of the LXX to coin new words.[37] He seems to be saying that they have gone to extreme lengths in order to reflect the original with exactitude, without paying regard to the 'disertitudo, quae in Graeco sermone laudatur'. Origen also notes that the LXX sometimes leave Hebrew words untranslated. For

---

[35] See Neuschäfer, *Origenes*, pp. 112–13, and below, p. 23.

[36] *Hom. in Jer.* 18. 6. In fact, τροποφορέω is attested outside the LXX. However, it is a very rare word; see H. G. Liddell, R. Scott, and H. Stuart Jones, *A Greek–English Lexicon*[9], Oxford 1925–40, s.v. Hanson, *Allegory*, p. 173 n. 6, misinterprets this passage in thinking that according to Origen the *recentiores* have 'invented' a passage which they did not find in the LXX. But the text which Origen quotes is that of the LXX and a glance at the text of the *Hexapla* ad loc. reveals that the *recentiores* translate in a different manner.

[37] *Orat.* 27. 7. Cf. *Sel. in Ps.* 4: 5 (*PG* 12. 1144c). On the possibility that additional comments of Origen on this matter have been preserved by Jerome, see G. Q. A. Meershoek, *Le latin biblique d'après saint Jérôme* (LCP 20), Nijmegen 1966, pp. 33–7.

example, with reference to III Reg. 6: 23(22), he writes, τὰ μέντοι δύο χερουβεὶμ ἐν τῷ δαβεὶρ ἦν, ὅπερ οὐ δεδύνηνται ἑρμηνεῦσαι κυρίως οἱ μεταλαμβάνοντες εἰς Ἑλληνισμὸν τὰ Ἑβραίων. καταχρηστικώτερον δέ τινες ναὸν αὐτὸν εἰρήκασιν τοῦ ναοῦ τιμιώτερον τυγχάνοντα (Comm. in Jo. 10. 282–3). R. P. C. Hanson believes that this passage constitutes a criticism of the LXX, in that they 'did not know the meaning of the Hebrew word'.[38] Sgherri on the other hand seems to think that Origen evaluates positively the prudence of the LXX in not attempting a rendering.[39] This latter view appears to be the correct one. When Origen says that the LXX 'were unable to translate κυρίως', he does not mean that they did not know the meaning of the word, but that it is impossible to give an exact rendering. Consequently, it is a translation that misleads us as to the precise meaning of the word.[40] That this is probably the correct interpretation of Origen's comment may be confirmed by a statement of Jerome: 'Origenes adserat . . . multo esse melius ininterpretata ponere, quam vim interpretatione tenuare' (Ep. 26. 2). Although Origen does not employ the term 'economy' in these passages, his clear conviction is that extraordinary measures have been taken to ensure the accuracy of the translation.[41]

---

[38] *Allegory*, p. 166 (the reference to I [III] Reg. 6: 16 is an error caused by confusion with a parallel passage, see below, n. 40).

[39] 'Sulla valutazione', pp. 22–3 n. 74.

[40] It is impossible to know which translators rendered the word דביר with ναός, since there are no Hexaplaric remains for the verse in question. Aquila and Symmachus employ the translation χρηματιστήριον in III Reg. 6: 16, but whether they used this term or ναός in III Reg. 6: 23 is a question that cannot be answered. Cf. Sgherri, loc. cit. (n. 39 above).

[41] On the other hand, J. Daniélou, *Origène*, Paris 1948, p. 142, Hanson, *Allegory* pp. 165–6, and Sgherri, 'Sulla valutazione', *passim*, have attempted to show that there are occasions where Origen 'criticizes' the LXX. With one possible exception (a comment on Ps. 118: 1–2, in M. Harl, *La chaîne palestinienne sur le Psaume 118*, i (Paris 1972 = SC 189), p. 188, cited by Sgherri, p. 10 n. 24), not a single one of their examples is convincing. Many of the passages which they cite are interpreted in quite different senses by Barthélemy, 'Origène'. In *Hom. in Lev.* 2. 5, a doubt about the translators is raised by other critics, not by Origen himself, as Sgherri, p. 11, implies. In *Cels.* 5. 48, Origen does not 'prefer' the Hebrew, as Sgherri, p. 15 n. 41, says, but reconciles it with the LXX (the participle παυόμενος in Origen's explanation is based on the word ἔστη in the text of the LXX; cf. Procopius of Gaza, *Comm. in Ex.* 4 (PG 87. 539–40)). See below, p. 25; cf. also Barthélemy, p. 259 with n. 83. Sgherri also reads too much into the texts when he claims, pp. 15, 22 n. 73 (with reference to *Sel. in Ezech.* 7: 27 (PG 13. 796a)), that Origen criticizes the LXX for omissions. In the passages cited by Sgherri, he either confesses his ignorance as to why they may have left something out, hypothesizes a different Hebrew *Vorlage*, or considers the possibility of textual corruption. Origen's remark in *Hom. in Ezech.* 6. 4, that the LXX have rendered

It follows from the preceding considerations that for Origen the fidelity of the LXX is dependent on both divine and human forces. On the one hand, although he does not speak formally of the inspiration of the LXX, or give voice to the story of the fantastic origin of the translation which developed out of the sober narration found in the *Letter of Aristeas*, he clearly believed that the reliability of the version was guaranteed by some kind of transcendent design. On the other hand, Origen was well aware that this reliability was also fostered by human translators.[42] However, our purpose here is not to determine the extent of the human and divine contributions in this process, nor to specify the exact nature of οἰκονομία.[43] It is rather to show that Origen's faith in the LXX as expressed in *Ep.* 1. 8(4) may not be dismissed as a repetition of the arguments of his opponents. He expresses complete confidence in the Greek text with regard to both the deviations from the original and the attempts to reflect it accurately. Indeed, his admonitions to pay attention to the smallest details of [Greek] biblical language which we read in the *Philocalia* would hardly make sense if this were not the case.[44]

On the basis of the preceding analysis it is clear that both tendencies which we have noted in Origen's specific pronouncements concerning his textual endeavours are confirmed in his exegetical writings. He seems to favour a 'pure' LXX, in that he expresses faith in the intentional aberrations of the LXX. On the other hand, he desires to 'correct' this text by reference to the Hebrew.

ad sensum is certainly not a criticism, as Hanson, p. 165, would have it. Cf. Barthélemy, p. 258 with n. 74. In *Hom. in Jer.* 15. 5, which Daniélou, loc. cit., seems to regard as a criticism of the translators, we in fact have a reference to a copyist's error. See P. Benoit, 'L'inspiration des Septante d'après les Pères', *L'homme devant Dieu*, i (*FS* H. de Lubac = Theol(P) 56), Paris 1963, p. 179 n. 64. For other examples of alleged criticism of the LXX, see above, n. 34, and below, n. 78. Harl, in her edition of *Philoc.* 1–20 (Paris 1983 = SC 302), p. 127, has probably done the right thing in passing over in silence such suggestions by Daniélou, Hanson, and Sgherri, and repeating the traditional view.

[42] According to Benoit, 'L'inspiration', pp. 173–4, the patristic belief in the inspiration of the LXX was based on, among other things, the conviction that the LXX were exceptionally well qualified as translators.

[43] On this question, see now Neuschäfer, *Origenes*, pp. 136–8.

[44] *Philoc.* 2. 4; 10. 2; 14. 1–2. Cf. the remarks of Harl in her edition of the text (Paris 1983 = SC 302), pp. 126–7. That these admonitions refer to the Greek text may be confirmed by the fact that Origen himself so often treats the Greek text as if it were the original. See Hanson, *Allegory*, p. 162.

From Origen's own perspective, this method is not self-contradictory. It simply rests on the assumption that one could distinguish between intentional changes on the part of the original translators and later textual corruption. Modern scholars, more modest in their approach to textual criticism, have found this assumption troubling. Yet that Origen made such an assumption need hardly be doubted. This is the same man who believed it was possible to distinguish between parts of the Bible which have a literal meaning and parts which do not.[45] Origen simply does not express himself extensively concerning the criteria to be employed in operating a distinction between intentional changes of the translators and textual corruption, neither with regard to the 'qualitative' changes, nor with regard to the 'pluses' and 'minuses'.[46]

Concerning the latter, the phenomenon is particularly acute. For we have seen that in his exegetical writings Origen almost always uses the longer text, that is to say, he comments on passages under both asterisk and obelus. What is the reason for this approach? Barthélemy has attempted to portray this practice as an intentional policy. He believes that Origen at least intuitively anticipated the view of Augustine as expressed in *De civitate Dei* 18. 43, according to which there were two revelations, one expressed via the Greek and another via the Hebrew. In this case, all 'pluses' must be regarded as authentic.[47] This would imply that Origen did not think it possible or desirable to distinguish between intentional aberration on the part of the LXX and textual corruption with regard to pluses and minuses, but that it was preferable to place the Hebrew and Greek texts side by side. Such a two-text approach naturally goes beyond his method as it may be understood from *Comm. in Mt.* and *Ep.* 1, where the focus is on the text of the LXX alone.

This view, however, cannot be accepted. First of all, Origen is known to comment on variants which lend themselves to meaningful exegesis, even if he regards them as scribal errors.[48] Thus, that

---

[45] See *Princ.* 4. 2. 5–3. 5 (= *Philoc.* 1. 12–21).

[46] Cf. now Neuschäfer, *Origenes*, p. 134, who notes that Origen rarely uses internal criteria in identifying interpolations.

[47] See 'La place de la Septante dans l'Église', *Aux grands carrefours de la révélation et de l'exégèse de l'Ancien Testament* (1967 = RechBib 8), pp. 14–18, 22–3.

[48] See *Hom. in Jer.* 14. 3 with 15. 5; Hanson, *Allegory*, p. 175.

he comments on both the Hebrew and Greek 'pluses' does not mean that he did not think they may have been due to textual corruption. Rather, the tendency to employ the longer text may be due not to specifically textual considerations, but to what may be termed an 'exegetical maximalism'. In his normal exegesis of the Bible Origen is reluctant to let possible nuances in meaning go unnoticed. His writings are characterized by the conviction that one passage of Scripture contains a multiplicity of senses.[49] Consequently, by expanding the size of his Bible he is able to expand the possibilities of exegesis.

In the textual sphere, Origen's practice of using the longer text is probably better explained as a conservative desire to 'play it safe', i.e. to avoid excluding even a possibly authentic passage from his Bible. That this was his motivation can be confirmed from a converse, yet parallel case concerning apocryphal books. Origen did think it was possible to extract from these books passages which are 'true'. Nevertheless, he advises against using these books 'ad confirmationem dogmatum' on account of the fact that some people are incapable of making such a distinction.[50] In other words, the fact that a distinction can be made does not necessarily mean that it should be made in every case.

In short, although Origen probably thought it was possible to distinguish between intentional change and textual corruption in the text of the LXX, he did not apply himself to such a task on a significant scale. He simply left open the degree to which the Hebrew text could be employed in correcting and the extent to which the LXX could stand in its 'pure' form. For this reason, the debate between Jerome and Rufinus was a legitimate one, and did not arise out of misunderstandings of Origen's position.[51] Indeed, the fact that the two great scholars of Origen's work had access to so much more of it than we do should make us slightly wary of attempting to formulate the question in another manner.

As we have seen, if the grounds of dispute were correctly drawn by Jerome and Rufinus, the conclusion that Origen's position was essentially 'LXX-centred' remains firm. It is the LXX that he

---

[49] See H. de Lubac, *Histoire et esprit* (Theol(P) 16), Paris 1950, pp. 139–40.

[50] *Comm. ser. in Mt.* 28 (23: 37–9 = GCS 38, p. 51). Cf. *Comm. in Cant.* prol. (GCS 33, pp. 87–8); Jerome, *Ep.* 107. 12.

[51] The position outlined here is thus in partial accord with that of Wendland, 'Zur ältesten Geschichte', pp. 273–4, and in complete disaccord with that of Barthélemy, 'Origène', pp. 260–1.

regards as his base-text both when it presents a translation of the
Hebrew and when it contains intentional aberrations from it (in
practice, so long as these do not represent 'minuses'). Providence
has ensured the reliability of both of these aspects of the version.
On the other hand, Origen believed that such a text was to be
'corrected' according to the Hebrew. This is the furthest he moves
towards recognition of the importance of the original. This position may imply the 'priority' of the Hebrew text, but caution is
required in assessing the purport of this 'priority'. For although
the Hebrew text may be seen as 'prior', it is none the less subordinate to the LXX. Origen makes use of the Hebrew text not for its
own sake, but for the sake of the LXX.

That Origen's approach was 'LXX-centred' may be confirmed
by both his own statements and his practice. In a discussion of
textual variants in Cant. 1: 2, he comments as follows:

Non autem lateat nos quod in quibusdam exemplaribus pro eo, quod nos
legimus: 'quia bona sunt ubera tua super vinum', invenimus scriptum:
'quia bonae sunt loquelae tuae super vinum', quod quamvis evidentius
significasse videatur ea ipsa, quae a nobis spiritali interpretatione disserta
sunt, tamen nos septuaginta interpretum scripta per omnia custodimus,
certi quod spiritus sanctus mysteriorum formas obtectas esse voluit in
scripturis divinis et non palam atque in propatulo haberi. (*Comm. in Cant.*
1 (1: 2 = GCS 33, pp. 100–1))

This passage is normally cited as evidence that Origen regarded
the LXX as inspired, a point which at this stage does not concern
us. Sgherri, however, arguing against this traditional view, raises
a doubt about Origen's statement which implies the centrality of
the LXX ('tamen . . . custodimus').[52] In his view, it is possible
that since Origen notes that the variant is found 'in quibusdam
exemplaribus', he may have in mind a variant reading within the
manuscript tradition of the LXX, and not an opposition between
the LXX and the Hebrew or the *recentiores*. In this case, the
remark about the LXX may be an intervention of Rufinus in
which the translator is expressing his own views. This possibility
is most unlikely. For as Sgherri himself notes, Rufinus uses
phrases such as 'in quibusdam exemplaribus' rather loosely, even
in cases when it is much more logical to suppose that Origen is

---

[52] 'Sulla valutazione', pp. 11–13.

speaking of other translations.[53] But more importantly, Origen's statement that he always 'maintains' the text of the LXX may be authenticated by the fact that he makes a similar comment elsewhere. This comment survives in a Syriac fragment of his *Commentarii in Isaiam*, the relevant sentence of which is translated by Sgherri himself as follows: 'Ma ecco che noi diamo tutto secondo la traduzione dei LXX, non quasi non sapessimo che essa diverge in molte cose dall'Ebraico tramandato oggi e dal tenore dei rimanenti.'[54] Origen makes an analogous comment in *Homiliae in Numeros* 18. 3. After noting a variant which he says he has found 'in Hebraeorum codicibus', he continues, 'quibus quamvis non utamur, tamen agnoscendi gratia dicemus'. In this passage as well, Sgherri would like to attribute the phrase 'quibus . . . utamur' to Rufinus.[55] In view of the Syriac fragment, however, such a suggestion must be rejected.[56] In fact, the three statements which we have considered are not dissimilar to the affirmation which Origen makes in *Ep.* 1. 9(5), namely, that he has concentrated his efforts on the text of the LXX. All of these assertions should be taken at their face value, since they correspond to Origen's actual practice. In the words of Hanson, 'The form of the Old Testament which Origen uses in the vast majority of his scriptural references is the LXX version.'[57] Sgherri as well acknowledges that Origen uses the LXX 'come testo normale della Scrittura nella sua esegesi'.[58]

III

In this final section concerning Origen, which may be read as a kind of appendix, we shall consider in more detail the views of

---

[53] Ibid., p. 6 n. 16. Cf. p. 3 n. 4; p. 7 n. 20. Sgherri's remark (pp. 12–13) that there is only partial opposition between the Hebrew text and the LXX because the latter is based on a consonantal text identical to the Masoretic Text is gratuitous. For Origen probably has in mind an opposition between the LXX and the *recentiores*, and a difference in vocalization will have been enough to cause this.

[54] *Aug* 14 (1974), p. 252 n. 74.   [55] 'Sulla valutazione', p. 3 n. 4.

[56] Indeed, Sgherri, loc. cit. (n. 55 above), gives no valid reason for rejecting the phrase, outside of the fact that Rufinus 'tende, in polemica con Girolamo, a mettere in buona luce i LXX presso Origene, mentre Girolamo ha fatto l'opposto: "Aquila Hebraeam exprimens veritatem"' (*Hom. in Cant.* 2. 4). However, the context of this passage reveals that Jerome's remark is parenthetical and informative. It has no place in the controversy about the biblical text which broke out between him and Rufinus. Jerome knew very well to what extent he could cite Origen as a precedent for his own use of the Hebrew (see below, pp. 59–63; cf. p. 25), and it is most unlikely that he is trying to pass off as Origen's the phrase 'Hebraea veritas'.

[57] *Allegory*, p. 162.   [58] 'Sulla valutazione', pp. 26–7.

Nautin and Barthélemy, who have called into question the idea
that Origen's position was fundamentally 'LXX-centred'. According to the former, Origen was aiming at the original Hebrew text,
and according to the latter, he placed the Greek and Hebrew texts
on equal footing, anticipating the view later formulated by
Augustine.

With regard to the view of Nautin, we have already noted that
he rejects Origen's statements in *Ep.* 1 as 'smoke in the eyes', and
is willing to take seriously only the affirmations made in *Comm.
in Mt.*, where Origen says he is attempting to correct the text of
the LXX. But Nautin believes that this is only part of the truth.[59]
He appeals to Origen's exegesis in order to show that he actually
had the goal of arriving at the original Hebrew text of the Bible.
He makes three observations to support his case. First of all, he
notes that Origen often employs the *Hexapla* not as a criterion for
deciding between variants of the LXX, 'mais simplement de savoir
ce qu'il y avait dans l'hébreu'. Secondly, he brings examples to
show that Origen knew that 'les divergences entre la Septante et
les "autres éditions" ne sont pas toutes dues à des fautes de copie
dans les exemplaires de la Septante mais peuvent être inten-
tionnelles de la part des traducteurs'. And finally, he claims that
Origen was aware that 'le texte hébreu traduit par les autres
éditions pouvait avoir lui-même des fautes'.[60]

We shall examine the second and third points first. Nautin,
taking *Comm. in Mt.* 15. 14 as his starting point, has discovered
that Origen does not always proceed in accordance with the principles presupposed by that passage, namely, (*a*) that the LXX
always rendered their Hebrew *Vorlage* in a literal fashion, and (*b*)
that the Hebrew text has remained unchanged. He seems to have
assumed that since Origen sometimes followed principles different
from those presupposed by *Comm. in Mt.*, he went beyond the
goal specified by that text. But this assumption is flawed, and
Nautin has not proved by these two points that Origen was interested in arriving at the original Hebrew text, but in fact only that
he did not assume the universal validity of the two principles
noted, even if he was attempting to establish the original text of
the LXX.[61] That he had the latter goal is clear from a number of
indications.

---

[59] *Origène*, pp. 349–50.   [60] Ibid., pp. 351–3.
[61] See Barthélemy, 'Origène', p. 252.

First, Origen's awareness that the LXX did not always attempt to arrive at a literal rendering is a positive and not a negative factor in his evaluation of the version. In other words, he does not ascertain the intentional aberrations on the part of the translators in order to discard them in favour of the original, but to retain them. So much is clear from our previous discussion, in which we have seen, for example, that οἰκονομία is a positive concept, related to and perhaps deriving from Providence. It may be that Nautin's rather hasty dismissal of Origen's statements in *Ep.* 1 has caused him to misinterpret the relevance of those passages which, at least we have tried to demonstrate, may be most easily understood in the light of that text. However, that Origen evaluated in a positive sense intentional aberrations of the LXX is also clear from the first example which Nautin cites in the present context. In this passage (*Sel. in Ps.* 2: 12 (*PG* 12. 1116c–17a)), Origen considers two possible explanations for the addition of the word δικαίας in the LXX: intentional change (οἰκονομία) and scribal error. He provides exegesis for both possibilities. He first explains the passage incorporating the addition, on the assumption that there has been an intentional change. He then provides an exegesis for the second possibility, scribal error, and does not take the word into consideration. The clear implication is that if there was intentional change on the part of the translators the addition is to be accepted, not rejected, i.e. the change is seen in a positive light. Accordingly, when in *Hom. in Jer.* 16. 5 (the second text cited by Nautin) Origen considers both the possibility that the LXX have deleted the word πρῶτον intentionally (οἰκονομήσαντες) and that there has been a scribal error, and then goes on to discuss the passage taking the word into account, it is likely that he is explaining the passage only according to the possibility that there has been a scribal error.[62]

Nautin's third point, namely, that Origen was aware that the Hebrew text was also subject to corruption, is more relevant to his argument but not without problems. In fact in neither of the two passages which Nautin cites (*Sel. in Ps.* 3: 8 (*PG* 12. 1129b–c) and *Sel. in Ezech.* 7: 27 (*PG* 13. 796a)) do we have proof that Origen was interested in the original of the Hebrew more than he

---

[62] Sgherri, 'Sulla valutazione', pp. 14–15, in his desire to force Origen to choose between the Hebrew and the Greek, fails to appreciate the logical process involved in these passages.

was interested in the original of the LXX. For Origen mentions
the possibility that the Hebrew text has undergone corruption
only in so far as it provides a possible explanation for the diver-
gence in the LXX from the current Hebrew text. He also considers
the possibility that the translators made the changes intentionally,
so it seems that he was more concerned with determining the
origin of the LXX reading than arriving at the original Hebrew
text.

We may now return to Nautin's first point, that is, his claim
that Origen often cites readings from the Hebrew or the *recentiores*
when he does not have the intention of correcting an error or (it
may be added) filling in a 'minus' in the LXX. This point requires
further consideration, for it implies that Origen employed the
Hexapla for more than just the reconstruction of the Hexaplaric
LXX. That this was the case may be accepted, but it does not
necessarily follow that Origen accepted the priority of the Hebrew
text or attempted to arrive at its original form.

First, on many of the occasions where Origen cites the Hebrew
or the *recentiores* apparently for their own sake, the 'priority' or
'centrality' of the LXX is in fact in no way diminished. For he
often employs the Hebrew or the *recentiores* for the purpose of
explaining the LXX, that is to say, he uses the original language
text, and the more literal translations of it, to explain a translation,
not vice versa. This use of the Hebrew and the *recentiores* has
various forms.[63] In two of the four examples which Nautin cites
as evidence that Origen was interested in the Hebrew for its own
sake, the *recentiores* are in fact employed in order to clear up
ambiguities in the LXX by limiting the connotations attributable
to words employed in the latter version.[64] Conversely, Origen may
cite the later versions to extend the sense of a word.[65] On other
occasions Origen mentions the *recentiores* in order to corroborate
interpretations which he has propounded on the basis of the Greek
of the LXX. For example, in *Comm. in Gen.* 1: 16–18 (= *Philoc.*
14. 1), another text cited by Nautin, Origen bases his interpretation on a grammatical distinction between εἰς ἀρχάς and ἄρχειν. He

---

[63] Cf. Sgherri, 'Sulla valutazione', pp. 23–4 n. 77.

[64] The passages are *Prol. in Psalt.* 1. 15 (ed. G.(W.) Rietz, *De Origenis prologis
in Psalterium quaestiones selectae*, Jena 1914, p. 8 = *PG* 12. 1072b–c); *Sel. in Ps.*
2: 1–2 (*PG* 12. 1101c–d).

[65] See the examples cited by Sgherri, 'Sulla valutazione', p. 24 n. 77.

employs Aquila, who also translates with a noun and an infinitive, to confirm the validity of that distinction.[66] In other instances, when the LXX leave Hebrew words (especially proper names) untranslated or leave unclear their etymologies, Origen may go to the *recentiores* for explanations.[67] The use of the Hebrew and the *recentiores* which we have considered in this paragraph, far from proving that Origen was interested in arriving at the original Hebrew text, in fact merely substantiates something which we already know from the indirect testimony of Jerome, namely, that Origen 'interdum linguae peregrinae quaerit auxilia' (*QHG* prol.).

On the other hand, we must consider a number of passages which seem to indicate that Origen gave equal weight to both the LXX and the Hebrew or the *recentiores*. This phenomenon is most clearly manifest in the many cases, collected by Sgherri, in which Origen forges the components of the various versions together to form one interpretation.[68] He uses the different versions as blocks in constructing a single edifice. On numerous other occasions Origen extracts different meanings from the different versions, without attempting to merge them.[69] However, one needs to be careful in formulating conclusions with regard to Origen's textual position on the basis of this phenomenon. For he normally takes a positive view of all versions and variants which he cites, and this precludes any process of textual judgement.[70] In other words, Origen does not employ the *Hexapla* as would a modern scholar, using a comparative system to work back to the original text. He rather works 'forward' to arrive at a sense which for him is worthy of divine inspiration.[71]

[66] Other examples where Origen employs the *recentiores* or the Hebrew to confirm interpretations given on the basis of the LXX include *Hom. in Gen.* 2. 1 (Greek = GCS 29, pp. 26–7), and *Comm. in Mt.* 14. 16 (GCS 40, pp. 321–2).

[67] See the examples cited by Sgherri, 'Sulla valutazione', p. 22 n. 74. Cf. *Comm. in Mt.* 14. 16 (GCS 40, pp. 322–3). Origen is also generally interested in knowing the form of the name as well as the translation or etymology. See, e.g., *Cels.* 6. 25, where he employs the *recentiores* (or perhaps the Greek transliteration of the Hebrew) to discuss the word Leviathan, which underlies δράκων in the LXX in Ps. 104(103): 26. However, Origen had a special interest in proper names which need not necessarily have entailed an interest in the Hebrew text for its own sake. See *Cels.* 1. 24–5; 5. 45–6; cf. the remarks of Augustine, *Doct. Chr.* 2. 23.

[68] 'Sulla valutazione', pp. 2–4.

[69] See Sgherri, 'Sulla valutazione', pp. 4–6.

[70] Cf., with regard to Origen's treatment of textual variants in the New Testament, B. M. Metzger, *StPatr* 12 (1975 = TU 115), pp. 342–3.

[71] The features of Origen's textual approach noted in this paragraph have been recently discussed by Neuschäfer, *Origenes*, pp. 118–19, 129–30. He would explain

In short, neither the attempt to arrive at the original text of the Bible nor even the assertion of the priority of the Hebrew is a component of either of the two approaches which we have described in the two preceding paragraphs. On the other hand, it would seem that if Origen sometimes gives equal weight to both the LXX and to the Hebrew or the *recentiores*, he goes beyond a 'LXX-centred' outlook. This fact appears to constitute support for the view of Barthélemy, according to which Origen favoured a sort of 'dualisme biblique' in a manner similar to Augustine.[72] However, it seems doubtful that such an attitude was the motivating factor of the exegetical approach which we are considering, even if it offers an attractive explanation.

In the first place, Origen's dependence on the later versions, i.e. at least three different texts, is such that it seems to have obviated a sustained, comprehensive perception of the Hebrew text as a separate entity. For he does not normally employ the *recentiores* as a means to understanding the Hebrew, but bases his exegesis on a very literal reading of the Greek.[73] The reason for this may be that his reliance on the letter of the Greek text, which as we have mentioned above (p. 17) is a feature of his exegesis of the LXX, was unconsciously retained when he moved over to treat the other versions. Whatever the explanation for the phenomenon, the consequence is that a 'vue stéréoscopique' of the biblical text is often difficult for Origen to acquire. For example, there are cases where the LXX and two additional translations are either fused together or expounded separately, each of the three having equal weight.[74] Elsewhere, Origen propounds a double exegesis when Aquila and the LXX translate the same Hebrew

them by appealing to an imperial 'Schulphilologie', in which the epigones of the great Hellenistic scholars contented themselves with a simple enumeration of variants without arriving at the stage of textual judgement. This explanation, however, is not fully satisfactory. For Origen's objective is not to summarize material after the manner of an *epitomator*, and his point of arrival is not a *non liquet*. Rather, he employs the variants constructively in progressing towards the sense of a passage. Finally, in either case, this aspect of Origen's treatment of textual variants should not be classified under the rubric of 'Bewertungskriterien', as it is by Neuschäfer, pp. 118–19.

[72] See, in the present context, 'Origène' p. 259. Cf. 'La place', pp. 14–18, 22–3, and the preceding section of this chapter.

[73] Cf. Sgherri, 'Sulla valutazione', p. 4; Neuschäfer, *Origenes*, pp. 384–5 n. 141.

[74] See, e.g., *Sel. in Ps.* 29: 8 (*PG* 12. 1296a–b); *Comm. in Mt.* 16. 16 (GCS 40, p. 531); *Sel. in Gen.* 41: 43 (*PG* 12. 133d–136a). This last example is discussed below, pp. 101–3.

word differently, so the stereoscopic view does not derive from a textual dualism.[75] In fact, before Jerome there does not seem to have existed in the Church an appreciation of the importance of the Hebrew text taken as a whole and in its own right, and consequently, there were no real attempts to come to terms with it. Indeed, it is significant that the idea of the 'dualisme biblique' did not develop until after Jerome, and is probably best understood as a reaction to his efforts, be it in the formulation of Augustine or Barthélemy himself.[76]

Secondly, it is important to remember that a 'Hebrew + LXX' dualism does not emerge as a decisive principle in Origen's textual achievement (the Hexaplaric LXX) nor in his exegesis, both of which must be described as fundamentally 'LXX-centred'. The concept rather suggests itself on account of the fact that he sometimes seems to give equal weight to the LXX and the *recentiores* in exegetical writings. Since this is the case, if another cogent explanation can be found for the phenomenon, it would probably be preferable to claiming that Origen intuitively anticipated Augustine. Such an explanation may be found in another aspect of Origen's attitude to Scripture, namely, that which we have characterized above as a sort of 'exegetical maximalism'. The different versions provide him with another opportunity to elicit further meanings from the text.[77] But since he obviously could not comment on all the versions for every verse, Origen chooses such versions as may provide him with useful exegetical material for any given verse.[78] We have noted above that he is quite content

[75] *Comm. in Cant.* (Greek) 2 (1: 13 = GCS 33, pp. 168–9). The word in question is דוֹד, which the LXX render as ἀδελφιδός and Aquila as πατράδελφος.

[76] Barthélemy's formulation of the idea may be found in 'La place'. The only way in which one could attribute a doctrine of 'dualisme biblique' to Origen would be to reject the theory of Jellicoe mentioned above, p. 7, and conclude that Origen favoured the use of two Greek versions of the Book of Daniel. But this will have been the result of respect for tradition rather than of a deliberate policy, for he favoured no such practice with respect to the rest of the Old Testament.

[77] The *recentiores* serve a similar purpose in the exegesis of Didymus the Blind. Note the remark of L. Doutreleau in the introduction to his edition of the *Commentarii in Zachariam* found at Toura (Paris 1962 = SC 83), p. 48: 'Les variantes qu'ils [sc. the *recentiores*] apportent sont un enrichissement, puisqu'elles permettent des explications nouvelles.' Cf., with regard to Latin exegetes, B. Marti, *Übersetzer der Augustin-Zeit* (Studia et testimonia antiqua 14), Munich 1974, p. 51.

[78] Since this is the case, it will not be surprising that the *recentiores* sometimes offer readings which prove more useful for Origen than the version of the LXX. See, e.g., *Hom. in Jer.* 20. 5; *Prol. in Psalt.* 1. 13 (ed. Rietz, pp. 7–8 = PG 12. 1069c–1072b), cf. below, n. 107; *Fr. in Jer.* 14 (GCS 6, pp. 204–5); *Fr. in Lam.* 96 (GCS

to employ more than one of the *recentiores* without being concerned about which one represents the Hebrew. We have also seen
that Origen's use of the *recentiores* is primarily exegetical rather
than textual. It is therefore likely that the motivation for such a
use is to be found in the exegetical and not the textual sphere.[79]

BETWEEN ORIGEN AND JEROME

It will be evident from the preceding discussion that conflicting
tendencies are perceptible in Origen's work. On the one hand,
there was his commitment to Church tradition. On the other hand,
there were the more 'scientific' aspects of his Hexaplaric recension
of the LXX and the *Hexapla*. In the period following Origen's

6, p. 270). But such passages are rare, and do not betray a negative attitude towards
the LXX, but only a 'more positive' attitude towards the other versions. Those
scholars, such as Sgherri, who represent Origen as rejecting one text when he
gives an exegesis of another, are attempting to read textual choices into contexts
where they are not at issue. The same should probably be said of the recent
attempt by Neuschäfer, *Origenes*, pp. 119–21, 130–1, to show that Origen, in a
manner similar to that of pagan exegetes, 'evaluates' variants of the various Greek
versions on the basis of 'Bewertungskriterien' such as clarity and 'Ausdrucksstärke'
(*ἔμφασις*), and *νοῦς* (i.e. the extent to which a version corresponds to the actual
sense of a given passage). As we have already indicated, however, there is ample
evidence from Origen's own writings to show that he did not regard clarity as a
criterion for selecting the 'better' text. See the passages cited above in n. 34.
Indeed, Neuschäfer himself, pp. 283–5, points out that the consciousness of [i.e.
the respect for] the *ἀσάφεια* of the text is deeper [and more constant] in Origen
than in his pagan counterparts. For this reason, one cannot assume that clarity
was a 'Bewertungskriterium' for him on the basis of pagan parallels. With regard
to *νοῦς*, Neuschäfer, p. 131, acknowledges that this term is used in pagan philology
for the most part to introduce exegetical interpretations and not as a criterion in
evaluating variants. This is all the more reason for us to assume that Origen
employs the term in presenting nuances of exegesis and not textual choices. See
also above, n. 71.

[79] The view that Origen's use of the *Hexapla* in his commentaries is primarily
exegetical is visible already in a statement of Jerome found in the preface to his
translation of Origen's *Hom. in Cant.*: 'primum septuaginta interpretes, deinde
Aquilam, Symmachum, Theodotionem et ad extremum quintam editionem . . .
magnifice aperteque *disseruit*' (GCS 33, p. 26). Some have gone one step further
in claiming that Origen's actual objective in composing the *Hexapla* was partially
or largely exegetical rather than textual. See J. Morinus, *Exercitationum biblicarum
de Hebraei Graecique textus sinceritate libri duo*, Paris 1669, i. 4. 1. 3–4 (pp. 87–8);
and now J. Wright, 'Origen in the Scholar's Den: A Rationale for the Hexapla',
Origen of Alexandria: His World and His Legacy (Christianity and Judaism in
Antiquity 1), ed. C. Kannengiesser and W. L. Peterson, Notre Dame, Ind. 1988,
pp. 48–62.

death, as the discussions concerning the position of the LXX intensified, both tendencies were influential.

As we have seen, in *Ep.* 1. 8(4–5), Origen defends the version of the LXX on the basis of the fact that it had been sanctioned by tradition. However, this view seems to have undergone further development during the period between Origen and Jerome. For we find that Christians formed a clearer notion of the exact character of the chain of tradition by which the version of the LXX came down to them. In particular, it was thought that this chain of tradition had a specifically gentile orientation and that accordingly the LXX represented the true biblical text as a sort of 'Bible of the Gentiles'.[80]

What is the basis of this idea? It is well known that the Fathers believed that the authors of the New Testament, the Apostles, used the version of the LXX in citing the Old Testament.[81] However, it was also claimed, no doubt on the basis of this same belief, that the Apostles chose the version of the LXX for transmission to the Gentiles. That is, they not only used the version for themselves, but also commended it to the Gentiles for use by them.[82] Eusebius, for example, defending his use of the LXX as the basis of his *Chronicon*, notes that the universal [i.e. gentile] Church uses the version of the LXX because it was transmitted to it by the Apostles.[83] Theodore of Mopsuestia, in a similar defence of his own use of the LXX, cites the fact that the Apostles gave the Old Testament to the Gentiles in that version (*Comm. in Soph.* 1: 4–6). It is Rufinus, however, who explains the full significance of the apostolic use of the LXX. For he points out that the Apostles, even though they were quite capable of making their own translation, chose to use and pass down one which was already in existence, that of the LXX (*Apol. adv. Hier.* 2. 37–8). That is to say, the Apostles did not choose the LXX just because it was there,

---

[80] The following discussion (pp. 29–34) may be compared with that of Benoit, 'L'inspiration', pp. 174–9. Generally, I regard the two ideas which he discusses separately (pp. 174–7, 177–9) as intimately connected.

[81] See, e.g., Irenaeus, *Haer.* 3. 21. 3.

[82] Cf. Benoit, 'L'inspiration', pp. 177–9. However, he does not distinguish clearly between these two ideas.

[83] *Chron.*, ed. J. Karst, Leipzig 1911 (= GCS 20), p. 45. The Greek text has been preserved by G. Syncellus, *Ecloga chronographica*, ed. A. Mosshammer, Leipzig 1984, p. 100. For a convenient juxtaposition of both the (Latin translation of the) Armenian and the Greek texts, see A. Schoene's edition of *Chron.*, i, Berlin 1875, p. 96.

but their choice was conscious and deliberate. Thus, this version was specifically selected by the Apostles for transmission to the Gentiles, and accordingly obtained the status of the 'Bible of the Gentiles'.

In addition, however, this status seems to have received a sort of confirmation from the circumstances of the translation itself. That is, the version was initiated not by Jews, but by a gentile king: Ptolemy Philadelphus. In *Praeparatio evangelica* 8. 1. 6–7, Eusebius writes that God, with a view to the conversion of the Gentiles, prompted Ptolemy to sponsor the translation. For the Jews, motivated by jealousy, would not have willingly given the Old Testament to the Gentiles. Eusebius thus appears not only to regard the making of the translation as a divinely engineered preparatory step to the conversion of the Gentiles, but he also seems to see the role of the gentile king in its creation as a sort of prefiguration of that event.[84]

Accordingly, there developed the idea of a sort of gentile chain of transmission of the Old Testament, which began with the seventy translators, and extended via the Apostles to the gentile Church. In *Hom. in Heb.* 8. 4 (*PG* 63. 74), a remarkable passage, John Chrysostom seems to allude to such a chain of transmission, while referring to additional links in it. In presenting something of a history of the 'preservation' of the Old Testament, he begins with Moses and the Prophets, proceeds to the restoration of the Scriptures by Ezra,[85] and moves on to the 'economy' of the version of the LXX. He then relates that Jesus took up the writings from the LXX, the Apostles from Jesus, and the Gentiles from the Apostles. It would appear, therefore, that gentile Christians began to formulate a conception of their own chain of tradition, in a manner similar to that of the Rabbis. The chain of tradition to which the Rabbis appeal is well known, and is presented at the beginning of *Pirkei Avot*. According to this latter text, the Torah

---

[84] By emphasizing this aspect of the 'gentile' participation in the project of the translation, Eusebius would appear to go beyond Irenaeus, *Haer.* 3. 21. 1–2, and Clement, *Str.* 1. 149. 2–3. Cf. J. Chrysostom, *Hom. in Gen.* 4. 4 (*PG* 53. 43), who also sees significance in the fact that the version of the LXX was accomplished by the agency of a non-Jew.

[85] For this tradition, see IV Esr. 14, and cf. *b. Suk.* 20a; *Sif. Dev.* 48 (ed. H. S. Horovitz and L. Finkelstein, Berlin 1939, p. 112). For additional patristic references, see J.-D. Kaestli in the volume edited by him and O. Wermelinger, *Le canon de l'Ancien Testament*, Geneva 1984, pp. 72–83. Cf. also below, n. 88.

was handed down from Moses to Joshua, to the Elders, to the Prophets, to the men of the great synagogue, to Antigonus of Sokko, and finally to the 'pairs', which culminate in the schools of Hillel and Shammai. In this manner the Torah reaches the Tannaim. On comparing the two chains of transmission, it is evident that they diverge from one another not at the time of Jesus, but some three centuries earlier. This is because the branch of tradition represented by the LXX was 'left hanging' by normative Judaism, and at the same time was retroactively incorporated into the gentile Christian chain. The reasons for this latter development, as we have seen in the two preceding paragraphs, seem to have been apostolic sanction of the version of the LXX for gentile use, and the gentile role in the initiation of the version.

The reliability of the gentile chain of transmission was reinforced through reference both to the origin of that chain and to its point of arrival or purpose. The reinforcement of the chain at the point of origin was achieved via the use of the concept of oral tradition. This concept is of course more familiar in the Jewish than in the Christian context. For it is well known that according to the Rabbis, the oral as well as the written Torah was handed down via the chain of transmission described in *Pirkei Avot*.[86] Indeed, there was sometimes more emphasis on the oral tradition, for in the rabbinic view, this part of the tradition was given to the Jews alone and could not be appropriated by the Gentiles. According to Rabbi Judah b. Shalom, a Palestinian *amora* of the fifth generation, God gave the oral law because he foresaw a time when the Gentiles would translate the written Torah into Greek and claim that they, not the Jews, were Israel. When faced with the rival claimants, God would accord recognition only to those who possessed his secret knowledge (מסתורין). 'What is this? The Mishna, which was given orally.'[87]

It seems, however, that Christians formulated a particularly sophisticated response to this claim. According to Hilary of Poitiers, *Tractatus super Psalmos* 2. 2–3 (cf. 'Instructio' 8), it was the seventy translators who were the recipients of a secret, apparently

[86] See W. Bacher, *Die exegetische Terminologie der jüdischen Traditionsliteratur*, i. *Die bibelexegetische Terminologie der Tannaiten* (= *Die älteste Terminologie der jüdischen Schriftauslegung*), Leipzig 1899, pp. 106, 197.

[87] *Tan.* Ki-Tissa 34. Cf. *Tan.* Va-Yera 5; *Tan. B.* Va-Yera 6, Ki-Tissa 17; *Pes. R.* 5 (ed. M. Friedmann, Vienna 1880, p. 14b); *Shem. R.* 47. 1; *Bem. R.* 14. 10; and the discussion in E. E. Urbach, *Chazal*², Jerusalem 1971, p. 271.

oral, tradition, which extended back to Moses: 'erat autem iam a Moyse antea institutum, in synagoga omni septuaginta esse doctores. nam idem Moyses, quamvis verba Testamenti in litteras condidisset, tamen separatim quaedam ex occultis legis secretiora mysteria [cf. above, מִסְתּוֹרִין] septuaginta senioribus, qui doctores deinceps manerent, intimaverat.' The knowledge of this tradition allowed them to produce the most accurate translation of the Scriptures. And, as Hilary puts it, 'ex eo fit, ut qui postea transtulerunt [i.e. the *recentiores*] . . . magnum gentibus adtulerint errorem, dum occultae illius et a Moyse profectae traditionis ignari ea, quae ambigue lingua Hebraea commemorata sunt, incerti suis ipsis iudiciis ediderunt.' In other words, the oral tradition was indeed appropriated by the Gentiles, for it was preserved in the gentile, not the Jewish chain of transmission.[88] And it was not only appropriated, but it was incorporated into the written Greek text. Thus, the version of the LXX contained not only the biblical message, but the correct interpretation of it. In this case, the original Hebrew text would appear to be superfluous. The result of this appropriation of the oral tradition was, as stated, that the reliability of the gentile chain of transmission was reinforced at its base or point of origin.

The reliability of the chain was reinforced in a second sense,

---

[88] The text from Hilary has been discussed by N. J. Gastaldi, *Hilario de Poitiers: Exegeta del Salterio* (Institut catholique de Paris. Thèses et travaux de la faculté de théologie: Série patristique 1), Paris 1969, pp. 98–102, and more recently by M. Milhau, *Aug* 21 (1981), pp. 365–72. However, both writers fail to appreciate the significance of the passage within the context of the Jewish-Christian debate concerning the text of the Old Testament. Milhau thinks that Hilary's discussion reflects the influence of Origen and Irenaeus. But it is easier to argue that the suggestion put forward by Hilary (or his source) is an elaboration of material in *Hom. Clem.* 2. 38. 1; 3. 47. 1 (cf. *Clem. ep. Petr.* 1. 2; 3. 1–2), or some related source, according to which Moses transmitted to 70 elders an entirely oral tradition, which included law (νόμος) and explanations or solutions (ἐπιλύσεις). It seems that in the view of Hilary, however, only the explanations were given orally. Both traditions may also be related to the story in IV Esr. 14 (cf. above, n. 85), in which Ezra, when 'restoring' the Scriptures, was instructed to transmit 24 [canonical] books to all the people, but 70 additional books only to the wise (note esp. IV Esr. 14: 6 (a reference to a similar action on the part of Moses), 26, 44–8). There are important differences, however, since in *Hom. Clem.* and in Hilary the reference is to oral and not written tradition, although some scholars have seen in the '70 books' of IV Esr. an allusion not to apocryphal or apocalyptic books (the more obvious interpretation, cf. Epiphanius, *Mens.* 5, 10), but rather to an early recording of the oral tradition (see L. Ginzberg, *JJLP* 1 (1919), pp. 34–7; A. Kaminka, *MGWJ* 76 (1932), p. 510). Moreover, in *Hom. Clem.* and Hilary the non-biblical material is employed in order to interpret the canonical writings, and not as a separate tradition.

through reference to its point of arrival or purpose. For the gentile chain of transmission of the Old Testament did not represent just any tradition. It was a tradition guided by divine Providence, in order that the Gentiles be brought over to the true faith. In actual fact, this objective was undertaken by the Apostles. However, it was really a function of the entire chain of tradition. And since the LXX were part of the chain, the purpose of the Apostles, namely, the conversion of the Gentiles, must have been present in the version of the LXX as well. In other words, the LXX were not only a link in the chain of tradition, they also had a share in the 'divine economy' of that tradition.

How was this second reinforcement of the reliability of the gentile chain of transmission exploited in actual argument? It was claimed that a translation which God had employed to bring the Gentiles over to the recognition of the living God must be correct. However, this idea of 'correct' was understood in two senses. On the one hand, it is the accuracy of the translation and the exactness of the representation of the Hebrew text that is guaranteed by the place of the LXX in the divine economy. We should sooner believe that Aquila or Symmachus have made errors than the LXX, who have produced their version for the salvation of mankind. Such an idea, although perhaps prefigured in Philo, *De vita Mosis* 2. 36–40, is first explicitly formulated by Eusebius in *PE* 8. 1. 6. He explains that God, foreseeing the conversion of the Gentiles, made sure that an accurate translation was available well in advance.[89] Thus the gentile chain of transmission of the Old Testament was a reliable one; that is to say, those who had a role in it did indeed transmit what they had received.

On the other hand, Christians were also conscious of the fact that their chain of tradition, in which the LXX played a key role, was dynamic. For it involved the transfer of the heritage of the old Israel, the Jews, to a new Israel, the Gentiles. Accordingly, it would be conceivable that any changes in the original message might be connected specifically with this transfer, and indeed motivated by it. And since the transfer of the message was part of the divine economy, the changes would naturally be as well. In other words, the position of the version of the LXX as the 'Bible

---

[89] Eusebius here again may be elaborating ideas found in Irenaeus, *Haer.* 3. 21. 2–3. For Irenaeus, however, the accuracy of the version of the LXX seems to be less dependent on the purpose for which the version was intended than on other considerations.

of the Gentiles' guaranteed not only the accuracy of the translation. It also guaranteed the reliability of any changes which the translators made with respect to their original. For it was thought that the version of the LXX represented a special dispensation for gentile Christians, which went beyond a mere translation. This second principle, although perceptible in Origen (*Hom. in Lev.* 12. 5), seems to have been first explicitly stated by Epiphanius.[90] However, it is most eloquently formulated by Augustine: 'even if one finds something in the Hebrew text which differs from what they [sc. the LXX] have written, I think one must cede priority to the divine dispensation which was accomplished through the latter translators. . . . it is possible that they have translated in the manner which the Holy Spirit, who guided them and gave one voice to them all, judged to be appropriate for Gentiles' (*Doct. Chr.* 2. 22). Here again, the implication is that the Hebrew text has been rendered obsolete.

Despite the development of such a sophisticated view of the tradition by which the Old Testament was transmitted to the Church, and a corresponding strengthening of the position of the LXX within the Church based on a heightened consciousness of that tradition, there can be no doubt that at the same time Origen's Hexaplaric recension of the LXX and his *Hexapla* raised the question of the Hebrew text for Christian scholarship in an unprecedented manner. First, as already noted, the importance, if not the priority of the Hebrew is implied in the Hexaplaric LXX, where it is employed as a criterion in correcting the LXX. Secondly, the inclusion of additional Greek versions of the original could imply that the LXX did not have a monopoly on the correct translation. Thirdly, the fact that the Hebrew text itself was contained in the synopsis might suggest to some that it was a worthy object of study. Nevertheless, it appears that the established position of the LXX within the Church, particularly as the awareness of the process by which that position had been achieved was deepened, may have prevented these implications of Origen's textual achievements from being fully understood.

The Hexaplaric text of the LXX was endorsed by Origen's successors in Caesarea, Pamphilus and Eusebius, and achieved

[90] *Mens.* 6. Cf. H. Karpp, '"Prophet" oder "Dolmetscher"', *Festschrift für Günther Dehn*, Neukirchen Kreis Moers 1957, p. 109.

a fairly wide influence.[91] However, this text did not achieve any kind of official status, nor did its appearance deter further recensional activity. At the end of the fourth century, Jerome tells us that recensions which circulated under the names of Lucian and Hesychius, both of whom flourished in the latter part of the third and early part of the fourth century, enjoyed dominant positions in Asia and Egypt respectively. The Origenian recension, on the other hand, held the field only in Palestine and its vicinity. This situation, in which three eastern regions each followed a different text, is described by Jerome as a 'trifaria varietas' (*Praef. in Par.* (*IH*) 9–12). There has been considerable debate concerning the existence and character of the 'Lucianic' and 'Hesychian' recensions.[92] Nevertheless, at least with regard to the 'Lucianic recension', recent research has shown that 'Hebraization' played only a minor role.[93] It would appear, therefore, that the propagation of the Origenian recension did not lead to the view that the Hebrew text had a central role to play in serious textual endeavours. In fact, even where the Hexaplaric text was received, it was not always understood to imply the priority or even the importance of the Hebrew. For example, Epiphanius seems to have thought that Origen's purpose was to prove the exactitude of the Scriptures used in the Church, i.e. the LXX (*Mens.* 2; cf. 17). Similarly, for Rufinus, Origen's intention in introducing the critical signs had been simply to indicate 'ea quae per alios interpretes sive perempta fuerant seu etiam abundantius prolata' (*Apol. adv. Hier.* 2. 40).

Although the *Hexapla* itself did stimulate interest in the *recentiores*, many serious biblical scholars did not make extensive use of them.[94] The Cappadocian Fathers, followers of Origen in many respects, do not employ these versions in any systematic fashion.[95] Didymus the Blind, whose use of the *recentiores* is attested by

[91] See D. S. Wallace-Hadrill, *Eusebius of Caesarea*, London 1960, pp. 60–1; Nautin, *Origène*, pp. 354–7. Jellicoe, *The Septuagint*, p. 146, notes that another supporter of the Hexaplaric LXX was Basil of Caesarea.

[92] For a recent treatment of these recensions, see Munnich, *La Bible grecque*, pp. 168–72.

[93] See the conclusions of J. Ziegler as conveniently summarized by (J.-)D. Barthélemy, 'Les problèmes textuels de 2 Sam 11,2–1 Rois 2,11 reconsidérés à la lumière de certaines critiques des *Devanciers d'Aquila*', *1972 Proceedings: IOSCS/Pseudepigrapha* (1972 = SCSt 2), ed. R. A. Kraft, pp. 64–70.

[94] Cf. Augustine's remark in *Civ.* 18. 43 that most Greeks were unaware of the existence of versions other than the LXX.

[95] The assessment of B. de Montfaucon, *PG* 15. 118d, is essentially correct, if somewhat overstated (cf. H. Weiss, *Die grossen Kappadocier Basilius, Gregor von Nazianz und Gregor von Nyssa als Exegeten*, Braunsberg 1872, pp. 36–40).

Jerome in *Adversus Rufinum* 2. 34, in fact refers to them only sparingly.[96] Even Theodore of Mopsuestia does not seem to have utilized them outside of his *Comm. in Ps.*[97] When these versions are cited, they are used for the most part in the same manner as by Origen, viz. not as the means to arrive at the original Hebrew, but as additional aids in understanding the LXX.[98] Indeed, this method of employing the *recentiores* is explicitly endorsed by some Fathers.[99] The same practice is mentioned by Jerome when he discusses the use of the later versions on the part of the Greeks (*Praef. in Is.* 19–21).

There were of course cases when the LXX and the *recentiores* were at variance. The interesting point to note is that this opposition stimulated less curiosity about the original text than attempts to prove the greater authority of the LXX. For the most part, non-philological considerations are involved. For example, it was pointed out that the LXX undertook their version before the birth of Jesus, so there was no question of prejudice on their part.[100] The later translators, on the other hand, corrupted the biblical testimonies which referred to Christ.[101] Indeed, it is the view of Epiphanius that Aquila undertook his version with precisely such a purpose in mind (*Mens.* 15). The Fathers also appealed to the number of seventy translators as opposed to only three *recentiores*.[102] What is more, the LXX were all in agreement, whereas the later translators often disagreed among themselves.[103] So much

[96] Cf. Jay, *L'exégèse*, p. 125. Generally, the new commentaries discovered at Toura have contributed little to our knowledge of the *recentiores*.

[97] See J.-N. Guinot in the introduction to his edition of Theodoret, *Comm. in Is.* (Paris 1980 = SC 276), pp. 53–4 n. 4.

[98] See H. Kihn, *Theodor von Mopsuestia und Junilius Africanus als Exegeten*, Freiburg im Breisgau 1880, pp. 91–2, on Theodore; Guinot, op. cit., pp. 54–5, on Theodoret; M. Simonetti, *RSLR* 19 (1983), pp. 39–40, on Eusebius. Cf., with regard to Ambrose, L. F. Pizzolato, *La dottrina esegetica di sant'Ambrogio* (SPMed 9), Milan 1978, pp. 215–20.

[99] Hilary, *Psal. 118* He 13 (see the new edition and translation of Milhau (Paris 1988 = SC 344), pp. 214–16); Augustine, *Doct. Chr.* 2. 22. Cf. Bar Hebraeus, *Scholia in Vetus Testamentum* prol. (based ultimately on a Greek source?).

[100] See Hilary, *Psal.* 2. 3; Chrysostom, *Hom. in Mt.* 5. 2 (*PG* 57. 57); Theodoret, *Comm. in Is.* 3 (7: 14). Note already Irenaeus, *Haer.* 3. 21. 1, 3.

[101] See Chrysostom, loc. cit.; Augustine, *Ep.* 82. 34; Theodoret, loc. cit.

[102] Epiphanius, *Mens.* 17; Chrysostom, loc. cit.; Theodoret, loc. cit. A similar argument was employed by Augustine against the version of Jerome in *Civ.* 18. 43, and by Theodore of Mopsuestia against that of 'the Syrian' in *Comm. in Soph.* 1: 4–6.

[103] See Epiphanius, *Mens.* 17; Chrysostom, loc. cit.; Augustine, *Ep.* 28. 2; Theodoret, loc. cit.

did these views take hold that a tradition developed according to which Origen placed the LXX in the middle of the *Hexapla* in order to refute the other translations.[104]

On the other hand, it has been pointed out by Barthélemy that there are a few occasions in Eusebius' *Comm. in Ps.* where the Father prefers the *recentiores* to the LXX on the basis of a clearer Christological or messianic allusion, and similar instances in the *Comm. in Is.* have been noted by M. Simonetti.[105] However, no textual consequences are drawn from such observations. It is true that this phenomenon is cited by Jerome in his defence of the 'Hebraica veritas', although he tries to emphasize that the allusions to Christ are to be found in the Hebrew as well as in the *recentiores*. Nevertheless, it seems unlikely that this aspect of the exegesis of Eusebius represents a significant step beyond the position of Origen in the direction of that of Jerome.[106] First of all, Origen himself was hardly unaware that the versions of the *recentiores* were sometimes more suitable for a Christian interpretation.[107] Secondly, as we shall see below, the recognition of this fact on the part of Jerome was less a central moment in his 'conversion' to the Hebrew text than an incidental feature of Eusebius' exegesis which he exploited for his own ends.[108] And in general, we have already seen that Eusebius accords a privileged position to the version of the LXX on the basis of the fact that it was approved by the Apostles, and served as a vehicle for the conversion of the Gentiles according to divine plan. Indeed, he expresses his own preference for the LXX against the Hebrew in a quite unambiguous fashion in the *Chronicon*, and also alludes on occasion to the 'unanimity' of the LXX.[109] His textual position was probably not

---

[104] See Epiphanius, *Mens.* 19. Cf. Filastrius, *Diversarum haereseon liber* 142. 4.

[105] Barthélemy, 'Eusèbe, la Septante et "les autres"', *La Bible et les Pères*, Paris 1971, pp. 53–6; Simonetti, *RSLR* 19 (1983), pp. 40–1. Cf. Wallace-Hadrill, *Eusebius*, p. 62; Barnes, *Constantine*, p. 102.

[106] This seems to be the view of Barthélemy, 'Eusèbe', pp. 63–5.

[107] See *Prol. in Psalt.* 1. 13, in Rietz, op. cit. (n. 64 above), pp. 7–8 (= *PG* 12. 1069c–1072b), and the comments of the latter, pp. 36–7. Cf. Barthélemy himself, 'Eusèbe', pp. 51–3. Note a similar awareness on the part of Eusebius of Emesa, *CS* G 189.

[108] See below, pp. 64–7.

[109] *Chron.*, ed. Karst, pp. 39–40, 44–5. Eusebius refers to the 'unanimity' of the translators in *DE* 5. Prooem. 35, and in a Greek fragment of *Chron.* cited by Wendland in his edition of the *Letter of Aristeas* (Leipzig 1900) pp. 128–9 (the corresponding (translation of the) Armenian text is found on p. 37 of Karst's edition). However, Eusebius need not be following the legendary account of a

very far removed from that of Origen, as is apparent from his part in the propagation of the separate Hexaplaric LXX, and his use of Origen's recension in his commentaries.[110]

The presence of the Hebrew text in the *Hexapla* does not seem to have stimulated the Greeks to come to terms with the original language of the Bible any more than the presence of the various translations. To what extent such an interest was lacking among the Greeks can be measured from how little is preserved of the Hebrew column(s) of the *Hexapla* in proportion to what remains of the *recentiores*. This failure to appreciate the significance of the original can also be seen from the way in which even those Fathers who are said to have known Hebrew apply their knowledge of it. For it is generally employed as are the *recentiores*—that is, to throw light on the LXX.[111]

In contrast to this general tendency stands the approach of certain members of the Antiochene school. In particular, Eusebius of Emesa shows an interest in the Hebrew text perhaps unparalleled in any Greek Father. Nevertheless, in actual practice Eusebius does not seem to have accorded a real priority to the Hebrew, since he shows just as much interest in 'the Syrian' text, and still uses the LXX as the central text of his exegesis. In addition, he seems to have approached the Hebrew text via indirect means.[112]

miraculous unanimity between translators working in separate cells, as Wendland seems to think (cf. also H. Gelzer, *Sextus Julius Africanus und die byzantinische Chronographie*, ii. 1, Leipzig 1885, p. 39). Rather, in view of the fact that he generally avoids mention of this legend, it seems more prudent to follow B. Donatus and conclude that the reference is to a unanimity which was achieved on the basis of consultation between the translators. In his rendering of the phrase, ἑβδομήκοντα δ' οὖν ἄνδρες ἀθρόως Ἑβραῖοι συμφώνως αὐτὰς μεταβεβλήκασιν, which appears in the passage of *DE*, Donatus seems to see in the word ἀθρόως a reference to that consultation which, as related in the *Letter of Aristeas* 302, was the source of unanimous versions. See *PG* 22. 347–8c. And in fact, the use of the word συμφώνως reflects the phraseology of the same passage of the *Letter of Aristeas* (cf. §§ 32, 39). Nevertheless, the context of the statement in *DE* indicates that unanimity is cited by Eusebius as a reason to prefer the version of the LXX to other versions, just as it is by the writers cited above, n. 103. For this reason, the suggestion of Nautin, *Origène*, p. 321, that Epiphanius' explanation of the order of the *Hexapla* (see above, pp. 36–7) may go back to Pamphilus and Eusebius should be seriously considered.

[110] See Wallace-Hadrill, *Eusebius*, p. 61. For Eusebius' use of the Hexaplaric LXX in his *Comm. in Is.*, see Ziegler in his introduction to the edition of that text (Berlin 1975 = GCS Eusebius, ix), pp. xxxv-xxxvi.

[111] Cf. G. Jouassard, *StPatr* i (1957 = TU 63), p. 312 n. 1.

[112] The method of Eusebius of Emesa will be discussed in detail below in the third section of Ch. 5.

More importantly, however, the insights of Eusebius were not developed or elaborated within the Antiochene school. While his method was pursued to a degree by his pupil Diodore of Tarsus, the pupil of the latter, Theodore of Mopsuestia, perhaps the most influential of all representatives of the Antiochene school, seems to have reacted against it.

Whether this is because he rejected the arbitrary fashion in which Eusebius and Diodore employed the LXX, the Hebrew, and 'the Syrian' is not certain. Yet it is clear that he gradually formulated a more monolithic approach. On the one hand, he expressly acknowledges the priority of the Hebrew.[113] Nevertheless, he thought that access to the Hebrew was to be best obtained via the version of the LXX, because in his view this was the most accurate and literal translation. Indeed, it is the literal character of the LXX that sets it above the work of Symmachus.[114] His high regard for the reliability of the LXX with respect to accurate representation of the Hebrew is also clear from his intimation that those who prefer the version of 'the Syrian' to that of the LXX in a passage of Habakkuk have abandoned the Hebrew text (*Comm. in Hab.* 2: 11). In general, the version of 'the Syrian' was viewed in a particularly negative light by Theodore. It is his view that 'the Syrian' translator came up with what we should probably term 'exegetical' renderings when he did not understand the Hebrew text (*Comm. in Hab.* 2: 11, *Comm. in Soph.* 3: 2). That is, Theodore seems to have regarded these readings as insignificant *lectiones faciliores*. That he took such a harsh stance concerning 'the Syrian' is noteworthy, and in all probability it was stimulated by what in his view was an excessive use of that version on the part of Eusebius of Emesa and Diodore.[115] Finally, Theodore

---

[113] *Comm. in Ps.* 35: 2a (ed. R. Devreesse, Città del Vaticano 1939 (= StT 93), p. 195).

[114] See *Comm. in Ps.* 55: 7 (ed. Devreesse, pp. 365–6).

[115] It is now generally agreed that the version of 'the Syrian' to which Theodore refers is not different from the text cited by other exegetes as ὁ Σύρος, and that this text was an 'Old Syriac' translation or the Peshitta itself rather than a Greek version. See H. N. Sprenger in the introduction to his edition of Theodore's *Comm. in XII Prophetas* (Wiesbaden 1977 = GOF/5. Reihe: Biblica et patristica 1), pp. 79–83; Guinot, op. cit. (n. 97 above), p. 49 n. 1; H. J. Lehmann, 'The Syriac Translation of the Old Testament—as Evidenced around the Middle of the Fourth Century (in Eusebius of Emesa)', *Scandinavian Journal of the Old Testament* 1987. 1, pp. 66–86; id., 'Evidence of the Syriac Bible Translation in Greek Fathers of the 4th and 5th Centuries', *StPatr* 19 (1989), pp. 366–71.

ridicules the translation of Jerome as the product of a person without adequate knowledge of Hebrew and incompetent as an exegete.[116] Effectively, therefore, while acknowledging the supreme authority of the Hebrew, Theodore seems to have ruled out access to that text via means other than the LXX, such as a plurality of versions or direct consultation. The result is a return to a stricter dependence on the LXX on 'scientific' grounds. Indeed, Theodore bases his system of exegesis on a close analysis of the linguistic characteristics of the LXX, on the assumption that it was in this version that the original was reflected most accurately.[117]

In short, we find that in the Greek world, between the time of Origen and Jerome, there was little movement in the direction of the Hebrew text. Despite the questions raised by various aspects of Origen's textual work, the furthest most were prepared to go was to adopt the position of the master. If the Antiochenes ventured beyond, they did so in a restricted fashion. It was in fact only in the Latin world that the implications of the *Hexapla* and the Hexaplaric LXX were fully understood.

[116] Theodore's criticisms of Jerome survive in Photius, *Bibliotheca*, cod. 177 (121b–122a). Cf. Kihn, *Theodor*, pp. 90–1; F. Cavallera, *Saint Jérôme: Sa vie et son œuvre*, i. 2 (SSL 2), Louvain 1922, p. 115.

[117] For the 'system' of Theodore, see R. Devreesse, *Essai sur Théodore de Mopsueste* (StT 141), Città del Vaticano 1948, pp. 58–68; Chr. Schäublin, *Untersuchungen zu Methode und Herkunft der antiochenischen Exegese* (Theoph 23), Cologne 1974, pp. 95–147 (esp. pp. 123–36). This system, and other aspects of Theodore's views noted above, are already visible in *Comm. in Ps.*, his first work (for the chronology, see J. M. Vosté, *RB* 34 (1925), pp. 70–2). Accordingly, it is possible that his use of the *recentiores* (and indeed 'the Syrian') in this commentary (as compared with a neglect of these versions in subsequent exegetical writings, see above, p. 36 with n. 97) is a remnant of the methods of his teachers. Theodore himself does characterize *Comm. in Ps.* as the work of a beginner (see Devreesse, *Essai*, p. 28). Cf., on this question, L. Pirot, *L'œuvre exégétique de Théodore de Mopsueste*, Rome 1913, pp. 102–4, and Sprenger, op. cit. (n. 115 above), pp. 72–4.

2

Jerome and the Problem of the Text of the Old Testament

◆ ◆ ◆

THE 'CONVERSION' TO THE HEBREW

Jerome began the study of Hebrew at an early point in his career. Living the life of a hermit in the desert of Chalcis during approximately the years 375–7, he began learning Hebrew from a Jewish convert to Christianity.[1] His continuing work in the language is attested by his remarks in the preface to the translation of the *Chronicon* of Eusebius, a work which he produced in Constantinople around 380.[2] But it was during his stay in Rome (*c*.382–5) that Jerome seems to have consolidated his knowledge of Hebrew and began propagating his position concerning the importance of the Hebrew text for biblical study. This is most evident from the letters which he wrote during this period.

In perfecting his knowledge of Hebrew, Jerome exploited all possible resources. First of all, he seems to have concentrated his efforts on collecting whatever information was available about Hebrew matters from Christian Greek exegetical sources. For some of his letters reveal dependence on these sources.[3] Nevertheless, most of the letters in which this dependence is visible concern matters which require a knowledge of Hebrew even for readers of the Greek text. The subject of *Ep.* 26 and 29 is Hebrew words which appear in the Greek and Latin versions in transliterated form, such as *amen* and *ephod*. Similarly in *Ep.* 25, Jerome explains the different Hebrew names of God. These names are also found in transliteration, in most cases in the LXX and in any case in the

---

[1] Jerome describes his first Hebrew studies in *Ep.* 125. 12. Concerning his stay in the desert of Chalcis, see J. N. D. Kelly, *Jerome: His Life, Writings, and Controversies*, London 1975, pp. 46–56; J. H. D. Scourfield, *JThS* 37 (1986), pp. 117–21.

[2] For the date, see Cavallera, *Saint Jérôme*, i. 2, p. 20.

[3] See Nautin, *Origène*, pp. 284–8; Marti, *Übersetzer*, pp. 152, 155, 161–2, 165.

recentiores.[4] The Hebrew alphabet, the subject of *Ep*. 30, is known
to the Greek reader from Ps. 118. In other words, Greek material
was available in cases where a knowledge of Hebrew was important
for the understanding of the Greek text. That Jerome found such
material insufficient for a comprehensive study of the Hebrew text
seems clear from the fact that he also employed a more direct
approach. He undertook a collation of Aquila's version with the
Hebrew text (*Ep*. 32), and borrowed certain manuscripts from
a local synagogue (*Ep*. 36. 1). Indeed, Jerome's immersion in
Hebrew was so intense during these years that he claims that his
Latin had suffered as a result of his studies.[5]

And Jerome did not merely attempt to acquire a knowledge of
Hebrew for himself. He began putting forward in his letters his
position that the Hebrew text is the key to understanding the
Scriptures. When faced with exegetical questions raised by his
correspondents, he gives them answers based on the Hebrew text
(*Ep*. 20; 28; 34). Errors of other commentators are attributed to
their ignorance of Hebrew or failure to inform themselves about
Hebrew matters (*Ep*. 34. 3; 37. 3). Finally, Jerome's phraseology
indicates that the emotional fervour with which he embraced the
Hebrew text goes back to at least the 'Roman' period. Now, it
may be true that the expression 'Hebraica veritas' is first attested
in the preface to the *Quaestiones Hebraicae in Genesim*, written
c.391–2.[6] Nevertheless, the concept is already present in the
Roman letters. In *Ep*. 20. 2, we read the statement, 'ex Hebraeis
codicibus veritas exprimenda est.' At the end of the same letter,
in which he employs the Hebrew text extensively, he notes, 'con-
decet ob veritatem laborare paulisper et peregrino aurem adcom-
modare sermoni' (*Ep*. 20. 6). Elsewhere, after explaining the sense
of the Hebrew expression 'leem aasabim', he writes, 'cum ita se
veritas habeat, . . .' (*Ep*. 34. 2). That Jerome's crusade was at least

---

[4] Cf. Basil, *Eun*. 2. 7 (*PG* 29. 585a)

[5] *Ep*. 29. 7. Irenaeus, in a similar vein, asks his addressee not to expect a high
quality of language [i.e. Greek] from one who lives 'among the Celts' (*Haer*.
1. prol.). The existence of such a precedent, however, does not in and of itself
invalidate the legitimacy of similar sentiments expressed by others, and therefore
need not cast doubt on the sincerity of Jerome's claim.

[6] Cf. Jay, *L'exégèse*, p. 89, who points out that the expression 'veritas Hebraici
sensus' appears in *Comm. in Eccl*. 8: 13. Note also the preface to this commentary,
where Jerome characterizes the Hebrew text as the 'fons veritatis'. The work is
generally dated to *c*.388.

partially successful is clear from the fact that some of his students began to study the Bible in the original.[7]

Why did Jerome attach so much importance to the study of the Hebrew text when no one before him in the Greek Church had done so? It seems that there can only be one explanation for this. He was part of a culture in which sensitivity to a foreign language was an integral element. The Romans had developed one of the most sophisticated bilingual cultures in the history of man. Jerome was heir to that culture, and in fact, as is clear from the researches of P. Courcelle, was perhaps its most significant representative in his own epoch.[8] The Greeks, on the other hand, did not possess such a level of sophistication when it came to the study of foreign languages. Their culture had always been monolingual.[9] Indeed, this seems to be what Jerome has in mind when he notes that Origen undertook the study of Hebrew 'contra gentis suae naturam'.[10] We should therefore not be surprised if it was a Latin rather than a Greek who realized the full implications of the fact that the Bible was written in Hebrew.[11]

That it was a fundamental difference in approach to linguistic matters that separated Jerome from almost all of the Greek Fathers can be determined from an examination of the major factors which led him to appreciate the importance of the Hebrew text in the first place. What were these factors? One way to go about

---

[7] See *Ep.* 29. 1; 39. 1. For the position defended in the preceding paragraphs, see also A. Allgeier, *Bib* 12 (1931), pp. 456–66. Cf. F. Stummer, *Einführung in die lateinische Bibel*, Paderborn 1928, p. 91.

[8] *Les lettres grecques*, pp. 37–115. Cf. G. Bardy, *La question des langues dans l'Église ancienne*, i, Paris 1948, pp. 206–7.

[9] See H. I. Marrou, *Histoire de l'éducation dans l'antiquité⁶*, Paris 1965, pp. 374–9. Cf. Schäublin, *Untersuchungen*, pp. 124–5.

[10] *Vir. ill.* 54. Jerome is probably dependent on the testimony of Porphyry as reported by Eusebius, *HE* 6. 19. 7, according to which Origen was a 'Hellene'.

[11] It is interesting to note that he who came closest to Jerome in depth of linguistic sensitivity was Eusebius of Emesa, also a representative of a bilingual culture. Yet neither the work of Eusebius nor that of Jerome led to any attempt on the part of the Greeks to develop a Hebrew philology. Concerning the legacy of Eusebius, see above, pp. 39–40, and below, pp. 131–3. With regard to Jerome, it may be said that with few exceptions (see Barthélemy, *ThZ* 16 (1960), pp. 342–53), his work had little or no influence in the East. See Jouassard, *StPatr* 1 (1957 = TU 63), pp. 312–13. In the Latin world, on the other hand, Augustine, although loath to give up belief in the inspiration of the LXX (see *Civ.* 18. 42–3), did at least recognize the problem. In *Doct. Chr.* 2. 16, he writes as follows: 'contra ignota signa propria magnum remedium est linguarum cognitio. et Latinae quidem linguae homines . . . duabus aliis ad scripturarum divinarum cognitionem opus habent, Hebraea scilicet et Graeca.'

answering this question is to see which of the arguments which he employs in the 390s to defend his use of the original appear already in the writings of the earlier period. Two themes stand out.

In the preface to *QHG*, written *c*.391–2, he appeals to the differences between the LXX and the *recentiores* in justifying his own use of the original. The key to understanding this argument, however, lies in a pronouncement made some ten years earlier. In the preface to his version of Eusebius' *Chronicon*, in order to show how difficult translation can be, Jerome claims that Aquila, Symmachus, and Theodotion, while producing vastly different versions, decided to translate anew precisely because they were unsatisfied with the extent to which the translation of the LXX diverged from the original. In other words, he was at this time also aware of the great differences between the LXX and the *recentiores*. Indeed, his extensive experience of such differences is attested in *Ep.* 18b, which dates to roughly the same period.[12] For Jerome, however, in contrast to most Greek Fathers who lived in a 'post-Hexaplar' world, these lateral differences were indicative of a great gap between version and original. It would seem logical to conclude that his awareness of this gap was a chief factor in impressing upon him the urgency of a return to the Hebrew at this early date.

The principle which Jerome applies here goes back to Origen. In his textual work on the LXX, Origen established that when one is faced with variations of translation in a given text, one must return to the original.[13] However, the point of departure for Origen was the variant readings in the LXX, and his point of arrival was a corrected version of that text. For Jerome, on the other hand, the point of departure was the differences between the LXX and the *recentiores*. These differences led him to conclude that the foundation for any serious biblical research was the Hebrew text. Contrary to prevalent custom, he seems to have been instinctively willing to put the *recentiores* on an equal footing with the LXX.

That the reason for this was his experience with translations from Greek to Latin is suggested by the same preface to the

---

[12] For the date, see Cavallera, *Saint Jérôme*, i. 2, pp. 21–2; Kelly, *Jerome*, p. 78.

[13] Jerome's awareness of Origen's method as described in *Comm. in Mt.* 15. 14 is evident from his *Praef. in Evang.* 14–16, where we find an echo of the former passage. See the note of E. Klostermann in his edition of *Comm. in Mt.* (Leipzig 1935–7 = GCS 40), p. 387.

Chronicon. For he discusses the question of Old Testament versions within the context of his discussion of translation from Greek to Latin. In practice as well, he puts all translation in the same category and applies 'Origen's principle' to different kinds of text in the same manner. This is most clearly manifest in the language which Jerome employs in this period. He refers to original texts of every sort in like manner as 'fontes', whereas translations or opinions based on them are characterized as 'rivuli' or the equivalent.[14] The Hebrew text is described as 'fons' in *Ep.* 20. 2 and 34. 4, just as the Greek text of the New Testament is in *Praefatio in Evangelia* and *Ep.* 27. 1. In the same period or slightly later, in the preface to his translation of Didymus' *De spiritu sancto*, he claims that his own version will allow the reader to distinguish the 'fontes' from the adaptation of Ambrose, described as 'rivuli'.[15] Still later, in 388, he describes the Hebrew text as the 'fons veritatis', whereas the translations are represented as 'rivuli opinionum' (*Comm. in Eccl.* prol.). Probably around the same date, he uses similar language with respect to his revision of the Psalter based on the Hexaplaric LXX, contrasting the 'fons' to the 'turbulentus rivus' of the Old Latin version (*Praef. in Ps.* (*iuxta LXX*) 15–17). This last example is important, for it shows that when Jerome applied 'Origen's principle' to the current Latin versions of the Old Testament, he was aware that the LXX constituted the 'fons' (cf. *Helv.* 8 (*PL* 23. 200d–201a)). If, therefore, the principle could be equally applied to both the Latin and the Greek versions of the Old Testament, why was Jerome so much more preoccupied with the Greek versions than he was with the Latin, even at this early period in his career? The answer to this question lies in the second theme to which we have alluded above (p. 44).

This second theme is closely related to the first. In his *Praef. in libros Salomonis* (*IH*), written *c*.396, Jerome notes that while his own version has been translated from the original source, the Old Latin has been 'poured into the third jar' (ll. 24–5), i.e. it is removed two degrees from the original. He mentions the same phenomenon in his *Praef. in Evang.*, which dates to *c*.384, pointing out that the Old Testament 'tertio gradu ad nos usque pervenit' (ll. 16–18). This fact probably constituted a key factor in his original 'conversion' to the Hebrew. For he seems to refer to it in

---

[14] For the use of this imagery, see Marti, *Übersetzer*, p. 157.

[15] See the new edition of this preface published by Doutreleau, *ΑΛΕΞΑΝΔΡΙΝΑ* (*FS* C. Mondésert), Paris 1987, p. 306.

the preface to the translation of the *Chronicon*. While discussing
the intelligibility of the Bible, he notes, 'haec cum Graece legimus,
aliud quiddam sonant, cum Latine, penitus non haerent.'[16] It
seems again that Jerome's ability to grasp the extent of the 'ver-
tical' gap separating the Latin from the Greek allowed him to
reach an awareness of the gap between the Hebrew and the Greek
which was more profound than that of the Greek Fathers. The
return to the Hebrew was a result of that awareness.[17] In addition,
the 'double distance' between the Hebrew and the Latin led him
to believe that translations are ideally made from original texts
and not from texts that are themselves translations. As he would
later argue, if the Latin version of the New Testament is based
on the Greek original, so must the Latin version of the Old
Testament be based on the Hebrew original (*Ep.* 112. 20; cf. *Ep.*
71. 5; 106. 2).

One final observation may be in order here. The return to the
Hebrew undertaken by Jerome should also be seen as a character-
istically Latin solution to what may be termed the 'literary problem'. It is well known that cultivated Greek and Latin readers
had a good deal of difficulty finding literary merit in the Bible.
This was chiefly because of the extremely low level of biblical
style as it appears in Greek and Latin form.[18] Christian writers,
as E. Norden has pointed out, formulated two different responses
to this problem.[19] The standard approach, which has its roots in
the New Testament itself, was to admit the absence of art in the
biblical style, yet to insist that form is of limited relevance in
comparison with content. It is the greatness of the biblical message
that one should consider, and the Bible was written in a simple
style in order that its teachings would be accessible to all. State-

---

[16] For a different interpretation of this passage, see Meershoek, *Le latin*,
pp. 22–3.

[17] In other Latin writers before Jerome, we do find an awareness of the gap
between the Latin and the Greek, and even inklings of a consciousness of the gap
between the Greek and the Hebrew. See the passages from Hilary cited by
Meershoek, *Le latin*, p. 28, and the passage from Ambrose (*Psal.* 37. 49) cited by
Marti, *Übersetzer*, p. 60 (in view of the late date of the latter passage, it may reflect
the influence of Jerome). Yet these writers were generally content with a return
to the Greek.

[18] See now G. Rinaldi, *Biblia gentium*, Rome 1989, pp. 168–70, 171–2, 173–5.

[19] *Die antike Kunstprosa*, Leipzig 1898, pp. 521–8. Although Norden presents
his discussion under the rubric, 'Theorien über die Sprache des Neuen Testaments', many of the passages cited by him in fact relate to the language of Scripture
in general, or to the language of the Old Testament in particular.

ments to this effect are found in many Christian writers, and it is
not surprising that they are echoed by Jerome as well.[20] But there
was also a second approach, which involved the claim that the
Bible did in fact possess literary quality. It was with regard to this
claim that Jerome made his real contribution. Of course already
Philo and Josephus had said that Hebrew poetry was written in
metre, and this assertion was repeated by later writers.[21] In a
similar vein, Origen tells Celsus that the Jewish writings were
composed in a respectable style in the original Hebrew.[22]

However, statements such as these had little or no impact in
the Greek world.[23] Indeed, the extent to which they were ignored
is indicated by subsequent events. In the year 362, Julian the
Apostate prohibited Christians from teaching classical literature
and bid them turn to the exposition of Matthew and Luke.[24] In
response, Apollinaris of Laodicea, later Jerome's teacher, and his
father undertook to rewrite the Bible in a variety of Greek literary
genres.[25] In other words, Greek-speaking Christians essentially
accepted the proposition that the Bible did not constitute a work
of literature.[26] Indeed, this admission is consistent with the first
approach to the 'literary problem' outlined by Norden. And a
'literary' solution to the problem was not to be sought by turning
to the original, but by transforming the Greek Bible and rewriting
it in a style and in literary forms acceptable to classical tastes. The
Greeks were for the most part simply unable to accept 'barbarian'
works of literature as such. Not so the Latins. Just shortly after

[20] See Meershoek, *Le latin*, pp. 4–10.

[21] For a dossier of the Jewish-Hellenistic and patristic passages concerning this
question, see S. Euringer, *Die Kunstform der althebräischen Poesie* (BZfr 5. 9–10),
Münster in Westfalen 1912, pp. 7–17. Note the pre-eminent position occupied
by statements of Jerome. For further discussion of these, see G. Castellino, *Bib*
15 (1934), pp. 505–16. I am indebted to my colleague, Alan Cooper, for these
references.

[22] *Cels.* 7. 59. The passage is noted by Marti, *Übersetzer*, p. 90. Cf. Eusebius,
PE 11. 5. 2.

[23] It is true that the 'Versuche aus dem ἄτεχνον ein τεχνικόν zu machen' were
carried forward by Theodore of Mopsuestia (see Schäublin, *Untersuchungen*,
pp. 109–23) and Hadrian, and as Norden has noted, op. cit. (n. 19 above),
pp. 526–8, by Augustine. Yet these authors essentially undertook to collect rhetorical figures and σχήματα as they appear in Greek and Latin form, and not to arrive
at an appreciation of the literary merits of the Hebrew.

[24] For references to the sources concerning Julian's school law and discussion,
see B. C. Hardy, *ChH* 37 (1968), pp. 131–43.

[25] See Socrates, *HE* 3. 16; Sozomen, *HE* 5. 18.

[26] See L. Alonso Schökel, *RF* 157 (1958), p. 469.

Apollinaris produced his works, Jerome undertook his campaign for a return to the Hebrew. And Jerome's efforts may be seen as a Latin parallel to those of Apollinaris. For although the latter writer may have had the practical intention of training Christians in proper Greek, he probably had an apologetic objective as well, namely, to show the world that Christians did possess a respectable literary patrimony. Jerome had a similar goal, yet advocated a different approach. For from an early period he emphasizes that the Bible, if read in the original Hebrew, had great literary appeal.[27] And that such statements go beyond lip-service is clear from his attempt to formulate judgements on the style of individual authors.[28]

In fact, it is even possible that Jerome's original decision to learn Hebrew was based on a simple aesthetic need to read decent literature rather than on his desire to ward off sensual thoughts, as he himself claims, or on scholarly and text-critical considerations, as modern writers have thought.[29] For he acknowledged his disgust with biblical [Latin] style and his preference for classical authors, and dreamed his famous dream (in which he repented and vowed to put aside his Cicero) either shortly before or indeed during his residence in the desert, when he first undertook the study of Hebrew.[30] So it may be that in order to compensate for the loss of the enjoyment which he derived from the Latin classics, he turned to the Hebrew original. For he will have instinctively known that in this manner he could recover the literary beauty of the Bible which had been lost through the Greek and Latin transla-

---

[27] See *Praef. in Chron.* (GCS 47, pp. 3–4), and *Ep.* 48. 4. It would appear from the latter passage ('quae si legere volueris . . . apud nos scatere vitiis') that Jerome did not believe that the occasional difficulty of the biblical text detracted from the elegance of the Hebrew style, as might be inferred from the remarks of Meershoek, *Le latin*, pp. 17–18. Similarly, the 'barbaries' of the Hebrew may have had an adverse effect on the Latin style (Meershoek, pp. 23–4), but not on the appeal of the original itself.

[28] See *Praef. in Is.*; *Praef. in Jer.*; *Praef. in Ez.* Note also the comments on specific passages cited by J. Barr, *BJRL* 49 (1966–7), pp. 292–5. Alonso Schökel, *RF* 157 (1958), pp. 469–71, has neglected this evidence concerning Jerome, and, citing Augustine's assertion in *Doct. Chr.* 4. 41 to the effect that the Hebrew text does possess literary quality, attributes a breakthrough to that Father. Yet, as we have seen, simple statements of this sort are also found in Origen and Eusebius. And, in actual practice, Augustine does not follow through on the implications of his statement, but uses a different method. See above, n. 23.

[29] Jerome, *Ep.* 125. 12; Allgeier, *Bib* 12 (1931), p. 458; Barr, *BJRL* 49 (1966–7), pp. 285–6; Kelly, *Jerome*, p. 50.

[30] See *Ep.* 22. 30, and, for the date of the events described, Kelly, *Jerome*, p. 41.

tions. Having been schooled in the great Latin tradition, he was capable of appreciating the aesthetic merits of works in a language not his own.[31]

JEROME AND THE HEXAPLARIC SEPTUAGINT

In the preceding section of this chapter, we have tried to argue two main points: (*a*) that Jerome became convinced of the necessity for a return to the Hebrew text at an early point in his career, and (*b*) that this attitude was based on an approach to texts in foreign languages which was fundamentally different from that of the Greek Fathers. This picture stands in some contrast to the more widespread view of Jerome's development, especially with regard to the first point.[32] For it is normally believed that although he did realize the relevance of the Hebrew text at an early stage, his real 'conversion' did not occur until around the year 390, just before he began his translation *iuxta Hebraeos*. What is more, this 'conversion' was based more on a disillusionment with the LXX translation than on a positive evaluation of the Hebrew.

This view is based principally on the fact that between the Roman period and the commencement of *IH*, i.e. *c.*385–91, Jerome undertook to revise the Old Latin versions of the Old Testament on the basis of the Hexaplaric LXX. It is thought that he began this revision because he believed in the inspiration of the LXX. He later gave up that belief, probably around 390–1, and consequently abandoned the revision and embarked upon *IH*. It is at this point that we must see the conversion. Those who propose this explanation for the Hexaplaric revision appeal to three passages written before 391, in which Jerome expresses his faith in the version of the LXX by saying that it was approved by the Apostles and, indeed, that it was inspired.

This view of Jerome's development is found in various forms,

---

[31] The fact that at first Jerome found the sounds of the Hebrew language rather harsh (see *Ep.* 125. 12; *Praef. in Dan.* 11–15; *Comm. in Tit.* 3: 9) does not constitute an argument against the suggestion put forward in this paragraph. He was surely aware that this feeling was due to the strangeness of the language, and was something that he had to overcome. That he indeed did overcome it is clear from the fact that in his circle there developed the practice of singing the Psalms in Hebrew. See *Ep.* 39. 1; 108. 26.

[32] The view of Allgeier, cited above, n. 7, is a notable exception.

but it has been articulated most fully by L. Schade and W. Schwarz.[33] According to the former, Jerome did not begin to lose confidence in the LXX until the writing of *QHG*. In Schade's view, this work was in fact occasioned by Jerome's first doubts about the traditional version. In the process of writing it Jerome was 'converted', although his position continued to harden through the 390s and early 400s. Schwarz, on the other hand, sees a more decisive turn-about during the preparation of the revision of the *VL* and pays less attention to the process after *IH* was begun. A similar position has been adopted by J. Gribomont in an article on Jerome in the volume prepared as a continuation to J. Quasten's *Patrology*.[34]

Yet this view appears to be beset with many difficulties.[35] First of all, the evidence of the Roman letters has not been appreciated. This appears to be because Schade and his followers have concentrated excessively on Jerome's negative position *vis-à-vis* the LXX while neglecting his positive evaluation of the Hebrew. Indeed, Schade's main intention in proposing the theory of progressive development was to acquit Jerome of the charge of an inconsistent attitude towards the LXX.[36]

---

[33] Schade, *Die Inspirationslehre des heiligen Hieronymus* (BSt(F) 15. 4–5), Freiburg im Breisgau 1910, pp. 141–53; Schwarz, *Principles and Problems of Biblical Translation*, Cambridge 1955, pp. 26–34. Cf. also P. W. Skehan, 'St. Jerome and the Canon of the Holy Scriptures', *A Monument to Saint Jerome*, ed. F. X. Murphy, New York 1952, pp. 271–9.

[34] 'Girolamo', *Patrologia*, iii, ed. A. di Berardino, [Turin] 1978, p. 214. The view that Jerome abandoned the Hexaplaric revision in favour of *IH* is widespread. See D. De Bruyne, *RBen* 31 (1914–19), p. 229; H. F. D. Sparks, 'The Latin Bible', *The Bible in its Ancient and English Versions*, ed. H. W. Robinson, Oxford 1940, p. 113; Kelly, *Jerome*, p. 159. Cf. Grützmacher, *Hieronymus*, ii, p. 96; B. Kedar, *EB(B)* 8 (1982), col. 831; Jay, *REAug* 28 (1982), p. 212. Note also the view of H. J. White, *DB(H)* 4 (1902), p. 875 (cf. J. Brochet, *Saint Jérôme et ses ennemis*, Paris 1905, pp. 45–6), according to which Jerome did complete the Hexaplaric revision, but that this project seemed to him a half-way measure and led to an appreciation of the Hebrew.

[35] Here again, the position defended in this section owes something to views voiced in the first half of the present century by Allgeier. See esp. *ThGl* 18 (1925–6), pp. 671–87, and *Die Psalmen der Vulgata* (SGKA 22. 3), Paderborn 1940, pp. 63–6. Nevertheless, there are many differences, and the specific problem with which Allgeier was concerned, the relative chronology of Jerome's three editions of the Psalter, is not at issue here.

[36] *Die Inspirationslehre*, p. 141. In like manner, it appears that C. Estin, *RB* 88 (1981), p. 206 n. 23, has also failed to take account of the Roman letters. For she seems to suggest that the emotional fervour with which Jerome embraced the Hebrew text is visible only from *c*.390.

Secondly, the passages which are cited as evidence that Jerome had faith in the LXX before 390 are not unequivocal. One of these passages is found in *Praef. in Evang.* 16–19, where Jerome writes as follows: 'neque vero ego de Veteri disputo Testamento, quod a septuaginta senioribus in Graecam linguam versum, tertio gradu ad nos usque pervenit. non quaero quid Aquila, quid Symmachus sapiant, quare Theodotion inter novos et veteres medius incedat; sit illa vera interpretatio quam apostoli probaverunt.' The key phrase here is constituted by the words, 'sit illa . . . probaverunt'. Most scholars refer this phrase to the LXX, and accordingly take it as an indication that Jerome thought the LXX had given the 'true' translation, on the basis of the fact that it was approved by the Apostles.[37] Schwarz on the other hand thinks that Jerome is advocating the use of the Apostles as a criterion to judge between the LXX and the *recentiores*.[38] It seems that this latter view is the correct one. For Jerome was already aware at this early period that the Apostles often cite the Old Testament according to the Hebrew rather than the Greek. This fact would later become one of his stock arguments in his defence of the Hebrew text and his own version.[39] In *Ep.* 20, which was written in the same period as the revision of the Gospels, we read what may almost be considered as a precursor to the later argument. In this letter, he justifies his use of the Hebrew text to elucidate a problem in the Gospels in the following manner: 'restat ergo, ut omissis opinionum rivulis ad ipsum fontem, unde ab evangelistis sumptum est, recurramus. nam quomodo illud neque in Graecis neque in Latinis codicibus possumus invenire: "ut conpleretur id, quod dictum est per prophetas: Quoniam Nazaraeus vocabitur", et illud: "Ex Aegypto vocavi filium meum", ita et nunc ex Hebraeis codicibus veritas exprimenda est' (*Ep.* 20. 2). It is especially revealing that the verses to which he refers are Mt. 2: 23 and 2: 15. These verses recur more frequently than any others in the prefaces and other later texts where Jerome invokes the form of Old Testament quotations in the New in order to defend his return to the Hebrew text.[40] In view of this fact it seems unlikely that the sentence in

---

[37] See, e.g., Karpp, '"Prophet"', p. 110 n. 18; Benoit, 'L'inspiration', pp. 182–3 n. 84; Müller, *Scandinavian Journal of the Old Testament* 1989. 1, p. 114. Cf. Wendland, 'Zur ältesten Geschichte', p. 281 n. 3; Grützmacher, *Hieronymus*, i, p. 223; Skehan, 'St. Jerome', p. 272.

[38] *Principles*, pp. 27–8. [39] See below, pp. 63–4.

[40] See Schade, *Die Inspirationslehre*, p. 154 with n. 4.

Praef. in Evang. should be taken as an indication of Jerome's faith in the LXX.

The other two passages in question both come from the preface of Jerome's revision of the Paralipomena according to the LXX. At the end of this preface Jerome notes that although some passages are not contained in the Hebrew they have been added by the LXX 'vel ob decoris gratiam vel ob spiritus sancti auctoritatem'. It should be noted that Jerome does not state here that the entire LXX is inspired but only *some* of those passages which represent 'pluses' over against the Hebrew. I would not argue against the possibility that he indeed at one time held this view. However, even if this is the case, it cannot explain the preparation of the revision of the *VL* on the basis of the Hexaplaric LXX. First, in the *Praef. in libros Salomonis* (*iuxta LXX*), Jerome notes that he has employed the obelus so that readers will know 'quid redundet' in the LXX version. In the same preface, he characterizes the passages under obelus as 'superflua'. It is therefore clear that the publication of the revision was not dependent on a belief in the inspiration of the 'pluses', for it is definitely absent in this case. Secondly, such a belief would not necessitate an entire version, but only the insertion of those passages under obelus in *IH*. This method Jerome adopted in his translation of Daniel with regard to the major 'pluses' of the LXX.[41]

In the same preface to the Paralipomena, Jerome emphasizes the presence of a great number of errors in the proper names. He takes care to point out, however, that these errors are to be attributed to copyists, and not to the LXX, 'qui spiritu sancto pleni, ea quae vera fuerant transtulerunt'. This sentence is normally understood as an indication of Jerome's belief in the inspiration of the LXX version.[42] So it would appear. However, if we are always to take what Jerome says at its face value, we must accept that he held this view as late as 395–6, when he wrote the preface to his version of the same book *IH*.[43] In this preface, he

[41] See his *Praef. in Dan.* 20–3.

[42] In addition to Schade, *Die Inspirationslehre*, pp. 142–4, and Schwarz, *Principles*, pp. 28–30 (on p. 28, he dates the preface to '*not* before 395', but it is clear from p. 31 that he must mean either 'before 395' or 'not before 385'), see J. Schmid in his edition of the correspondence between Jerome and Augustine (Bonn 1930 = FlorPatr 22), p. 10, and Benoit, 'L'inspiration', pp. 180–1.

[43] The date of this preface is dependent on the date of *Ep.* 57, to which there is a reference. See L. H. Cottineau, 'Chronologie des versions bibliques de S.

implies that the original LXX version was infallible. For he says that if it had been preserved in its original form, there would be no need for him to produce a new version. This amounts to the same as saying that the LXX version is inspired, for inspiration essentially means freedom from error.[44] However, according to both Schade and Schwarz, Jerome did not believe in the inspiration of the LXX as late as 395–6, but they fail to explain this passage.[45] We shall attempt to argue in the following section of this chapter that in *Praef. in Par.* (*IH*) Jerome is not expressing his own view, but constructing an argument on the basis of his opponents' premisses. If this is the case, a similar explanation may be in order for the earlier statement. It is possible that in defending the LXX from the possible charge of committing banal errors, something which he does throughout his career,[46] Jerome has employed hyperbole. This would be understandable in a preface in which the pro-Hebrew element is strong. It is also possible that the remark is to be understood in connection with the statement in the same preface which we already examined, in which only some additions of the LXX are regarded as inspired.[47]

Thirdly, it is not at all clear when, if ever, Jerome stopped work on the Hexaplaric revision, nor is it known why he may have done so. Although many believe that the work was never finished, some scholars accept the possibility that he may have completed the project, but that most of it has been lost.[48] Indeed, Jerome himself tells Augustine that he has lost most of it 'ob fraudem

Jérôme', *Miscellanea geronimiana*, Rome 1920, p. 65; Nautin, *REAug* 19 (1973), pp. 82–3; id., 'Hieronymus', p. 310.

[44] This point has been emphasized by H. Sasse, 'Sacra Scriptura: Bemerkungen zur Inspirationslehre Augustins', *Festschrift Franz Dornseiff*, Leipzig 1953, pp. 268–9.

[45] Skehan, on the other hand, 'St. Jerome', p. 272, would explain the passage as a remnant of Jerome's early faith in the original text of the LXX.

[46] See *Ep.* 65. 9; *Comm. in Ezech.* 2 (5: 12–13 = CChr.SL 75, p. 60). Cf. *Comm. in Ezech.* 12 (40: 5–13 = CChr.SL 75, p. 559); *Ep.* 106. 2.

[47] I would be wary of accepting the idea that Jerome's favourable opinion of inspiration as articulated in this passage is merely a reproduction of the views of his addressees. This idea was first propounded by Erasmus (see *PL* 29. 421–2) and has often been repeated, e.g. by E. Mangenot, *DB(V)* 5 (1911), col. 1627, and Kelly, *Jerome*, p. 159 n. 23. In contexts such as the present one, Jerome will not normally use views which are not his own without a particular reason (cf. Wendland, 'Zur ältesten Geschichte', p. 280). What that reason is in the present case may have eluded us.

[48] See White, *DB(H)* 4 (1902), p. 875. Cf. Brochet, *Saint Jérôme*, pp. 44–5; Stummer, *Einführung*, p. 88; Jellicoe, *The Septuagint*, p. 252.

cuiusdam'.[49] However, even if Jerome did not finish the project, we have no way of explaining why, any more than we can explain why he left the revision of the New Testament unfinished.[50] This is true all the more when we remember that there is no solid evidence concerning the exact absolute chronology of the different books of the revision, even if we do know that individual books preceded their counterparts which were translated from the Hebrew.[51] Therefore, an overlap of the Hexaplaric revision and *IH* with regard to some books is not to be excluded.[52] In short, in no way can we be sure that Jerome abandoned the Hexaplaric revision in favour of *IH*. In fact, the information available suggests that he continued to support the Hexaplaric LXX after the publication of *IH*. From reading his *Ep.* 106, one gets the impression that he even made a concerted effort to promote the Hexaplaric revision in the West. It is difficult to date this letter, but there can be no doubt that it was written after the commencement of *IH*, for the latter version is mentioned in it.[53] Recently scholars have preferred a time frame as late as 404–10.[54] In addition, P. Jay has shown that Jerome put forward at least an informal Latin version of the Origenian recension in the *Comm. in Is.*, a work which may be dated to the years 408–10.[55]

Accordingly, it seems difficult to explain the rise and fall of the Hexaplaric revision on the basis of a youthful belief in the inspiration of the LXX which was later abandoned. However, if our view of a 'conversion' to the Hebrew early in Jerome's career is correct, how is one to explain this project? Rather than return to accusing

---

[49] *Ep.* 134. 2. See White, loc. cit. The view voiced by Bardy, *La question*, p. 263 (cf. Cavallera, *Saint Jérôme*, i. 1, p. 147; W. H. Semple, *BJRL* 33 (1950–1), p. 114), according to which this loss was the cause of Jerome's abandonment of the revision is pure speculation. We do not know when the loss took place, for the letter was written around 416 (see Schmid, op. cit. (n. 42 above), p. 8), i.e. only four years before Jerome's death.

[50] Gribomont, *MD* 62 (1960), p. 48, attributes the abandonment of the revision of the New Testament as well to Jerome's enthusiasm for the 'Hebraica veritas'.

[51] See Cottineau, 'Chronologie', pp. 54–5.

[52] See Stummer, *Einführung*, p. 90; B. Altaner and A. Stuiber, *Patrologie⁸*, Freiburg (im Breisgau) 1978, p. 397.

[53] *Ep.* 106. 86. This point is noted by Cavallera, *Saint Jérôme*, i. 2, p. 46. Those before Cavallera who attempted to date the letter to an earlier period, e.g. Ohrloff, *ZDP* 7 (1876), p. 282 n. 1, and Grützmacher, *Hieronymus*, i, p. 85, iii, p. 222 n. 2, had not taken this passage into account.

[54] Altaner, *VigChr* 4 (1950), pp. 246–8. He is followed by Kelly, *Jerome*, p. 285.

[55] See *L'exégèse*, pp. 114–19, and, for the date of composition, p. 66.

Jerome of inconsistency, it seems more prudent to view his revision of the LXX within the context of a more sophisticated approach to the problem of the biblical text on his part.

It must be remembered that despite his belief in the centrality and priority of the Hebrew text, Jerome was a member of a Church in which the LXX was the accepted version. That he was quite aware of this fact is clear from his own statements.[56] Since all theological and exegetical discussion took place on the basis of that translation, he was not about to burn his LXX and cut himself off from the rest of the Christian world. In fact, there is an abundance of evidence to show that it was not his policy to pretend that the LXX did not exist. For example, he appears to have normally employed it in his sermons.[57] In writings from all periods of his career he often cites the Bible according to the LXX/*VL*.[58] Therefore, his statement to Rufinus that he could not forget what he learned in his youth (*Ruf.* 2. 24) is an accurate reflection of the situation.

We may draw two important conclusions from Jerome's recognition of the importance of the LXX. In the first place, he was probably not a one-dimensional man who saw in the LXX only a version which was in conflict with his 'Hebraica veritas'. He will have been interested in LXX problems for their own sake without always being consumed by the Hebrew/LXX opposition. Starting with this assumption, we will find that his motives for the preparation of the Hexaplaric revision become much clearer. As we have seen in the previous section of this chapter, Jerome was aware that the Latin Old Testament was a translation from the Greek rather than the Hebrew. Consequently, if he was going to apply 'Origen's principle', according to which versions must be revised on the basis of their *Vorlage*, to the Latin Old Testament, it was logical to return to the Greek. There are, indeed, many places where Jerome discusses the errors consequent upon translation from Greek to Latin, and the sorry state of the Latin manuscripts.[59] How necessary a revision was and how welcome Jerome's efforts in this direction were is attested by Augustine (*Ep.* 71. 6;

---

[56] See *Ep.* 57. 11; *Ruf.* 2. 35; *Comm. in Is.* 18 (65: 20 = CChr.SL 73A, p. 763). Cf. Jay, *L'exégèse*, pp. 119–20.

[57] See *Praef. in Par. (IH)* 36–7; *Ruf.* 2. 24.

[58] Cf. Jay, *L'exégèse*, pp. 92–3; Jellicoe, *The Septuagint*, p. 254.

[59] *Ep.* 34. 5; prefaces to Esth. 2–6, Jos. 11–12, Libri Salomonis (*iuxta LXX*).

82. 35). Jerome himself takes pride in his revision throughout his career, always stressing that his work constitutes an 'emendation'.[60]

More importantly, however, Jerome's Hexaplaric revision must be understood not in terms of a LXX versus Hebrew opposition, but rather in the context of the rivalry between the recensions of the LXX. For, as we have seen, the Hexaplaric LXX had not achieved universal recognition in the East, where there were three competing recensions. In the West, at least as a recognized entity, it was almost without influence before Jerome's revision.[61] Consequently, at the time of its publication the Hexaplaric revision was anything but a neutral proposition. It was an attempt by Jerome to extend in the West the influence of the recension of the LXX which he believed to be correct. That this was his view is evident from *Ep.* 106. 2, where he describes the Hexaplaric LXX as 'incorrupta et inmaculata septuaginta interpretum translatio', and compares it with the corrupt κοινή, which he identifies with the recension of Lucian.[62] In other late writings, he refers to the Hexaplaric recension as 'emendata et vera exemplaria Septuaginta'[63] or even 'ipsi Septuaginta'.[64] Jerome therefore took a firm position regarding the rivalry between the recensions, and maintained that position throughout his life.[65]

---

[60] Prefaces to Ps. (*IH*) 31–3, Libri Salomonis (*IH*) 22–3, Par. (*IH*) 35–6; *Ep.* 71. 5; *Ruf.* 2. 24; 3. 25.

[61] In *Civ.* 18. 43, Augustine writes, 'et multi codices has notas [sc. the Hexaplaric signs] habentes usquequaque diffusi sunt et Latini.' However, this diffusion of the Latin Hexaplaric LXX must be the consequence of Jerome's efforts and will not have taken place before that time. It should be kept in mind that *Civ.* 18 was written in 425 (see Bardy's introduction to the translation of *Civ.* by G. Combès (Paris 1959 = BAug 33), pp. 29–30), i.e. almost forty years after the appearance of the first books of Jerome's revision. In addition, we learn from Augustine, *Ep.* 28. 2, that all African churches were very anxious to get Jerome's Hexaplaric revision. The request would not have been so urgent (cf. Augustine, *Ep.* 71. 4, 6) if there had been a diffusion previous to that time. This enthusiasm on the part of the Africans will also explain why there were 'multi codices' by 425. On the other hand, since the second 'et' of the phrase quoted must be rendered 'even', it may be that in using the word 'multi' Augustine is referring more to Greek than to Latin codices, and has simply derived his information from Jerome, *Ep.* 112. 19.

[62] Cf. *Praef. in Evang.* 23–7, where already Jerome pours scorn on the recensions of Hesychius and Lucian.

[63] *Comm. in Is.* 16 (58: 11 = CChr.SL 73A, p. 671).

[64] *Comm. in Ezech.* 1 (4: 4–6 = CChr.SL 75, p. 47). Cf. *Comm. in Is.* 16. prol. (CChr.SL 73A, pp. 642–3).

[65] In view of the evidence presented in the preceding part of this section, the fact that Jerome may use a non-Hexaplaric recension in his references to the

But, in the face of the 'trifaria varietas', why did Jerome view the Hexaplaric recension as the correct one? The reason can only be its closer proximity to the Hebrew. This much is clear from *Ep.* 106. 2, where he says, 'quidquid ergo ab hac [sc. the Hexaplaric recension] discrepat, nulli dubium est, quin ita et ab Hebraeorum auctoritate discordet.' That is, in the view of Jerome, there is no recension nearer to the Hebrew text than the Hexaplaric.[66] Indeed, there are many occasions in the letter where he mentions readings which are common to his own [Hexaplaric] LXX and the Hebrew but are not shared by the κοινή/Lucianic text.[67]

That Jerome had the same motive for choosing the Hexaplaric recension as the basis for his revision some twenty years earlier can be inferred from what remains of the revision itself. For scholars have found that Jerome subjected the Hexaplaric LXX to even further 'Hebraization'.[68] He clearly believed that the more Hebraized a recension was, the better. His own statements in *Praef. in Par. (iuxta LXX)* confirm this. Here he says that he employed a Jewish scholar from Tiberias to help him correct the version, and he challenges anyone who would find fault with his work to verify its correctness with the Jews. Such appeals are normally to be found in the prefaces to *IH*.[69] The implication is therefore that the Hexaplaric recension was to be evaluated on the

version of the LXX in *Comm. in Jer.* should not be taken as evidence that he considered the Hexaplaric recension to have been superseded, as it is by W. Mckane, *Selected Christian Hebraists*, Cambridge 1989, pp. 40–1. Rather, the phenomenon may be due to the fact that Jerome did not have available a Latin text of the recension, and the preparation of a new, even informal version (see above, p. 54), was not possible owing to the conditions under which the commentary was written. For these, see Kelly, *Jerome*, pp. 326–7.

[66] The statement of H. Dörrie, *ZNW* 39 (1940), p. 62, that Jerome equates the Hebrew text with the Hexaplaric recension is thus not quite exact.

[67] *Ep.* 106. 4 (cf. 5), 13, 44, 56, 70, 75 (with reference to Ps. 118: 109), 77. In these passages, Jerome does not explicitly characterize his own 'Septuagintal' readings as Hexaplaric and only on occasion does he say that the 'Greek' readings of his correspondents are derived from the κοινή. However, a comparison of the readings cited with the material collected by Rahlfs in his edition of the Greek text of the Psalms (Göttingen 1931 = *Septuaginta*: [*Vetus Testamentum Graecum auctoritate academiae scientiarum Gottingensis editum*], x) reveals that the 'Septuagintal' readings of Jerome are in accord with Hebraizing (i.e. Hexaplaric) readings, whereas the 'Greek' readings of the correspondents agree for the most part with 'Lucianic' readings.

[68] C. P. Caspari, *Das Buch Hiob* (*Christiania Videnskabs-Selskabs Forhandlinger* 1893. 4), Christiania 1893, pp. 43–8; A. Vaccari, *Bib* 8 (1927), pp. 466–7; Stummer, *Einführung*, pp. 86–7.

[69] See the prefaces listed below, n. 78.

basis of its proximity to the Hebrew text. In short, it was not his work on the Hexaplaric LXX which led him to appreciate the Hebrew text, but his appreciation of the original which led him to support the Hexaplaric LXX.

This brings us to the second conclusion (see above, p. 55) which we may draw from Jerome's recognition of the place of the LXX in the Church: he was a realist who was willing to accept progress in whatever measure it might be obtainable. This circumstance constitutes an additional explanation for Jerome's revision of the LXX according to the Origenian recension. That is, he was ready to make compromises with conservative attitudes towards the LXX in order that his own position might achieve maximum possible influence. Over the years he developed a multifaceted policy by which to increase the recognition of the importance of the Hebrew text in the Church, by whatever means possible. The attempt to diffuse the Hexaplaric recension is a component of that policy, for he regarded that recension as an important step in the right direction. As we shall see straightaway, this realistic approach is visible not only in Jerome's support for the Hexaplaric recension, but also in the presentation to the public of *IH*.

THE VERSION *IUXTA HEBRAEOS*

In putting forward and defending his translation 'according to the Hebrew', Jerome reveals himself as the master polemicist. Nevertheless, the structure of his arguments is not always easy to follow, and the discussion in this section represents an attempt to unravel some of the threads of his logic. First of all, Jerome presents the version on two different levels. On the one hand, his consciousness of the prestige which the LXX enjoyed in both Greek and Latin Christendom led him to put forward the version not as a replacement for the LXX, but as a complement to it. On the other hand, we have already seen that on the basis of fundamental convictions regarding the relationship between translation and original Jerome came to prefer the Hebrew to the LXX version. Indeed, as he sees it, his preference depends on nothing less than 'studium veritatis' (*Ep.* 106. 78). Inasmuch as he saw his own version as a closer representation of the original than the LXX, Jerome could not regard his version as a mere complement to the LXX.

In no less than six prefaces Jerome claims that he has not come to reprehend or destroy the LXX.[70] He rather describes *IH* as a supplementary version, and cites the *recentiores* as a precedent. In *Praef. in Is.* 19–21, Jerome appeals to the fact that scholars have employed these versions in order to arrive at a clearer understanding of the LXX, which, as we have seen, is an accurate description of the way in which the Greeks normally used the later translations.[71] Accordingly, Jerome suggests the same role for his own version (*Ep.* 112. 20; *Praef. in Jos.* 9–11). Elsewhere he claims that his motive for publishing the translation was to protect Christians from Jewish ridicule and accusations that they were ignorant of the true Scriptures.[72] We should understand this characterization of *IH* as an apologetic tool in a similar sense. For one would not have to discard the LXX to employ his version in this fashion. We know that arguments of this type did find at least one convert. For Augustine became persuaded of the value of *IH*, but only in the capacity of an auxiliary version (*Ep.* 82. 34–5; *Civ.* 18. 43).

We find, however, that Jerome also appeals to other roles played by the *recentiores* in order to justify his own version. First of all, he refers to the passages under asterisk in Origen's Hexaplaric LXX, and constantly emphasizes that these passages were read in church.[73] Secondly, he often calls attention to the fact that the Book of Daniel was read by the Christians not according to the version of the LXX, but that of Theodotion.[74] We sometimes get the impression that he appeals to this ecclesiastical usage of the *recentiores* in order to argue the point mentioned above, only *a fortiori*. That is, if the *recentiores* are read in church, surely his own translation can be used as an auxiliary version.

On a different plane, however, this use of the *recentiores* on the part of Christians is exploited by Jerome to prove that the version of the LXX is inadequate, and that this fact has been recognized by the Church. According to him, Origen would not have made

---

[70] Ps. (*IH*) 31–2; Sam. et Reg. 58–9; Job (*IH*) 37–8; Libri Salomonis (*IH*) 22–3; Jos. 6–7; Pent. 34–5. Cf. *Ruf.* 2. 34; *Ep.* 112. 20.

[71] See above, pp. 24–5, 36.

[72] *Praef. in Is.* 30–1; *Ruf.* 3. 25. Cf. *Praef. in Ps.* (*IH*) 18–22, 33–5; *Praef. in Jos.* 19–20.

[73] See the prefaces to Job (*IH*) 41–8; Esdr. et Neh. 32–6; Par. (*IH*) 12–19; *Comm. in Dan.* prol.

[74] *Praef. in Dan.* 1–3; *Praef. in Jos.* 23–4; *Ruf.* 2. 33; *Comm. in Dan.* prol., 1 (4: 5a).

the additions had the LXX been satisfactory. As he puts it, 'quae fuit stultitia, postquam vera dixerint, proferre quae falsa sunt?' (*Praef. in Jos.* 25–6). Of course there were those, such as Rufinus, who claimed that Origen composed the Hexaplaric LXX for apologetic purposes only.[75] Clearly it is Jerome's point that the passages under asterisk were read in church (i.e. were accepted as valid by Christians) that constitutes his response to such a view. For him, this acceptance was an admission that the LXX had made omissions.[76] Jerome himself viewed these omissions with grave concern, as may be seen from his treatise *De optimo genere interpretandi*, where he notes, 'sacrilegium est vel celasse vel ignorasse mysterium.'[77]

Jerome took the logic a step further. In his *Praef. in Job (IH)* 9–10, he claims that if one admits omissions on the part of the LXX, one must also admit errors on the part of the same translators. The clear implication of this statement is that it is legitimate not only to supplement the LXX, but also to replace them. And, indeed, it is in this context that we must understand his reminders that the Church read Daniel according to the version of Theodotion. For this fact constitutes a precedent for the rejection of the LXX in favour of the *recentiores*.

In other words, Jerome justifies his own version by pointing to three ways in which the *recentiores* were employed. First of all, they were used exegetically in order to explain the sense of the LXX. Jerome would have his version used in the same way by those who believe in the infallibility of the LXX. Moreover, the later versions were used textually, and that in two ways: (*a*) as a supplement to the LXX and (*b*) as a replacement for them. Jerome appeals to these latter two uses for two reasons. On the one hand, he wants to make the same point as he makes by appealing to the exegetical usage, only *a fortiori*. However, there can be no doubt that his main intention is to show that the inadequacy of the LXX has to an extent been acknowledged within the Church, so that his own attempt to replace that version will not be seen as such a revolutionary project. And it should be stressed that the argument is based not on Jerome's own endorsement of the Origenian recen-

---

[75] See above, Ch. 1 n. 9.

[76] See *Praef. in Job (IH)* 5–7, where Jerome writes that Origen made insertions in the text of the LXX from Theodotion, 'probans defuisse quod additum est'.

[77] *Ep.* 57. 7. See also *Comm. in Ezech.* 1 (1: 13–14).

sion, but on the at least *de facto* endorsement of that recension (including the passages under asterisk) within the Church, and the use of Theodotion's version of Daniel on the part of Christians.[78]

In his *Praef. in Par.* (*IH*), Jerome puts forward a different kind of text-critical argument. In this preface, he says that if the version of the LXX had been preserved in its original state, there would be no need for him to make a new translation, implying, incidentally, that in its original state the translation was infallible, although he avoids stating this explicitly. He points out, however, that the text of the LXX circulates in different forms in different regions ('pro varietate regionum'), and claims [on this basis] that the original version ('germana illa antiquaque translatio') has suffered textual corruption. He goes on to describe the 'trifaria varietas', according to which three eastern regions, Asia, Syria, and Egypt, each follow a different recension, the Lucianic, Hexaplaric, and Hesychian respectively. Jerome here exploits the 'trifaria varietas' in order to argue that the original version of the LXX is not extant. For this reason, as he sees it, a return to the original Hebrew is necessary.[79] In other words, he has applied 'Origen's principle' to the rival recensions of the LXX, including that of Origen himself.

Jerome here implies that there is no such thing as a 'pure LXX',

[78] It is a presupposition of Jerome's arguments that his version is philologically on the same level as the *recentiores*. It seems that there were those who were unwilling to accept such a proposition. For example, we have seen that Theodore of Mopsuestia apparently refused to believe that Jerome's Hebrew was on a comparable level. See above, pp. 39–40 with n. 116. In order to refute such criticisms, Jerome often appeals to his readers to verify the accuracy of his version with the Jews. See the prefaces to Esdr. et Neh. 31–2; Sam. et Reg. 69–73; Ps. (*IH*) 27–8; and cf. *Praef. in Par.* (*IH*) 19–21. Probably as a result of the incident in Oea, described by Augustine, *Ep.* 71. 5, where the verdict of the Jews went against him, Jerome suggested that critics ask Jews from different localities. This would obviate the possibility of conspiracy for him or against him. See *Praef. in Pent.* 43–4; *Comm. in Ezech.* 10 (33: 23–33 = CChr.SL 75, p. 475). Cf. *Ep.* 112. 20–2. It may be that Augustine took up his challenge, for in *Civ.* 18. 43 he reports that the Jews gave a very positive evaluation of Jerome's work.

[79] That this is the thrust of the argument is clear from the context as well as the parallel in *Praef. in Esdr. et Neh.* 21–3, where Jerome writes, 'si quis autem septuaginta vobis opposuerit interpretes, quorum exemplaria varietas ipsa lacerata et eversa demonstrat—nec potest utique verum adseri quod diversum est—. . .', even if there are different opinions concerning the exact translation of some of the phraseology. Compare Semple, *BJRL* 48 (1965–6), p. 237, with Dörrie, *ZNW* 39 (1940), pp. 66–8.

and relinquishes his position that the Hexaplaric LXX constituted the 'ipsi Septuaginta'. For he represents the latter recension as one of the three major corrupt forms of the LXX. Some scholars have seen this passage as evidence of an evolution in Jerome's position, according to which he lost his faith in the Origenian recension.[80] But we have seen in the previous section that Jerome held his view concerning the authenticity of that recension throughout his life. And, indeed, two other considerations should make one wary of appealing to the idea of progressive development in explaining the contradiction. First of all, he also implies in this passage that the original version of the LXX was infallible, when there is abundant evidence to show that he did not believe in the infallibility of that version at the date of this preface, c.396. It will suffice to cite *Ep.* 57. 7, where Jerome would pardon the LXX, 'ut homines', for an error, and apply to them Jac. 3: 2, where it is written, 'multa peccamus omnes'.[81] Secondly, as we noted immediately above, the textual argument based on the Hexaplaric recension is based not on Jerome's own position concerning it, but on the acceptance of the recension by Christians. Accordingly, it would be logical to conclude that here as well he is constructing an argument based on the premises of his opponents. As he would say, he is arguing γυμναστικῶς rather than δογματικῶς.[82]

But what, then, is the point of abandoning the Origenian recension? It will be recalled from the final section of the previous chapter that neither this recension, nor Jerome's understanding of how it was to be used, was universally endorsed. Consequently, the argument based on the use of the recension (including the passages under asterisk) in church could not be of comprehensive application. On the other hand, an argument based on an ostensibly objective view of all the major recensions, as well as on the infallibility of the original translation of the LXX, could appeal to those who were not partisans of the Hexaplaric LXX. In other

[80] Dörrie, *ZNW* 39 (1940), pp. 68–9, 84 n. 70; Semple, *BJRL* 48 (1965–6), pp. 232–3 (with pp. 230, 237). Cf. the latter writer, *BJRL* 33 (1950–1), pp. 114–15; Brochet, *Saint Jérôme*, pp. 44–6; E. F. Sutcliffe, 'Jerome', *CHB*, ii (1969), pp. 95–6.

[81] This letter is mentioned in *Praef. in Par.* (*IH*) 21, so there can be no doubt about the relative chronology. Attribution of error to the LXX is attested at least as early as *QHG*. See, e.g., 4: 6–7; 14: 5. Cf. 26: 32–3; 31: 7–8, 41. For such accusations in later works, see Schade, *Die Inspirationslehre*, pp. 151–2.

[82] Cf. *Ep.* 49. 13. On this passage, see H. Hagendahl, *Latin Fathers and the Classics* (SGLG 6 = *GUA* 64. 2), Gothenburg 1958, pp. 158–9.

words, Jerome's principal text-critical argument is double edged. If one accepts the Hexaplaric recension, one must admit that the translation of the LXX is flawed. If one accepts neither the Hexaplaric recension nor this troubling implication which results from such an acceptance, one must put all recensional activity in the same boat, even if one need not discard the idea of the infallibility of the LXX. In this case, however, one must admit the irretrievability of that version. Either way, one is led to acknowledge the necessity of *IH*.[83]

So much for 'scientific' text-critical arguments. Jerome still had to deal with a more emotional issue: the established position of the version of the LXX within the Church. For it seemed to many Christians that Jerome, by translating the Bible anew, was scoffing at a Christian institution.[84] Indeed, he was accused of producing a Jewish Bible.[85] The position of the LXX as the traditional Bible of the Church had been greatly strengthened by the view that had developed for the most part after the time of Origen, viz. that the version of the LXX was a key link in a specifically gentile chain of transmission of the Old Testament, and indeed constituted a special dispensation for gentile Christians.[86]

In an attempt to undermine this view, Jerome employs a two-pronged attack. On the one hand, he attempts to deprive the LXX of their position in the gentile chain of transmission of the Old Testament. We have seen that for most Fathers this position was dependent on the view that the Apostles selected and sanctioned the translation of the LXX for transmission to the Gentiles. And this view was in turn based on the common assumption that the version of the LXX was the source of the citations of the Old Testament in the New.[87] Accordingly, Jerome focuses his attention on these citations. He makes the audacious claim that the Apostles, when they quote the Old Testament, follow the Hebrew rather than the LXX. This he sometimes qualifies by saying that they may follow the version of the LXX provided that it is in accord

---

[83] Neuschäfer, *Origenes*, pp. 319–20 n. 40, while correct in his criticism of Dörrie, has failed to see this two-edged aspect of the textual argument.

[84] See Rufinus, *Apol. adv. Hier.* 2. 36–7. Cf. Augustine, *Ep.* 71. 4.

[85] See Rufinus, op. cit., 2. 36, 38, 39, 41. Note also the accusation of Theodore of Mopsuestia as preserved in Photius, *Bibliotheca*, cod. 177 (122a).

[86] See above, pp. 29–34.　　　　　　　　　　[87] See above, pp. 29–30.

with the Hebrew.[88] He pays particular attention to those passages which contain testimonies of Christ.[89]

Modern scholars have taken Jerome to task for his argument, claiming that it is objectively false.[90] However, the evidence concerning Old Testament citations in the New Testament is rather complex, in that many quotations follow neither the Hebrew nor the LXX. And if one attempts to make a judgement on the basis of sense in these cases, there is often room for dispute.[91] Indeed, the great variety in the form of these citations was one of the factors that led Kahle to posit his thesis that there never was a single, original, Greek translation, but a multitude of such translations.[92] In other words, Jerome has simply exploited the complex nature of the situation in a manner favourable to his own position. If he overstates his case, this is in order that he may deprive the LXX of their entry ticket to the gentile chain of transmission of the Old Testament, which was apostolic approval.

In an attempt to substantiate his position, Jerome provides an explanation for the fact that the LXX 'omitted' Old Testament testimonies of Christ which are nevertheless present in the New Testament. He claims that the translators did not want to reveal to Ptolemy the mysteries by which the coming of Christ was promised, in order that the Jews would not seem to him to worship a second god. For the king, as a follower of Plato, admired them specifically because of their monotheism. Accordingly, the translators hid allusions to the Trinity.[93] However, in furnishing this explanation for his view of the apostolic citations of the Old Testament, Jerome in effect launches a second prong of attack on the position of the LXX as the 'Bible of the Gentiles'. For in this manner he also undermines the idea that this version constitutes a special 'economic' dispensation intended for gentile Christians.

---

[88] *Ep.* 57. 11; *Ruf.* 2. 34. Cf. Jerome's description of his own procedure in *Comm. in Eccl.* prol.

[89] The passages involved and the places in Jerome's work where they are discussed have been collected by Schade, *Die Inspirationslehre*, pp. 153–6. Cf. his article in *BZ* 7 (1909), pp. 129–33; and A. Sperber, *JBL* 59 (1940), pp. 202–3.

[90] Benoit, 'L'inspiration', pp. 182–3; J. Braverman, *Jerome's 'Commentary on Daniel'* (CBQ.MS 7), Washington, DC 1978, p. 32.

[91] For the view of Jerome, see *Ep.* 121. 2. 7. Cf. C. Pesch, *De inspiratione Sacrae Scripturae*, Freiburg im Breisgau 1906, pp. 457–8 n. 1, 543–5.

[92] See *The Cairo Geniza*, pp. 249–52.

[93] See *Praef. in Pent.* 19–25. Cf. *QHG* prol. In describing Plato as a monotheist, Jerome is probably dependent on Eusebius, *PE* 11. 13.

He reduces this idea to its extreme by claiming that the version of the LXX was influenced not by a divine dispensation, but by the expectations of a pagan patron. The version does not represent a forward progression for gentile Christians, but a distortion for pagan Platonists. The 'Bible of the Gentiles' becomes the 'Bible of the pagans'. In short, Jerome transforms one of the most important themes underlying the position of the LXX in the Church into an argument for going beyond the LXX. He is able to accuse the LXX of hiding Christian mysteries, but without attributing to them an anti-Christian motive.[94]

In formulating this argument, Jerome was inspired by two different sources. On the one hand, we have already mentioned the phenomenon noted by Barthélemy, whereby Eusebius on occasion prefers readings of the *recentiores* because of clearer messianic or Christological connotations.[95] The Greek Father also sometimes comments that the LXX have hidden or alluded more obscurely to these mysteries.[96] However, this greater obscurity of the LXX does not seem to have been particularly significant for him. Barthélemy cites only one passage which contains a minimal attempt to explain it. In *Comm. in Ps.* 86: 6–7 (*PG* 23. 1049c), Eusebius says that the LXX have hidden a mystery because they were producing a translation for pagans, and Christ had not yet been born. However, he does not expand on this idea, and certainly does not regard the phenomenon as a reason to abandon the LXX. According to Barthélemy, 'un disciple d'Origène ne fera jamais de la clarté la norme suprême d'une traduction.'[97] Indeed, the great Dominican 'Septantiste' believes that Eusebius probably judged this feature of the LXX in a positive manner, and that he may have applied to the version of the LXX Origen's view of the obscurity of Scripture in general. That is, obscurity is a sort of pedagogic technique: it fosters gradual rather than immediate initiation into the profoundest mysteries.[98] Whether Eusebius did

---

[94] Cf. Augustine, *Ep.* 82. 34, who says he can see no reason why the LXX would omit or tamper with *testimonia* pertaining to Christianity.

[95] See above, p. 37.

[96] See Barthélemy, 'Eusèbe', pp. 56–7. He cites two passages: *Comm. in Ps.* 86: 6–7 (*PG* 23. 1049b–c); *Ecl.* 2. 5.

[97] 'Eusèbe', p. 56. Cf. above, Ch. 1 n. 34.

[98] See 'Eusèbe', pp. 58–9. One may add the fragment from *Comm. in Rom.* preserved in *Philoc.* 9. 3 to the passages there cited. Cf. also Clement of Alexandria, *Str.* 6. 126. 1.

in fact ascribe this technique to the LXX is not yet certain. Nevertheless, Barthélemy's suggestion finds added support from the fact that in *De doctrina Christiana* 4. 15, Augustine attributes the motive of edifying obscurity specifically to the LXX. And Augustine may be drawing on a Greek source still to be determined.

As we have seen above, however, Jerome interprets such obscurity in a different manner, and regards it as grounds for transcending the LXX.[99] He exploits for such a purpose a certain Jewish aggada, which is found in a number of rabbinic texts. According to this aggada, the Jewish scholars who prepared the translation for 'King Talmai' made a number of changes in the text.[100] Included in the changes listed are a few which would have the purpose of staving off polytheistic interpretations of the passages in question.[101] That Jerome is dependent on this aggada is clear from the fact that he explicitly cites a Jewish source in *Praef. in Pent.* 21, and so much has also been noted by Barthélemy.[102] However, Jerome 'Christianizes' the aggada in a rather sophisticated manner in order to suit his own purposes. Whereas the Rabbis see the changes in a positive light, inasmuch as they prevent Ptolemy from arriving at an incorrect—polytheistic—understanding of the original, Jerome casts them in a negative light. In his view they prevent Ptolemy from arriving at the correct—trinitarian or Christological—understanding of the original. For the Rabbis, the sense of the original has been preserved by an intelligent non-literal rendering. Indeed, from *b. Megilla* 9a it would seem that the changes were regarded as divinely inspired.[103] For Jerome, the original text has been perverted to suit the whims of

---

[99] That *Praef. in Is.* 11–13 may be an allusion to the explanation of the obscurity of the LXX ascribed by Barthélemy to Eusebius (cf. 'Eusèbe', pp. 57–8) does of course not alter this fact.

[100] For recent discussions of this aggada, including full references to the rabbinic sources, see K. Müller, 'Die rabbinischen Nachrichten über die Anfänge der Septuaginta', *Wort, Lied und Gottesspruch*, [i] (*FS* J. Ziegler, [i] = fzb 1), Würzburg 1972, pp. 73–93; E. Tov, *JSJ* 15 (1984), pp. 65–89.

[101] See Barthélemy, 'Eusèbe', pp. 61–3. Cf. Müller, 'Die rabbinischen Nachrichten', p. 80.

[102] 'Eusèbe', p. 60. Jerome's statements had already been discussed in connection with the aggada by H. Grätz, *ZRIJ* 2 (1845), pp. 430–2. Cf. also A. Geiger, *Urschrift und Übersetzungen der Bibel*, Breslau 1857, pp. 8–9.

[103] The original rabbinic view of the translation of the LXX was very positive. See the remarks of S. Zeitlin in the edition of the *Letter of Aristeas* of M. Hadas (New York 1951), p. 81 n. 110.

a Platonist. In short, Jerome takes a theme present in the exegetical works of Eusebius and a Jewish aggada, interprets each in the light of the other, and emerges with a new argument by which to contest the position of the LXX as the 'Bible of the Gentiles'.[104]

Jerome also took issue with the legend of the origin of the LXX, according to which the seventy(-two) translators, although working independently in separate cells, all produced the same version. The legend, which is attested from about the end of the second century of the Christian era, was not an insignificant source of prestige for the position of the LXX in the Church.[105] Jerome rejects the story, citing the testimony of Aristeas and Josephus.[106] This is of course well known to scholars. What needs to be emphasized here is that the rejection of the legend of the seventy isolated translators must be seen as a corollary of the belief that the LXX conspired to hide trinitarian mysteries from Ptolemy.[107] For the Egyptian monarch separated the translators with a specific objective in mind, as Irenaeus puts it, μήτι ἄρα συνθέμενοι ἀποκρύψωσι τὴν ἐν ταῖς γραφαῖς διὰ τῆς ἑρμηνείας ἀλήθειαν (*Haer.* 3. 21. 2). In other words, according to Irenaeus, Ptolemy attempted to obviate precisely what in Jerome's view did occur, namely, a conspiracy. Such a conspiracy would not have been possible had the translators been in separate cells.

Accordingly, the idea that the version of the LXX was a key link in a specifically gentile chain of transmission of the Old Testament and could therefore constitute some kind of special dispensation for gentile Christians was to be rejected. On the other

---

[104] Jerome was prepared to admit that the translation of the LXX was 'useful' in that it allowed Gentiles to know of Christ before he arrived (*Ruf.* 2. 35). However, it is not fair to say, on the basis of *Comm. in Is.* 8 (25: 6–8 = CChr.SL 73, p. 327), that Jerome attributes to the LXX 'le souci d'annoncer, au besoin par une traduction large, le transfert aux païens des réalités du salut' (Benoit, 'L'inspiration', p. 180). For if one reads the passage in question, it is clear that, according to Jerome, the LXX are merely translating *ad sensum* a concept already present in the Hebrew text.

[105] Benoit, 'L'inspiration', pp. 172–3, tries to deny this, but his arguments seem to represent an attempt to put the Fathers in modern dress. To take only one case, it is clear from *Civ.* 18. 42 that Augustine attached more than minor importance to the legend. A. Pelletier, in his edition of the *Letter of Aristeas* (Paris 1962 = SC 89), p. 98, notes that the legend continued to flourish well into the 13th cent. despite the criticisms of Jerome. If it was such an unimportant factor in the prestige of the LXX, why were Christians so loath to part with it?

[106] *Praef. in Pent.* 25–9. Cf. *Praef. in Par.* (*IH*) 17–18; *Comm. in Ezech.* 10 (33: 23–33 = CChr.SL 75, p. 475).

[107] The two themes appear together in *Praef. in Pent.* 19–29.

hand, Jerome attempts to portray his own version as a Christian Bible. As he says, his purpose is 'sacramenta ecclesiae puro et fideli aperire sermone' (*Praef. in Job (IH)* 46–7). As a matter of principle, Jerome seems to have believed that it was not possible to translate something which one did not understand (*Praef. in Is.* 15–16; *Praef. in Job (IH)* 22–3). Consequently, it was his view that the task of producing a Christian version was facilitated by the passage of time. For after the appearance of the Gospel, many of the mysteries of the Old Testament had become clear. The LXX, on the other hand, had no such good fortune: 'illi interpretati sunt ante adventum Christi et quod nesciebant dubiis protulere sententiis, nos post passionem et resurrectionem eius, non tam prophetiam quam historiam scribimus . . . quod melius intellegimus, melius et proferimus.'[108] Here Jerome has turned a motif normally cited in favour of the LXX against those translators. For it was claimed by some Fathers, Irenaeus and Hilary among them, that the credibility of the LXX was guaranteed by the fact that they had produced their version before Christ, and accordingly could not be accused of a pro-Christian bias.[109] Jerome, on the other hand, would have been delighted to be charged with such partiality.

In fact, it is for similar reasons that Jerome promotes his own *IH* as an advance on the *recentiores*. In the first place, he seems to have thought that because he lived after them it was possible for him to benefit from their work. For he claims that he is in a position to judge between them. This claim he makes in his *Praef. in Esdr. et Neh.* 39–44, where he also cites the case of a Greek scholar who, in his ignorance of Hebrew, had the misfortune of following the various translators when they were in error.[110]

More importantly, however, Jerome is a Christian, whereas

---

[108] *Praef. in Pent.* 35–9. Cf. also *Tract. Psal. I* 9 (CChr.SL 78, p. 28): 'mysterium quod omnibus retro saeculis fuerat occultum, nobis in fine apertum est.'

[109] For the passages, see above, Ch. 1 n. 100.

[110] It is most likely that the scholar in question is Apollinaris of Laodicea, who, according to Jerome, employed the *recentiores* 'non secundum scientiam' (*Ruf.* 2. 34). Cf. *Praef. in Ps. (IH)* 21–3, where it transpires that Sophronius, Jerome's addressee, was confused by the variety of translations (i.e. the three *recentiores*) and wanted Jerome to judge between them and/or translate anew. It would seem that Jerome saw his work as a combination of these two processes. In addition, Jerome was not above pointing out the practical value of his version. He tells readers that it is difficult and expensive to obtain the *recentiores*. See *Praef. in Esdr. et Neh.* 37–9. Cf. *Praef. in Jos.* 9; *Ruf.* 2. 34.

the *recentiores* are Jews or heretics, capable indeed of 'hiding' mysteries pertinent to Christ.[111] Here again Jerome is arguing γυμναστικῶς. For he exploits a motif which the Fathers normally employ in justifying the use of the LXX, viz. the denigration of the *recentiores* based on their Jewish origins, in order to justify his own version. He himself had the highest regard for the later translators, especially Aquila.[112] Indeed, his dependence on them in *IH* is well known.

We see, then, that in presenting *IH* Jerome is arguing on two planes. He promotes it both as an auxiliary version, which one could employ to better understand the LXX or to dispute with the Jews, and as a rival version to the LXX. The phrase 'rival version', however, should in turn probably be understood in two senses. Jerome sees *IH* first of all as a scientific version, in which he attempts to represent as accurately as possible the 'Hebraica veritas', the only true text. In his view, he has been just as successful in achieving this goal as all previous Greek translators, if not more so. Accordingly, as a scientific version, *IH* was produced at least on a theoretical level for Greeks as well as Latins.[113] In the second place, Jerome also seems to have envisaged an official and liturgical role for his version in the West. That is, he probably intended that *IH* replace the *VL*. The reason this conclusion is inescapable is that in preparing *IH* Jerome follows a procedure similar to the one he employs in the revision of the Gospels, and retains much of the style of the *VL*.[114] His statement in *Ep.*

---

[111] See *Praef. in Job* (*IH*) 41–8; *Comm. in Dan.* prol.; *Ruf.* 2. 33–4. Cf. *Praef. in Esdr. et Neh.* 32–6; *Ep.* 112. 19.

[112] See *Ep.* 28. 2; 36. 12; *Comm. in Is.* 13 (49: 5–6); *Comm. in Os.* 1 (2: 16–17). Jerome also thought that Aquila made a positive contribution to the Christian understanding of the Old Testament. See *Ep.* 32. 1; *Comm. in Abac.* 2 (3: 10–13 = CChr.SL 76A, p. 641). This belief was no doubt inspired by the aspect of Eusebius' exegesis which is discussed by Barthélemy in 'Eusèbe'.

[113] See *Praef. in Esdr. et Neh.* 36–7, and cf. *Vir. ill.* 134; *Ruf.* 2. 24. (Since the context of this last passage is a defence of *IH*, and the language is similar to that in *Praef. in Esdr. et Neh.* 33–7, it would seem that the reference is to a Greek translation of *IH*, not of *Comm. in XII Prophetas*, as Barthélemy, *ThZ* 16 (1960), p. 351, has suggested.)

[114] See Stummer, *Einführung*, pp. 117–19. Jerome claims to have followed a similar principle in the revisions of the New Testament and the LXX. See *Praef. in Evang.* 30–2; *Ep.* 106. 12, 30. It is also to be noted that in *Ep.* 48. 4 he describes *IH* with the words 'ecclesiastica interpretatio', though perhaps this should be translated as 'Christian translation'. Cf. above, pp. 67–8.

106. 46 (perhaps to be understood with reference to the Psalms only), that the version of the LXX was to be used in church, shows only that he was not trying to force the issue, and was probably looking for a 'draft'. And, in fact, we know that there were forward-looking Christians in the West who were willing to indulge Jerome, and that these included more than just his former circle in Rome. For in a letter of Augustine which dates to *c*.403, it is related that the bishop of the North African community of Oea tried, albeit unsuccessfully, to introduce Jerome's version into public worship.[115]

In short, in producing *IH* as a 'rival version' to the LXX, Jerome had different and even conflicting goals. One may characterize *IH* as a whole as a compromise between scientific and practical considerations.[116] This point should be borne in mind in any evaluation of the version.

We may summarize the result of the foregoing investigation. It will be clear first of all that Jerome became convinced of the centrality of the Hebrew text at an early point in his career. This conviction was to influence all his subsequent efforts with regard to the biblical text. For a Latin, however, the issues surrounding that text were complex, and did not always come down to a Greek versus Hebrew conflict. Other discussions were also taking place. That Jerome participated in such discussions and did not lose interest in LXX questions is clear not least from *Ep.* 106. Indeed, in conformity with the complexity of the situation, Jerome gradually developed a three-tier approach. His minimum or 'bottom-line' position was support for the Origenian 'Hebraized' recension of the LXX. He believed, however, that Christians could get a better idea of the original through a version which was closer to it than the traditional Greek version, so he made his own. But there were two ways in which Jerome went about promoting this text. On the one hand, he presented it as an auxiliary version, to be employed in the same manner as the *recentiores* were employed by the Greeks. Such a use of the version did not imply a negative view of the LXX nor faith in the 'Hebraica veritas'. That is, one could use the version quite profitably without sharing the views

---

[115] *Ep.* 71. 5. For the date, see Schmid, op. cit. (n. 42 above), p. 4.

[116] Cf. Stummer, *Einführung*, p. 99, and the remarks of Allgeier with regard to the Hexaplaric revision of the Psalms in *Bib* 11 (1930), p. 106.

of the translator. On the other hand, Jerome himself believed that the version of the LXX was flawed on the basis of the fact that it diverged too much from the original. He thought that his own version could (*a*) better serve anyone who would desire to understand and study the original, and (*b*) was indeed worthy of replacing the Latin versions of the LXX in the West. This was his 'top-line' position.

In a sense, Jerome's approach represents an attempt to come to terms with all three of the implications of the *Hexapla* as described above on p. 34. He tries to take his Latin public on an uphill guided tour of the mountain that was the *Hexapla*. The journey progresses from the Hexaplaric text of the LXX via the *recentiores* and his own *IH*, in an attempt to come as close as possible to the 'Hebraica veritas' itself. The faint-hearted could either stop at stage one, or continue on to stage two and obtain a better view of the LXX below. On the other hand, those like Paula and Eustochium, who desired to 'enter the libraries of the Hebrews' (*Praef. in Esth.* 7–8), would employ the *recentiores* and Jerome's version to gain a better understanding of the original. In fine, we would probably not be far from the truth in saying that Jerome's objective was to give as much of the *Hexapla* as possible to the Latin world, as he himself hints (*Praef. in Jos.* 7–10).

As far as the difference between Jerome's position and that of Origen is concerned, it emerges now with much greater clarity. Origen's position lies somewhere between the support of a 'pure' LXX and a Hexaplaric 'Hebraized' LXX. Jerome's position, on the other hand, is characterized by movement from a 'bottom-line' support of the Hexaplaric LXX to his 'top-line' support of a 'pure' Hebrew text. However, we are not able to say with certainty that we have a similar type of movement in the case of Origen. All we can do is establish the 'boundaries' of his position. For as we have seen, where he actually stood or in which direction he was moving was a subject of controversy already in the fourth century. What we can say, however, is that Origen's possible maximum was Jerome's minimum. Their positions overlap at support of the Hexaplaric LXX. But Jerome progressed beyond, attempting to reach the 'Hebraica veritas'. He began work where Origen left off.[117]

---

[117] For another attempt to 'rehabilitate' the reputation of Jerome in this regard, see now Jay, *L'exégèse*, pp. 89–126. Cf. Braverman, *Jerome's 'Commentary'*, p. 25.

It is necessary to emphasize, however, that Jerome's three-tier position was a tactical one and does not represent his own chronological development. For the evidence shows that his 'conversion' to the Hebrew was stimulated not by the Hexaplaric LXX, but by the *recentiores*, and that this conversion took place early in his career.[118] It was a conversion based primarily on an acute linguistic awareness and a recognition of the distance which separated the Latin Old Testament from the original Hebrew. A negative evaluation of the LXX version should probably be seen as secondary. Indeed, many of the anti-LXX motifs which we have considered in this section, rather than being factors which led Jerome to appreciate the centrality of the Hebrew, are better understood as arguments formulated at a time when he was already on the offensive, attempting to promote his own *IH* as a rival version to the LXX.*

[118] Jerome's first contact with the *recentiores* does not necessitate familiarity with the *Hexapla*. The versions were also circulating individually. See Vaccari, *Bib* 8 (1927), pp. 464–5 (citing *Ep.* 32. 1); Jay, *L'exégèse*, p. 417 (citing *Ruf.* 2. 34). It is also possible that Jerome's first exposure to these translations came through Greek commentaries.

* Two works came to my attention after the book was submitted to the press, viz. M. E. Schild, *Abendländische Bibelvorreden bis zur Lutherbibel* (QFRG 39), [Gütersloh] 1970, pp. 13–41; C. P. [Hammond] Bammel, 'Die Hexapla des Origenes: Die *Hebraica Veritas* im Streit der Meinungen', *Aug* 28 (1988), pp. 125–49. Both writers follow the standard view of a chronological evolution of Jerome's position concerning the text of the Old Testament. Indeed, Bammel would explain his later pro-Hexaplaric comments as an attempt to ingratiate himself with Epiphanius and his circle (pp. 141–2). Moreover, both scholars, by putting perhaps too much stress on the purely polemical context of Jerome's statements, end up by undervaluing the level of his argumentation. For they seem to be content to concentrate most of their efforts on summarizing in thematic (Schild, pp. 31–9) or chronological (Bammel, pp. 139–40, 143–6) order Jerome's arguments, and pay insufficient attention to the linkage between those arguments and the logic of his position as a totality.

3

The Version *iuxta Hebraeos* and the *Quaestiones Hebraicae in Genesim*

◆ ◆ ◆

When did the first volumes of the translation from the Hebrew begin to appear? This question may be answered on the basis of the following chronological data. From *Ep*. 48(49). 4, we learn that Jerome had already translated 16 books of the Prophets (= 3 major Prophets, 12 minor Prophets, and Daniel), Samuel and Kings, and Job. Nautin has recently dated *Ep*. 48 to early 394.[1] In *De viris illustribus* 134, Jerome states that his versions of the Prophets and the Psalms had already been translated into Greek by Sophronius. *Vir. ill.* was probably written in the spring of 393.[2] It is also well known that Jerome employs his versions of the minor prophets in his commentaries on five of them.[3] These commentaries were composed during the winter of 392–3.[4] In short, by early 394 Jerome had completed, according to a calculation based on page numbers of modern editions of the Masoretic Text, roughly 55 per cent of the Hebrew Bible. On the basis of this fact and the information from *Vir. ill.*, it must be concluded that the first translations based on the Hebrew date back to at least 392 if not 391. For as F. Stummer has noted, the statements which Jerome makes about the breakneck speed in which some of his translations were completed cannot be applied to his work as a whole.[5] Indeed, calculating on the basis of the old chronology

---

[1] *REAug* 20 (1974), pp. 254–5. This date has been accepted by Jay, *REAug* 28 (1982), p. 208. Cavallera, *Saint Jérôme*, i. 2, p. 43, had dated the letter to 393.

[2] See Nautin, *RHE* 56 (1961), pp. 33–5. This dating has generally been accepted (*pace* Kelly, *Jerome*, p. 174), despite the criticism of T. D. Barnes, *Tertullian*, Oxford 1971, pp. 235–6. See, e.g., Jay, *REAug* 28 (1982), p. 208 n. 1; P. Lardet in his edition of Jerome, *Ruf.* (Paris 1983 = SC 303), pp. 29*–30*; Duval, op. cit. (Introd. n. 4), p. 11. For Nautin's own response to Barnes, see *REAug* 20 (1974), pp. 280–4.

[3] See A. Penna, *S. Gerolamo*, Turin 1949, p. 171; Jay, loc. cit. (n. 1 above).

[4] See Nautin, *REAug* 20 (1974), p. 252; Jay, loc. cit. (n. 1 above).

[5] *Einführung*, pp. 97–8. Cf. Grützmacher, *Hieronymus*, ii, pp. 101–2.

(viz. that *Vir. ill.* was written in 392 and *Ep.* 48 in 393), Stummer has placed the start of Jerome's *IH* project in 390.[6] Applying the revised chronology to this reckoning, we arrive at the date of 391.

At approximately the same time, Jerome also published his *Quaestiones Hebraicae in Genesim.* The date of this work can be determined with a fair degree of accuracy. Jerome includes it in the catalogue of his own writings which he provides in *Vir. ill.* 135. A *terminus ante quem* is therefore readily available, since, as stated, *Vir. ill.* was probably completed in the spring of 393. The exact date of composition, on the other hand, must be established by reference to a statement found in another work, the translation of Origen's *Homiliae in Lucam.*

We may first turn to the date of this latter work. The translation is mentioned in *Vir. ill.* 135, so it too must have been published before the spring of 393. The *terminus post quem* may be determined from the preface. Jerome tells Paula and Eustochium that he has produced the version because of their dissatisfaction with a recent treatment of the same subject, which is known to be the *Expositio Evangelii secundum Lucam* by Ambrose.[7] The chronology of this work is in turn connected with that of the same writer's *Apologia prophetae David*, since in the former work he makes a reference to the latter (*Luc.* 3. 38). Recent scholarship has reached a consensus that *Apol. Dav.* was written after the massacre of Thessalonica, an event which took place in the spring of 390.[8] It is therefore unlikely that *Luc.* appeared before late 390, and it should probably be dated, as F. Claus believes, to 391.[9] We must then allow time for the work to arrive in Palestine and be read by Paula and Eustochium, and for Origen's *Hom. in Lc.* to be translated by Jerome. As Nautin has affirmed, it is unlikely that this could have taken place before 392.[10] The version of Origen's homilies should therefore be placed in 392 or early 393.

[6] *Einführung*, p. 92. Cf. Cottineau, 'Chronologie', p. 56: 'au moins avant 391'.

[7] See Rufinus, *Apol. adv. Hier.* 2. 25. Cf. A. Paredi, 'S. Gerolamo e s. Ambrogio', *Mélanges Eugène Tisserant*, v (StT 235), Città del Vaticano 1964, pp. 187–8.

[8] See F. Claus, 'La datation de l'*Apologia prophetae David* et l'*Apologia David altera*', *Ambrosius Episcopus*, ii (SPMed 7), ed. G. Lazzati, Milan 1976, pp. 177–92; F. Lucidi in his translation of *Apol. Dav.* and *Apol. Dav. II* (Milan 1981 = Opera omnia di sant'Ambrogio 5), pp. 25–8; P. Nautin, 'L'activité littéraire de Jérôme de 387 à 392', *RThPh* 115 (1983), p. 252. Cf. P. Hadot in his edition of *Apol. Dav.* (Paris 1977 = SC 239), p. 39.

[9] 'La datation', p. 179 n. 22. Cf. Nautin, 'L'activité', p. 252 n. 24; Lucidi, op. cit., p. 28.

[10] 'L'activité', pp. 252–3, 256.

In the preface to this translation, Jerome states that he has put aside his *Quaestionum Hebraicarum libri* in order to produce it. This statement, however, is difficult to interpret, for the following reason. The *Quaestionum Hebraicarum libri* are announced in the preface to *De nominibus Hebraicis* as a work to appear in the near future. In the preface to *QHG*, which includes only one book, Jerome declares that he will extend the series of *Quaestionum Hebraicarum libri* to the entire Bible. However, these additional books of *Quaestiones* on the rest of the Bible have not come down to us, so they were either lost or never completed. Accordingly, when in the preface to his translation of Origen's *Hom. in Lc.* Jerome writes that he has postponed the publication of his *Quaestionum Hebraicarum libri*, it is not clear whether he had not yet published a single volume of *Quaestiones*, and is explaining to his readers why he has not carried out his plans as announced in the preface to *Nom. Hebr.*, or whether he had already published his *QHG* and has set aside the elaboration of the further volumes of *Quaestiones* which are announced in the preface to *QHG*. Most scholars opt for the former possibility, and therefore believe that *QHG* was finished only after the publication of the translation of Origen's homilies.[11] G. Grützmacher and Nautin, on the other hand, believe that Jerome had already issued *QHG*, and that in the preface to the translation of Origen's homilies he is referring rather to *Quaestiones Hebraicae* on other biblical books.[12] Yet, in fact, since Jerome employs the plural 'libri' in the declaration of postponement, that declaration could just as easily refer to the entire series of *Quaestiones*, including *QHG*, as it could to the series of *Quaestiones* which was to follow *QHG*.

Nevertheless, it is possible to determine that *QHG* appeared either shortly after the translation of Origen's homilies, or shortly before. For if in his preface to *Hom. in Lc.* Jerome is speaking of *Quaestiones* which were as yet unpublished, including *QHG*, the latter work must have appeared after the publication of *Hom. in Lc.* and before *Vir. ill*, i.e. during the period 392–early 393. If, on the other hand, Jerome is referring to a work of which a part had

---

[11] O. Zöckler, *Hieronymus: Sein Leben und Wirken aus seinen Schriften dargestellt*, Gotha 1865, p. 174; Schade, *Die Inspirationslehre*, p. 148; Kelly, *Jerome*, p. 153. Cf. Penna, *S. Gerolamo*, pp. 135–6; H. Crouzel in his edition of Origen's *Hom. in Lc.* (Paris 1962 = SC 87), p. 77.

[12] Grützmacher, *Hieronymus*, ii, p. 80 n. 3; Nautin, 'L'activité', p. 256.

already appeared, that part must be *QHG*. For no other books of
Quaestiones were published before *Vir. ill*. In addition, the publication of such *Quaestiones* must have been quite recent, for in his
announcement of postponement Jerome makes clear that the
Quaestiones is the work that he has interrupted in order to produce
the translation. And it is difficult to imagine that he would have
completed *QHG* a long time beforehand, and then devoted a
considerable amount of time to other books of *Quaestiones* without
publishing them. In other words, if *QHG* preceded *Hom in Lc.*,
it will probably not have been by more than a year. The overall
conclusion will then be that *QHG* must have been published at
the earliest in 391 and at the latest in early 393.

This calculation can perhaps be confirmed from another indication. Recently, J. Divjak published a previously unknown collection of letters by Augustine.[13] The corpus also contains a letter
(no. 27) which Jerome wrote to Aurelius of Carthage in order to
congratulate him on his consecration as bishop, an event which
can be dated to January of 392 or 393.[14] Consequently, Jerome's
letter was probably written at the earliest in the middle of 392
and at the latest towards the end of 393. Among other things,
Jerome tells his correspondent that he is enclosing with his letter
copies of *QHG* and *Tractatus in Psalmos II* 10 (*Ep.* 27. 2). Apparently referring to these works, Jerome writes, 'si qua nunc scrip-
simus maturiora et aetati nostrae convenientia aestimare debes.'
It would seem, then, that at the time of the composition of the
letter, Jerome regarded these works as quite recent. How recent
of course cannot be determined. Yet it would not at all be surprising if by 'nunc' he means 'within the past year', since *Tract.
Psal. II* 10 should probably be dated to 392.[15]

It will be clear, therefore, that both *QHG* and the first translations
from the Hebrew appeared within a very short time of each other,
probably sometime during the period of 391–2. In view of such
chronological considerations, it would not be at all unreasonable
to assume that the composition of *QHG* was in some way related
to the genesis of *IH*. And, indeed, scholars have for the most part

---

[13] Vienna 1981 (CSEL 88); [Paris] 1987² (= BAug 46b).
[14] See J.-L. Maier, *L'épiscopat de l'Afrique romaine, vandale et byzantine* (Bibliotheca Helvetica Romana 11), Rome 1973, p. 262.
[15] See Nautin, 'L'activité', pp. 256–7.

made such an assumption. Nevertheless, there has not been general agreement on the exact nature of the relationship.

Already in the seventeenth century, Richard Simon proposed that *QHG* was to be understood as an apology for *IH*. He claimed that in *QHG* Jerome 'a combattu exprès la version grecque des Septante, pour autoriser davantage le texte hebreu, et en même tems sa nouvelle traduction sur ce texte'.[16] This view is probably the closest to being correct, yet it needs to be further elaborated. In addition, the view requires resurrection in a general sense, for it did not find favour with later scholars. The Maurist Jean Martianay objected vehemently to Simon's claim. He rejected the idea that the work was an attack on the LXX by citing Jerome's own statement in the preface to the effect that he was not condemning the LXX. As for the view that the work constituted an apology for his own version, the Maurist appealed to the fact that the publication of Jerome's translation of the Book of Genesis according to the Hebrew did not appear until many years later.[17]

The positive corollary of Martianay's view was not developed in depth until the present century, when Schade published his study on Jerome's concept of inspiration. According to Schade, as we have seen above, it was when Jerome began to sense that there were serious differences between the Hebrew text and the LXX that he started work on his *Quaestiones Hebraicae*. Indeed, this textual conflict was the catalyst for the work. At this point, in the view of Schade, Jerome still believed in the inspiration and infallibility of the LXX. It is this circumstance that explains why Jerome takes a conciliatory attitude towards both texts in the preface to *QHG*. Schade finds that in the first part of the work Jerome exhibits a more balanced view of the differences between the texts whereas in the second part his attitude shifts in favour of the Hebrew. He believes that both the announcement of the imminent publication of the *Quaestionum Hebraicarum libri* in *Nom. Hebr.* and the declaration of postponement of the same work in the translation of Origen's *Hom. in Lc.* refer only to *QHG* and not to other books of *Quaestiones*, and accordingly, that Jerome interrupted the composition of *QHG* in order to prepare both *Nom. Hebr.* and the version of *Hom. in Lc.* The change in his

---

[16] *Histoire critique du Vieux Testament*², Rotterdam 1685, p. 254. Cf. p. 396.
[17] See vol. ii of the Maurist edition of Jerome's works (Paris 1699), Prolegomenon ii. 1; pp. 558–9 (= *PL* 23. 1636d–38a).

attitude is therefore easier to explain. In any case, by the time he
had finished *QHG* he was convinced that a revision of the *VL*
based on the LXX was not the way forward and that it was
necessary to translate afresh using the Hebrew text as the base.
He therefore abandoned the Hexaplaric revision as well as his plan
to compose *Quaestiones Hebraicae* on all the books of the Bible.
Such an enterprise would in effect be made superfluous by the
new translation.[18] According to this reconstruction of events,
Jerome did not compose *QHG* as an apology for *IH*, but rather
it was the composition of this work that led to the idea of the
version. Schade's position on this matter has been recently taken
up by Gribomont.[19]

There is a series of reasons why such a view should be abandoned. First of all, *QHG* need not be seen as a defence of the
translation of Genesis in particular, but rather as an apology for
the new version in general. Accordingly, the fact that the translation of Genesis appeared only years after *QHG* cannot be regarded
as a serious objection to Simon's basic position. Indeed, it is well
known that Jerome published the volumes of *IH* not according to
the biblical order, but translated different books in the order in
which they were requested by his friends. It may be that he
desired to follow a more systematic approach in the publication
of the *Quaestiones*, and therefore began with Genesis.

Secondly, the appeal of Martianay and Schade to the preface of
QHG is perplexing. As we have noted, the latter scholar cites
Jerome's affirmation that his efforts should not be seen as a criticism of the LXX in order to support his view that Jerome still
believed in the inspiration of the LXX when he began work on
QHG. However, Schade's view rests on the assumption that
Jerome wrote the preface before rather than after he composed
the work itself, an assumption which would seem quite
unjustified.[20] But more importantly, it transpires from the preface
that the statement which Jerome makes about his position *vis-à-
vis* the LXX is a response to those who had already taken him to

---

[18] Schade, *Die Inspirationslehre*, pp. 144–9.   [19] 'Girolamo', pp. 214, 222.
[20] The view of Vaccari, *CivCatt* 1915. 4, pp. 415–16, that in antiquity the preface
was written *before* the composition of the work to which it was prefixed, or at any
rate that this was the practice of Jerome, cannot be sustained. See T. Janson, *Latin
Prose Prefaces* (SLS 13), Stockholm 1964, pp. 73–4, and with regard to Jerome in
particular, *Praef. in Is.* 4–6; *Praef. in Jer.* 11–14; *Praef. in Dan.* 20–3.

task for his criticism of that version. Since this is the case, the statement need not be understood any differently from similar statements which appear, as we have seen above, in many of his prefaces to *IH*, including those which contain such anti-LXX motifs as we have examined in the previous chapter. In fact, many of these same motifs are present in the preface to *QHG*. We find the arguments based on New Testament quotations, Ptolemy's Platonism, the details of the *Letter of Aristeas*, and the precedent of Origen. We saw that these arguments are characteristic of Jerome's prefaces to *IH* and other later texts in which he defends his version as a *fait accompli* and attempts to undermine the position of the LXX. Far from compelling us to believe that Jerome began *QHG* with a conciliatory attitude towards both the Hebrew and the Greek texts, the preface would rather induce us to associate the work with *IH*.

More importantly, however, one must consider the character of *QHG* itself. Throughout the entire work Jerome is completely partial to the Hebrew text. Schade's claim that his textual position gradually evolved during the composition of *QHG* from being pro-LXX or neutral to being anti-LXX is not at all borne out by the facts.[21] First of all, there is no lack of anti-LXX comments at the beginning of the work.[22] Secondly, some of the passages which Schade sees as neutral presentations of the evidence in fact show partiality to the Hebrew.[23] Finally, the evidence which Schade adduces to show that Jerome is 'defending' the LXX is unconvincing.[24] Of the three passages which he cites, one occurs near the end of the work (*QHG* 46: 26–7). But, in fact, in all of the three passages, Jerome merely explains why the LXX have a different reading without having made an error in translation. In *QHG* 14: 5 he simply says that the LXX have opted for a non-literal translation and in 23: 2 he attributes a corruption of a Hebrew

[21] For this claim, see *Die Inspirationslehre*, pp. 146–8.

[22] See, e.g., *QHG* 4: 6–7, 8; 14: 5. Schade himself, *Die Inspirationslehre*, p. 62, seems to think that Jerome attributes an error to the LXX in 19: 14–15.

[23] In *QHG* 14: 5, cited by Schade, *Die Inspirationslehre*, p. 147 n. 3, Jerome thinks that the LXX have misread the text. With regard to the age of Methuselah (discussed in *QHG* 5: 25–7), Jerome does not merely mention a difference in reading, as Schade, p. 147, would have it, but suspects an error in the MSS of the LXX (cf. *QHG* 5: 4). It is difficult to ascertain to which passages Schade is referring at p. 147 n. 1, for he cites the text according to the numbering of pages in P. de Lagarde's edition (Leipzig 1868) which contain more than one lemma.

[24] For this evidence, see *Die Inspirationslehre*, p. 147.

name to copyists rather than to the LXX. It is these passages that
should be described as neutral presentations of the evidence, for
on none of the three occasions does Jerome prefer the LXX
reading to that of the Hebrew. Indeed, there is not a single example
of such a phenomenon in the entire work. But more importantly,
such explanations of LXX readings without an accusation of error
may be found throughout Jerome's writings, including those of a
later period.[25] It seems difficult, therefore, to explain such comments as products of the period when Jerome still had faith in the
LXX. In fine, the work does not give the impression that it was
written by a man who 'volle chiarirsi le idee'.[26] The fact that
Jerome stubbornly supports the Hebrew throughout *QHG* should
come as no surprise, since, as we have attempted to show in the
previous chapter, his 'conversion' to the Hebrew text goes back
to at least his 'Roman' period.

Consequently, the view of Schade and Gribomont, according
to which the composition of *QHG* is seen as a sort of experiment,
must be abandoned. On the other hand, in many of the modern
biographies of Jerome one finds a sort of compromise position.
According to this view, while Jerome did compose *QHG* with the
intention of promoting the Hebrew text, or at least removing
mistrust of it, the work was nevertheless not intended as an apology for *IH*, but rather, together with the proposed series of
quaestiones commentaries, was superseded by *IH* and (in the view
of some) the full-scale commentaries.[27] Now, it may be that
Jerome's other exegetical works made the continuation of the
quaestiones series unnecessary.[28] However, the idea that *QHG* was
superseded by *IH* cannot be accepted. This is because the view
that *QHG* is simply an attempt to show the utility of the Hebrew
text or remove mistrust of it is itself incomplete and inadequate.
Rather, Jerome goes beyond this objective, and puts forward and
defends a system for interpreting that text. The system which he

---

[25] See the passages cited above, Ch. 2 n. 46.

[26] The expression is used by Gribomont, 'Girolamo', p. 214.

[27] For the combination of these two views, see G. Bardy, 'La littérature patristique des *Quaestiones et responsiones* sur l'Écriture sainte', *RB* 41 (1932), p. 357;
Grützmacher, *Hieronymus*, ii, p. 62; F. Cavallera, 'Les *Quaestiones Hebraicae in
Genesim* de saint Jérôme et les *Quaestiones in Genesim* de saint Augustin', *Miscellanea agostiniana*, ii, Rome 1931, pp. 360–1, together with *Saint Jérôme*, i. 1,
pp. 146–7. Cf. Zöckler, *Hieronymus*, pp. 171–3.

[28] Cf. Jay, *L'exégèse*, p. 196.

advocates may be termed a '*recentiores*–rabbinic philology', and, as we hope to show in Chapters 5 and 6, is presented as an alternative both to the standard LXX-based philology of the Greeks, and to the Greek attempts to go beyond a LXX-based system. It is of course this same '*recentiores*–rabbinic' philological system that underlies *IH*. In short, *QHG* is not so much a defence of specific translations or formulations present in *IH*, but rather a defence of the basic philological system which underlies the version.

Accordingly, if *QHG* constitutes a conscious presentation of such a system, then the view that the latter work was superseded by *IH* must also be discarded. For in this case the two works fulfil different functions, and must be seen as complementary. Indeed, the necessity of a philological apology for *IH* will be clear from the previous chapter. For we have seen exactly to what extent this project represented a new departure in Christian biblical scholarship. And it seems that for Jerome, just as the new translation required a 'novum scribendi genus' (*Praef. in Is.* 5–6), so it required evidence of a new philological system. That in his eyes *QHG* constituted such evidence seems clear from the preface to his *Nom. Hebr.*, where, as we have noted in the Introduction, he announces the forthcoming work as an 'opus novum et tam Graecis quam Latinis usque ad id locorum inauditum'.[29]

We may summarize briefly. It appears that both *QHG* and the first volumes of *IH* appeared at roughly the same time. In the preface to the former work Jerome defends the Hebrew text in a manner very similar to that in his prefaces to the latter. There is no section of *QHG* which reveals the spirit of a man feeling his way towards the solution of the conflict between the Hebrew text and the LXX. Indeed, we shall see that Jerome is putting forward a method of interpreting the original which constitutes an alternative to the version of the LXX and other systems of interpretation put forward by Greeks. In short, *QHG* must be seen as a justification of the basic philological system underlying *IH*. How does Jerome go about making his case? An appreciation of the literary genre which he employs will help us answer this question.

[29] Cf. the preface to *QHG* (ed. de Lagarde, p. 2, l. 3), where he refers to the work as an 'opus novum'.

4

The Literary Genre of the *Quaestiones Hebraicae in Genesim*

◆ ◆ ◆

The *Quaestiones Hebraicae in Genesim*, as is clear from the title, belongs to a branch or genre of literature known as ζητήματα, προβλήματα, or *quaestiones*. This literature had had an extremely long history prior to the time of Jerome. In 1927, A. Gudeman published an encyclopaedia article which remains fundamental for the study of the genre in question. In this article, he distinguishes two types of *quaestiones* literature, each of which had a different origin. One type is closely connected with the exposition of a literary text, and it is clearly this type that most concerns us. The second type is independent of a text, and was often employed in the treatment of philosophical questions. To this category belong many collections of προβλήματα attributed to Aristotle, a number of compositions by Plutarch, and many other works.[1]

The beginnings of the textual-exegetical ζητήματα are to be found in the criticisms of the Homeric poems which are attested as early as the sixth century BC. Originally, the critics were disturbed by and 'raised questions' about what was objectionable from a moral standpoint. As time went by, however, the grammar and style of the poems came under attack, and 'sachliche Widersprüche und Inkonsequenzen' were pointed out. In due course, others came along who undertook to defend the Homeric poems, and it became their task to 'solve' *(λύειν)* the difficulties raised by the critics. A very important stage in this process is constituted by chapter 25 of Aristotle's *Poetics*, which is entitled Περὶ προβλημάτων καὶ λύσεων. The author attempts to categorize the types of criticism which could be raised, and to put forward a system of refutation. Aristotle also produced a work entitled Ἀπορήματα Ὁμηρικά, which unfortunately has not come down to us.[2]

---

[1] Gudeman, Λύσεις, *PRE* i. 13. 2 (1927), cols. 2511–29. Also important is K. Lehrs, *De Aristarchi studiis Homericis*[3], Leipzig 1882, pp. 197–221, and see now O. Dreyer, 'Lyseis', *KP* 3. 16–17 (1968–9), cols. 832–3.

[2] For this paragraph, I am indebted to Gudeman, Λύσεις, cols. 2511–12.

It was in the Hellenistic and imperial periods that the genre of ζητήματα καὶ λύσεις reached its high point. According to a famous passage in the Homeric scholia, ἐν τῷ Μουσείῳ τῷ κατὰ Ἀλεξάνδρειαν νόμος ἦν προβάλλεσθαι ζητήματα καὶ τὰς γινομένας λύσεις ἀναγράφεσθαι (Porphyry, *Ad Iliadem I.* 682). We know the titles of numerous ζητήματα commentaries which were written between the third century BC and the second century of the Christian era.[3] The last great collection of Homeric problems and solutions was produced by Porphyry. It is believed that his Ζητήματα Ὁμηρικά constituted a sort of reservoir into which the material from all preceding periods flowed.[4] Although most of the Hellenistic and imperial collections have been lost, a good deal may be recovered from the Homeric scholia.[5] In addition, a portion of Porphyry's work survives in direct tradition, and these remains have been re-edited recently by A.R. Sodano.[6]

The *quaestiones* procedure was adopted by the Romans, and almost all of the extant material relates to Virgil. Some of this material is found in Gellius and Macrobius, but for the most part it is preserved in the commentary of Servius.[7] However, the problems which were perceived to exist in the *Aeneid* are both numerically fewer and qualitatively less pronounced than those relating to the Homeric poems. The reason for this lies largely in the nature of the literary works concerned. The Homeric poems are oral compositions and were produced in an age far removed from the classical or Hellenistic periods. From the former circumstance come inconsistencies and repetitions (cf. Josephus, *Ap.* 1. 12), and from the latter strangeness of language, content, and outlook. The *Aeneid*, on the other hand, was prepared as a written work by one man who lived in an age not so remote from that of his principal commentators.

The history of *quaestiones* literature in the early Church has been traced by G. Bardy.[8] The adoption of the genre on the part

---

[3] See Gudeman, Λύσεις, cols. 2512–14.

[4] See W. Schmid, *Geschichte der griechischen Literatur*, i. 1 (HAW 7. 1. 1), Munich 1929, p. 168. Cf. Schäublin, *Untersuchungen*, p. 60 n. 71.

[5] The standard edition of the Porphyrian scholia is that of H. Schrader (Leipzig 1880–90).

[6] *Quaestionum Homericarum liber I*, Naples 1970.

[7] See Gudeman, Λύσεις, cols. 2521–2. See also H. Georgii, *Die antike Äneiskritik aus den Scholien und anderen Quellen*, Stuttgart 1891; E. Thomas, *Scoliastes de Virgile: Essai sur Servius et son Commentaire sur Virgile*, Paris 1880, pp. 247–57.

[8] 'La littérature' (cf. C. Curti, *Dizionario patristico e di antichità cristiane* 2 (1983–4), cols. 2958–62). See also G. Heinrici, 'Zur patristischen Aporienliteratur',

of Christians was undoubtedly due to pagan influence.[9] Such influence was felt both directly and via the culture of Hellenistic Judaism, for the first ζητήματα commentary on the Bible seems to have been the *Quaestiones in Genesim et in Exodum* of Philo Judaeus.[10] However, one should add that the genre was especially suited for biblical exegesis. Much of the Old Testament, like the Homeric poems, is based on oral tradition, and goes back to an age very distant from the time of the ancient Christian commentators. Problems of inconsistency, offensive morality, and the like naturally came to the fore, just as in the case of Homer.

Both Theodoret and Augustine tell us that two sets of people were raising such questions about the Bible. On the one hand, the inconsistencies and other problems were pointed out by those who were inimical to the Old Testament. On the other hand, when pious Christians began to investigate the biblical text in a more than superficial manner, they too were disturbed by such problems.[11] Yet, as Bardy has shown, it seems that the former group, and specifically heretics, were the first to employ the *quaestiones* technique in a systematic fashion.[12] Marcion, for example, wrote his *Antitheses* primarily in order to point out the contradictions between the Old and the New Testaments. We also know from the testimony of Origen and Ambrose that Apelles, a disciple of Marcion, in a similar attempt to undermine the authority of the Old Testament, employed the *quaestiones* method in his Συλλογισμοί.[13] Pagan critics of Christianity followed the same procedure. Both Porphyry and Julian the Apostate put forward embarrassing questions about the Bible.[14] Pagan use of the

---

ASGW.PH 27 (1909), pp. 841–60; id., 'Scholien', *RE*³ 17 (1906), pp. 736, 738; H. Jordan, *Geschichte der altchristlichen Literatur*, Leipzig 1911, pp. 409–11; P. de Labriolle, *La réaction païenne¹⁰*, Paris 1950 (1948), pp. 487–508; H. Dörrie and H. Dörries, 'Erotapokriseis', *RAC* 6. 43 (1964), cols. 342–70; Schäublin, *Untersuchungen*, pp. 49–51, 55–60.

[9] See Schäublin, *Untersuchungen*, p. 56 n. 49.

[10] For the use of *quaestiones* methodology in the Jewish historian Demetrius, see J. Freudenthal, *Hellenistische Studien*, i, Breslau 1874, pp. 44–6.

[11] Theodoret, *Qu. in Oct.* prol.; Augustine, *Hept.* 7. 49. 1. Cf. Schäublin, *Untersuchungen*, pp. 57–8.

[12] 'La littérature' (*RB* 41), pp. 217–24.

[13] See the passages cited by Bardy, 'La littérature' (*RB* 41), pp. 220–2.

[14] For Porphyry, see A. B. Hulen, *Porphyry's Work Against the Christians: An Interpretation* (YSR 1), Scottdale, Pa. 1933, pp. 41–3; Cf. de Labriolle, *La réaction*, pp. 496–8. For Julian, see *Contra Galilaeos* 75b, 86a, 89a, 106e, 135c. These passages may be found in the edition of C.(K.) J. Neumann (Leipzig 1880 =

ζητήματα form in anti-Christian polemics is also attested in two texts attributed to Justin, *Quaestiones Graecae ad Christianos* and *Quaestiones et responsiones ad orthodoxos.*[15]

The orthodox writers took upon themselves the responsibility of answering or 'solving' the problems raised by the critics. They also went about formulating solutions to those questions which they themselves or their addressees/students had raised. The first work by an orthodox Christian writer which by virtue of its title qualifies as *quaestiones* literature is the Περὶ τῶν ἐν Εὐαγγελίοις ζητημάτων καὶ λύσεων of Eusebius of Caesarea.[16] His successor Acacius wrote six books of Σύμμικτα ζητήματα. This work is lost, but it is probable that the author was primarily concerned with scriptural problems.[17] The genre seems to have been particularly popular among Antiochene exegetes. We know from the testimony of Ebedjesus that Eusebius of Emesa wrote ζητήματα on the Old Testament,[18] and it is the view of R. Devreesse that the *catena* fragments on the historical books which are attributed to him indeed derive from a *quaestiones* work.[19] Chr. Schäublin has recently argued that the fragments of Diodore of Tarsus relating to the Octateuch originally belonged to a *quaestiones* commentary.[20] Theodoret composed *quaestiones* commentaries on the Octateuch and on Reigns and Paralipo-

---

Scriptorum Graecorum qui Christianam impugnaverunt religionem quae supersunt 3), pp. 167–8, 179, 182–3. Cf. de Labriolle, pp. 400, 495, 507.

[15] See Bardy, 'La littérature' (*RB* 42), pp. 215–19. Concerning the preservation of pagan criticisms of the Bible within Christian *quaestiones* works, see now Rinaldi, *Annali di storia dell'esegesi* 6 (1989), pp. 99–124.

[16] On this work, see Bardy, 'La littérature' (*RB* 41), pp. 228–36; Wallace-Hadrill, *Eusebius*, pp. 50–1, 74–7. The nature of the Προβλήματα of Tatian and a possible orthodox response on the part of his disciple Rhodo remains obscure. See Bardy, p. 223.

[17] See Bardy, 'La littérature' (*RB* 41), pp. 341–2; R. Devreesse, *Les anciens commentateurs grecs de l'Octateuque et des Rois* (StT 201), Città del Vaticano 1959, pp. 105–6. Cf. Petit's introduction to C. *Cois.*, p. c.

[18] *Catalogus* 36. For the text, various translations, and discussion, see É. M. Buytaert, *L'héritage littéraire d'Eusèbe d'Émèse* (BMus 24), Louvain 1949, pp. 38, 40–1. Cf. Bardy, 'La littérature' (*RB* 41), pp. 342–3.

[19] *Les anciens commentateurs*, p. 57. For the likelihood that some of this material has also been preserved in an Armenian version of a commentary attributed to Cyril of Alexandria, see below, p. 127.

[20] *Untersuchungen*, p. 49, *TRE* 8. 4–5 (1981), p. 765. Cf. Devreesse, *Les anciens commentateurs*, p. 155. Concerning a possible *quaestiones* composition by Theodore of Mopsuestia, see E. G. Clarke, *The Selected Questions of Ishō bar Nūn on the Pentateuch* (StPB 5), Leiden 1962, p. 10.

mena.[21] In the West, probably sometime during the pontificate of Damasus (366–84), the writer known as Ambrosiaster produced his *Quaestiones Veteris et Novi Testamenti*.[22] In addition to *QHG*, Jerome wrote a number of letters which belong to the same genre, and Augustine published a series of *quaestiones* commentaries.[23]

It will be clear from the foregoing that the exegetical-textual ζητήματα literature before Jerome is distinguished not merely by the question and answer format, but by the particular character of the questions. As H. Flashar puts it, a πρόβλημα is usually something knotty and complicated, the solution of which is indeed problematic. 'Nicht jede aufgeworfene Frage ist . . . ein 'Problema'. . . . Das Problema fragt nicht einfach, was der Fall ist, sondern es fragt nach den Gründen und Ursachen.'[24] Despite the fact that Flashar is concerned here primarily with the ζητήματα genre in its philosophical form, his words are none the less valid in the present context. For we have seen that the questions raised in the exegetical ζητήματα compositions normally entail 'problems' with or indeed attacks on the text concerned. In this regard, however, there arises a complication concerning Jerome's *QHG*. In the words of Bardy, 'Nous avons affaire beaucoup moins à une série de difficultés suivies de leurs solutions qu'à une chaîne d'explications de détails sur des passages controversés; l'auteur ne se propose pas de répondre à des objections, mais de fournir des éclaircissements sur les textes et leur signification littérale.'[25]

This statement is basically accurate, though slightly misleading. For there is no lack of cases in the text which can be classified only as standard *quaestiones*. Note the following passages from *QHG*:

> 4: 4–5:   unde scire poterat Cain quod fratris eius munera suscepisset Deus et sua repudiasset . . . ?

---

[21] For a recent study of portions of *Qu. in Oct.*, see Simonetti, *Annali di storia dell'esegesi* 5 (1988), pp. 39–56.

[22] On this work, see Bardy, 'La littérature' (*RB* 41), pp. 343–56; Courcelle, *VigChr* 13 (1959), pp. 133–69.

[23] The *quaestiones* productions of Jerome and Augustine are discussed by Bardy, 'La littérature' (*RB* 41), pp. 356–69, 515–37. On Augustine's *Quaestiones in Heptateuchum*, see W. Rüting, *Untersuchungen über Augustins Quaestiones und Locutiones in Heptateuchum* (FChLDG 13. 3–4), Paderborn 1916; and now A. Pollastri and F. Cocchini, *Annali di storia dell'esegesi* 5 (1988), pp. 57–76, 77–95.

[24] See the introduction in his German translation of the *Problemata physica* attributed to Aristotle (Berlin 1975² = Aristoteles: Werke in deutscher Übersetzung 19), p. 298.

[25] 'La littérature' (*RB* 41), p. 358.

5: 25–7: famosa quaestio et disputatione omnium ecclesiarum ventilata. . . . quo modo verum est quod octo tantum animae in arca salvae factae sunt?

12: 4: indissolubilis nascitur quaestio. . . . quo modo nunc post mortem Tharae Abraham exiens de Carra, LXXV annorum fuisse memoratur . . . ?

15: 16: quaeritur quo modo in Exodo scriptum sit . . .

19: 30: quaeritur quare cum primum fugae montis Segor praetulerit . . . nunc de Segor rursum ad montem migret.

37: 36: quaeritur quo modo postea uxorem habere dicatur [sc. Potiphar the eunuch].

None the less, Bardy is correct in identifying a problem, for there are many comments in *QHG* which do not appear to qualify as *quaestiones* in the conventional sense. For such passages contain neither the expression of a criticism nor the interrogative form. Bardy himself has proposed the following explanation to the dilemma: 'ne sont-ce pas après tout des problèmes réels [i.e. προβλήματα] que soulève la comparaison du texte hébreu et des versions grecques?'[26] It would seem that in Bardy's view it was Jerome's intention merely to raise questions without providing solutions. One could attempt to justify such a suggestion on the basis of some statements made by Augustine with reference to his own *Quaestiones in Heptateuchum*. For example, in the preface to this work he seems to emphasize that he is more concerned with establishing the nature of the problems than with finding the solutions. As he puts it, 'nonnulla enim pars inventionis est nosse quid quaeras.' Writing about *Hept.* some seven years after it had appeared, he notes, 'magis quaerenda proposui quam quaesita dissolvi' (*Retract.* 2. 81).[27]

Bardy cites both of these passages in his discussion of *Hept.*[28] And it may be that they inspired his suggestion regarding Jerome's *QHG*. But whether this is the case or not, it is a suggestion that is difficult to accept. In the first place, it is quite uncharacteristic of the *quaestiones* genre in its textual-exegetical form that a writer who is a partisan of the text on which he is commenting should

[26] 'La littérature' (*RB* 41), p. 358. That by 'Greek versions' Bardy means primarily that of the LXX seems clear from his remarks on p. 357.

[27] Cf. also *Hept.* 1. 145, and Rüting, *Untersuchungen*, pp. 202–27, who provides lists entitled 'Quästionen ohne Lösung' and 'Unentschiedene Quästionen'.

[28] 'La littérature' (*RB* 41), pp. 516–17.

raise questions about that text without providing the solutions. As we have seen, it was usually the opponents of the text who proceeded in this manner. On the other hand, those who would explain a text, i.e. the λυτικοί, were wont to find solutions for any problem that might be thrown at them. The manner in which Furius Bibaculus describes Valerius Cato is well known: 'summum grammaticum, optimum poetam, omnes solvere posse quaestiones' (Suetonius, *De grammaticis* 11). Similarly, for the Christian exegete, generally speaking, 'keine Schwierigkeit erscheint unüberwindlich. Nichts wird als unerklärbar anerkannt.'[29] In fine, the conventions of the *quaestiones* genre, together with the fact that Jerome in no way even intimates that his purpose is merely to raise questions, should make us wary of attributing to him intentions similar to those of Augustine.

In the second place, it is extremely unlikely that in Jerome's view the differences between the Hebrew and the Greek text constituted 'problems', as Bardy implies. For Jerome, it is the differences in the translations or among the manuscripts containing them that give rise to problems, and these must be 'solved' by reference to the original. As he writes in *Ep.* 106. 2, 'sicut autem in Novo Testamento, si quando apud Latinos quaestio exoritur et est inter exemplaria varietas, recurrimus ad fontem Graeci sermonis . . . ita et in Veteri Testamento, si quando inter Graecos Latinosque diversitas est, ad Hebraicam confugimus veritatem.' Moreover, as noted in the previous chapter, when it comes to comparing the Hebrew with the Greek, Jerome prefers the former throughout *QHG*. Indeed, we shall see that an important feature of this work is the attempt to solve problems which arise in the LXX by reference to the Hebrew. In short, 'la comparaison du texte hébreu et des versions grecques' will lead to solutions, not problems.

How then is one to confront the problem identified by Bardy? We shall employ two lines of approach. In the first place, one encounters in the history of *quaestiones* literature a phenomenon whereby the criticisms of a text and the refutations of such criticisms are not introduced by the standard question and answer format. Such cases have been termed by Gudeman as 'versteckte ζητήματα'.[30] The phenomenon is particularly pronounced in the

---

[29] Heinrici, 'Zur patristischen Aporienliteratur', p. 848.
[30] Λύσεις, cols. 2514–15.

exegesis of Virgil.[31] This point has obvious relevance for the case of Jerome, the former pupil of Aelius Donatus.[32]

With regard to specifics, H. Georgii has shown that many criticisms of the *Aeneid* are introduced with formulas which are not so obviously recognizable as 'Kritikformeln'.[33] Some of these are found in Jerome's *QHG*. For example, in *QHG* 13: 1-4, Jerome employs the phrase 'occurrit huic sensui illud, quod sequitur' to introduce an objection. Georgii finds that the forms of 'occurro' are often used with a similar function in Servius.[34] The forms of the word 'excuso' often point to criticisms both in Servius and in *QHG*.[35] The same holds true for the expressions 'nec miremur', 'nec mirum', and 'nullum moveat'.[36]

In addition, Georgii also finds a few passages in Servius where criticisms or problems are not explicitly expressed or clearly introduced by any formula, but are identifiable through an examination of the general context of the passage.[37] In other words, we sometimes find that the commentator gives us the solution without explaining the problem. This should come as no surprise to those familiar with *quaestiones* literature, for already in chapter 25 of Aristotle's *Poetics* we discover this phenomenon.[38] Similarly Ps.-Heraclitus, the author of a work of which the title is most probably Ὁμηρικὰ προβλήματα, sometimes puts forward an allegorical defence of Homer without specifying the exact nature of the criticism.[39] It has also been pointed out by E. E. Hallewy that the Rabbis often follow a similar procedure in their exposition of the Old Testament.[40] The most likely explanation for such a practice, in both classical and rabbinic exegesis, is that some προβλήματα were either so obvious or so well known that it became unnecessary to introduce them explicitly.[41]

---

[31] See Gudeman, Λύσεις, col. 2522. Cf. Thomas, *Scoliastes*, pp. 253-7.

[32] On Jerome and Donatus, see L. Holtz, *Donat et la tradition de l'enseignement grammatical*, Paris 1981, pp. 37-46, and the works there cited, especially those of F. Lammert.

[33] *Äneiskritik*, pp. 22-35.   [34] Ibid., p. 27.

[35] See *QHG* 12: 15-16; 19: 30; 25: 1-6; Georgii, *Äneiskritik*, p. 27.

[36] These expressions occur in *QHG* 21: 14; 30: 32-3; and 21: 15-17 respectively. For the use of similar phrases in Servius, see Georgii, *Äneiskritik*, p. 26.

[37] Ibid., p. 28.   [38] Note, e.g., 1461ª1-4; 1461ª10-12; 1461ª12-14.

[39] *Allegoriae* (= *Quaestiones Homericae*) 28. 1-3; 36; 75. 9-11. For the title of the work, see the introduction of F. Buffière to his edition of the text (Paris 1962), pp. vii-viii.

[40] *Tarb* 31 (1961-2), p. 157.   [41] Cf. Hallewy, ibid.

In view of these precedents, it will be quite understandable if we find a comparable phenomenon in Christian commentaries.[42] That it is present in *QHG* will be clear from an examination of individual passages within the context of earlier or contemporary Christian biblical exegesis. For example, according to Gen. 2: 17, God commands Adam not to eat from the tree of knowledge, and adds, 'in the day that you eat of it you shall die' (*VL* = 'morte morieris'). However, when Adam eats from the tree he does not die. Theodoret states the problem explicitly, τίνος ἕνεκα τοῦ θεοῦ εἰρηκότος, "ᾗ δ' ἂν ἡμέρᾳ φάγῃ ἀπὸ τοῦ ξύλου θανάτῳ ἀποθανῇ", οὐκ εὐθὺς ἀπέθανε τὴν ἐντολὴν παραβάς; (*Qu. in Gen.* 38). The same question is also discussed by several other exegetes.[43] Therefore, when Jerome comments briefly, 'melius interpretatus est Symmachus dicens: "mortalis eris"' (*QHG* 2: 17), there can be no doubt that he is commending the translator's solution to a well-known problem which he himself does not bother to explain. In Gen. 43: 34, we read that Joseph's brothers ate and drank with him: 'et biberunt et inebriati sunt cum eo.' Jerome comments, 'idioma est linguae Hebraicae, ut ebrietatem pro satietate ponat' (*QHG* 43: 34). In all likelihood, he is attempting to solve the problem constituted by unseemly behaviour, or ἀπρέπεια according to *quaestiones* terminology, on the part of a biblical hero.[44] So much is apparent from the context as well as from the following comment of Augustine, ad loc., 'solent hinc ebriosi adhibere testimonii patrocinium . . . propter Joseph, qui valde sapiens commendatur.'[45] That Jerome often supplies solutions only can be gleaned from another similar circumstance. Eucherius of Lyons, who employs *QHG* extensively in his *Instructiones*, sometimes

---

[42] As we have noted above, p. 85, Schäublin has asserted that the *catena* fragments of Diodore's exegetical work on the Octateuch were originally part of a *quaestiones* commentary. He explains the fact that the formal posing of the question is often missing by referring to the circumstance of transmission. The questions will have been excised in the process of epitomization, since it would not have been necessary to express them in the context of a *catena*. If, however, the reasoning presented here is correct, such an assumption would not be required.

[43] Philo, *All.* 1. 105; Isidore of Pelusium, *Epp.* 3. 252. Cf. Justin, *Dial.* 81; Irenaeus, *Haer.* 5. 23. 1–2; Origen, *Hom. in Gen.* 15. 2; Athanasius, *Inc.* 3. 5.

[44] For the term ἀπρεπές, see M. Carroll, *Aristotle's Poetics, c. XXV, in the Light of the Homeric Scholia*, Baltimore 1895, pp. 25–6; Gudeman, Λύσεις, cols. 2516–17; cf. Schäublin, *Untersuchungen*, pp. 78–9 (with references).

[45] *Hept.* 1. 144. Cf. the similar problem of the drunkenness of Noah in Gen. 9: 21. This problem is treated by Philo, *Quaest. in Gn.* 2. 68, and by Origen, *Sel. in Gen.* 9: 20–1 (*PG* 12. 109b–c; cf. Petit, 'Le dossier', p. 84 (no. 750)).

takes over Jerome's solutions while prefixing an explicit reference to the problem.[46] The reason for this phenomenon of 'hidden questions' in *QHG* most probably lies in a fact which we shall consider presently, namely, the close relationship between *QHG* and another patristic exegetical genre, the σχόλια or *excerpta*. In this genre, a tendency towards terseness prevails.

Despite the existence of 'hidden questions' in *QHG*, it is not possible to interpret every passage which does not constitute a standard *quaestio* as the solution to an unexpressed objection. Indeed, a large portion of the work must be explained in another manner. Here again, the most appropriate explanation will be one which may be justified in terms of the history of the genre. Now, although the outstanding characteristic of exegetical ζητήματα literature, as we have noted above, is the fact that the questions raised constitute objections, there developed a tendency according to which a wider range of inquiries came to be included in the collections. Such a tendency is visible in both the Homeric ζητήματα and Philo's *Quaest. in Gn. et Ex.* For example, exegetes ask what the difference is between two synonyms,[47] what the gender of a word is,[48] what a certain object is,[49] who certain people are,[50] etc. Indeed, we even find passages in which it is asked in a general way what a certain passage means.[51] Questions such as these are of course uncharacteristic of *quaestiones* literature in its traditional form, in that they represent attempts to determine 'was der Fall ist'.[52] However, the tendency is explained by the fact that the ζητήματα genre came to be used for didactic as well as for polemical purposes.

Keeping these points in mind, we shall not be surprised to find a similar tendency in patristic writings. Theodoret, for example, puts forward a fair number of such 'what' questions in his *Quaestiones in Octateuchum*. Sometimes he simply asks what a particular

[46] Compare, e.g., *QHG* 5: 2; 11: 29; 24: 9, with *Instr.* 1. 16, 21, 22, respectively.

[47] Porphyry, *Ad Iliadem E.* 533; Philo, *Quaest. in Gn.* 1. 62. Cf. Porphyry, *Ad Iliadem Z.* 491.

[48] Porphyry, *Ad Iliadem A.* 104.

[49] Ibid., *Λ.* 846; Philo, *Quaest. in Ex.* 2. 55, 60, 62, 80, 83.

[50] Philo, *Quaest. in Gn.* 1. 88. Note also Strabo, *Geographica* 16. 4. 27, where ἡ ζήτησις περὶ τῶν Ἐρεμβῶν is mentioned. For the question itself, see 1. 2. 34.

[51] Porphyry, *Ad Iliadem Z.* 77; *T.* 221; *Ψ.* 862; Philo, *Quaest. in Gn.* 1. 72; 2. 20, 22, 23; 4. 85, etc.

[52] For this phrase, see above, p. 86.

passage means.[53] At other times he raises more detailed questions. He asks about the ancestry of Melchizedek (*Qu. in Gen.* 65), and about the materials used in the construction of the Tower of Babel (*Qu. in Gen.* 59).

Jerome also took this wider view as to what constituted a *quaestio*. This may be seen from some of his 'Roman' letters to Marcella, specifically, *Ep.* 25, 26, 28, 29, and 34. That these letters constitute brief *quaestiones* tracts has been acknowledged by Bardy,[54] and so much may be confirmed by the terminology which Jerome employs in them. Note the following passages:

26. 1: quaesisti, quid ea verba . . . sonarent.
26. 5: et tibi aviditatem magis dilatae deberent facere quaestiones.
29. 1: famosissima quaestione proposita . . .
29. 2: posueras, quid sibi velit, quod in Regnorum libro primo scriptum est . . .; quaeris, quid sit ephod bad.
29. 3: . . . ut indissolubilem facerent quaestionem.
34. 1: mihi de eodem Psalmo proposuisti, qui esset panis doloris.
34. 3: illud quoque de eodem Psalmo interrogare dignata es, qui sint filii excussorum.

However, the questions involved here are 'what' questions, and do not constitute προβλήματα as defined by Flashar. For Jerome is concerned primarily with the meanings of a number of Hebrew terms and expressions, and the general exegesis of certain passages.[55]

Since in all forms of exegesis the object is to discover what a text means, to the extent that these 'what' questions appear in ζητήματα writings, the genre loses its distinctive character and begins to resemble other varieties of exegetical literature. And, in fact, scholars have noted that the *quaestiones* compositions of both Philo and Theodoret are not altogether different from ordinary

---

[53] *Qu. in Gen.* 75, 92, 98. One should not always, however, separate such questions (cf. also the passages cited in n. 51 above) from those in which an objection is explicitly expressed. For in the responses to these generally phrased questions one sometimes finds a more detailed formulation of the question in which an objection is expressed, or material which may be interpreted as a refutation of an unstated objection. This is true with regard to both Theodoret and Philo.

[54] 'La littérature' (*RB* 41), pp. 358–9.

[55] For a parallel to questions concerning the meaning of Hebrew words and other technical terms, see Ps.-Justin, *Qu. et Resp.* 86.

commentaries, in that sometimes both writers seem to be grafting rather extensive general expositions of the text on to an interrogative.[56] The result is that we have a sort of mixed genre, whereby something resembling a commentary is included within a collection of *quaestiones*. Such a mixing of genres will become more understandable when we remember that the reverse phenomenon is often encountered. That is, in the commentaries and homilies of Origen, Hilary, and Chrysostom, *quaestiones* methodology is employed on numerous occasions.[57]

Much of Jerome's *QHG* may be explained in terms of a mixture of genres, similar to that which we find in Philo and Theodoret. Jerome has merely taken the additional step of dispensing with the interrogative form on many occasions. However, in the context of a 'what' question, this cannot be regarded as a particularly drastic measure. For in many such instances the interrogative is close to being superfluous in an exegetical work in which the order followed is that of the text being discussed. In short, Jerome seems to have developed further a tendency which is visible in other *quaestiones* compositions.

In contrast to the works of Philo and Theodoret, it is not the commentary form that has intruded into *QHG*, but another form of exegesis, that termed *excerpta* or scholia. This genre was perhaps employed by Clement of Alexandria.[58] But it was first used extensively in the Christian world by Origen. Indeed, it is well known that according to Jerome's classification of the latter's exegetical works, the *excerpta* constitute one of the three literary forms which the Alexandrian Father employed, the other two being homilies and commentaries. In this classification, the *excerpta* are described as follows: 'primum eius opus excerpta sunt, quae Graece σχόλια nuncupantur, in quibus ea, quae sibi videbantur obscura aut habere aliquid difficultatis, summatim breviterque perstrinxit.'[59] Jerome probably had a similar purpose in

---

[56] For Philo, see G. Delling, *OLZ* 77 (1982), col. 567, and cf. Dörrie, 'Erotapokriseis', col. 344. For Theodoret, see G. W. Ashby, *Theodoret of Cyrrhus as Exegete of the Old Testament*, Grahamstown 1972, p. 116.

[57] For Origen, see E. de Faye, *Origène: Sa vie, son œuvre, sa pensée*, iii (BEHE.R 44), Paris 1928, pp. 156, 172; Bardy, 'La littérature' (*RB* 41), pp. 224–8. For Hilary, see J. Doignon, *Hilaire de Poitiers avant l'exil*, Paris 1971, pp. 332–42. For Chrysostom, see Jordan, *Geschichte*, p. 410.

[58] See Heinrici, 'Scholien', p. 737.

[59] This description is from Jerome's preface to his translation of Origen, *Hom. in Ezech.* (GCS 33, p. 318).

much of *QHG*. For if one were to give a reckoning of all the passages which could be classified as *quaestiones*, either expressed or 'hidden', there would still be left over a body of material which can only be described as scholia.[60]

The hypothesis of the mixed genre can be confirmed by the recent evidence of the Divjak letter mentioned above.[61] In this letter, Jerome refers to *QHG* as 'Quaestionum Hebraicarum in Genesin commentarioli' (*Ep.* 27. 2). The important word here is 'commentarioli'. For Jerome designates another of his works, a short commentary on the Psalms, by this same term.[62] In the preface of this work, he describes it as an adaptation of Origen's *Enchiridion*. It is well known that the latter title is another name for the same author's *Excerpta in Psalterium*.[63] It seems therefore that Jerome used the word 'commentarioli' with a similar if not the same sense as *excerpta* or scholia. This may be confirmed by Jerome's preface to his *Commentarii in Ecclesiasten*. Here he writes that he was requested by Blesilla, in his words, 'ut in morem commentarioli obscura quaeque dissererem'. It will be clear that he describes 'commentarioli' in essentially the same way as he describes Origen's *excerpta* in the passage cited above. It appears therefore that Jerome is acknowledging the mixing of genres in *QHG* by employing the term 'commentarioli' in the letter edited by Divjak.

It is even possible that Origen's procedure in his *Excerpta in Genesim* influenced Jerome as far as the mixing of genres is concerned.[64] For in this work many *quaestiones* have been incorpor-

---

[60] Bardy, 'La littérature' (*RB* 41), p. 358, also recognizes the 'scholia-like' appearance of *QHG*. However, as we have noted above, p. 87, he would explain such scholia as the 'raising of questions'. It should also be pointed out here that both Heinrici, 'Scholien', p. 736, and Bardy, p. 210, seem to classify ζητήματα literature as a subset of scholia. This is valid in so far as in both genres the practice is to comment only on selected texts. However, it is inherent in such a classification that the two are different genres. Indeed, Bardy, pp. 528–9, gives only brief mention in his survey to Augustine's *Expositio quarumdam quaestionum in Epistula ad Romanos* on the grounds that it constitutes scholia rather than ζητήματα καὶ λύσεις. Cf. Jordan, *Geschichte*, pp. 407–11, who treats the two genres under separate headings, and now Neuschäfer, *Origenes*, pp. 340–1.

[61] See above, p. 76.   [62] *Commentarioli in Psalmos* prol.; *Ruf.* 1. 19.

[63] See G. Morin's note in his edition of Jerome's *Commentarioli in Psalmos* (Maredsous 1895 = *AMar* 3. 1), p. 1 (= CChr.SL 72, p. 177); O. Bardenhewer, *Geschichte der altkirchlichen Literatur*, ii[2], Freiburg im Breisgau 1914, p. 120; Nautin, *Origène*, pp. 282–3.

[64] The remains of these *Excerpta in Genesim* are probably to be found among the *catena* fragments which are printed in *PG* 12. 92c–145b and elsewhere. See Devreesse, *DBS* 1 (1928), cols. 1106–7. Cf. id., *Les anciens commentateurs*,

ated.[65] Here again we have a mixture of genres of the reverse sort. That such Origenian influence is plausible is clear from the fact that the *Commentarioli in Psalmos*, written in roughly the same period as *QHG*, was, as we have mentioned, an adaptation of Origen's *Excerpta in Psalterium*.[66] However, if the composite make-up of *QHG* was determined by Origen's *Excerpta in Genesim*, the fact that Jerome inserted the word 'quaestiones' into his title (instead of simply calling it 'commentarioli' after the Origenian fashion) takes on special significance. For it will probably indicate that in Jerome's view the amount or, more probably, the importance of the *quaestiones* material in the work was such that the use of that word in the title was appropriate. In addition, Jerome may be intimating that his work was not to be considered an adaptation of a composition of Origen, but was to be placed alongside Antiochene works of similar titles. The relevance of this suggestion will be revealed in the following chapter.

Both of the genres which Jerome employs in this work were ideally suited for the aim which he pursues in *QHG*. This aim, as we have seen in the previous chapter, was to present a justification for *IH* and the philological system on which it is based. Jerome makes particularly effective use of the *quaestiones* genre. His method consists in putting forward solutions based on the Hebrew text (and his manner of interpreting it) for problems which were felt to exist in the Christian copies, i.e. in the LXX and the *VL*.[67] It seems most probable that it is to this approach that he alludes in the preface: 'studii ergo nostri erit . . . ea, quae in Latinis et Graecis codicibus scatere videntur, auctoritati suae reddere.' The use of the Hebrew text or the *recentiores* in order to solve exegetical difficulties was not a Hieronymian innovation. Such a technique had been employed by various Greek scholars. But Jerome

---

pp. 29–30. The fragments edited in *PG* have been surveyed critically and supplemented by Devreesse, *Les anciens commentateurs*, pp. 30–41, and Petit, 'Le dossier'.

[65] See *Sel. in Gen.* 5: 3; 7: 2, 15; 9: 1, 18; 41: 8b; 46: 7b; 47: 10; 48: 8–11 (*PG* 12. 104a, 105b, 105c, 105d, 108b, 133b, 141a, 141d–144a, 144d). Cf. Neuschäfer, *Origenes*, pp. 341–2.

[66] For the date of the *Commentarioli in Psalmos*, see Cavallera, *Saint Jérôme*, i. 2, p. 30; C. Estin, *Les Psautiers de Jérôme à la lumière des traductions juives antérieures* (CBLa 15), Rome 1984, p. 31.

[67] The presence of these 'Hebrew solutions' has been recognized by Cavallera, 'Les *Quaestiones*', pp. 360–1, and Penna, *S. Gerolamo*, p. 154.

practised this method in a more conscious and sophisticated fashion. Indeed, the extent to which he turned it into a systematic approach to Scripture is clear from a letter written some six years after the publication of *QHG*, in which he responds to a query from the presbyter Vitalis concerning a problem about the ages of Solomon and Ahaz when they fathered children. Jerome explains that in the present case he has had to forgo his customary methodology: 'et si quidem in his historiis aliter haberent septuaginta interpretes, aliter Hebraica veritas, confugere poteramus ad solita praesidia et arcem linguae tenere vernaculae; nunc vero . . . in sensu est difficultas.'[68] It is in fact in *QHG* that Jerome establishes the Hebrew text as his 'solita praesidia'. And by using 'Hebrew solutions' to provide a 'quick fix' to difficulties which other exegetes solve by more circuitous routes, he argues for a return to the Hebrew text based on internal considerations.

The scholia genre was also particularly appropriate for Jerome's main purpose in *QHG*. For it allows him to concentrate his attention on philological and textual matters. However, not all of his comments are directly related to problems of text, and the concern with etymological and geographical questions leads one to view *QHG* also as a sort of appendix to two other works which Jerome had prepared in the immediately preceding years, *De nominibus Hebraicis* and *De situ et nominibus locorum Hebraicorum*.[69] Both of these compositions are for the most part translations of Greek works, and in many passages of *QHG* Jerome takes the opportunity to put forward different views of issues treated in them. On other occasions he simply gives a fuller discussion or, indeed, employs additional sources to supplement the information given in *Nom. Hebr.* and *Sit.*[70] Nevertheless, in some of his remarks, and particularly those concerned with etymology, Jerome is anxious to demonstrate the relevance of Hebrew philology and the validity of his own approach to it.

[68] *Ep.* 72. 2. For the date, see Cavallera, *Saint Jérôme*, i. 2, pp. 45–6. Cf. Kelly, *Jerome*, p. 212.

[69] For the chronology of these two works, see Nautin, 'L'activité', pp. 253–6.

[70] There are many passages in *Sit.* where Jerome says he will give a different view or a fuller discussion in the *Quaestiones Hebraicae*. See, e.g., 43. 7–8, 13–16; 77. 7–9; 81. 3; 91. 2–6; 141. 12–13; 173. 7–8, 10–11. See also *Nom. Hebr.* prol.

5

Jerome and his Greek Exegetical Sources

◆ ◆ ◆

In his attempt to understand and interpret the Hebrew text, Jerome employed three kinds of sources: Jewish and especially Christian Greek exegetical writings, the *recentiores*, and rabbinic teachers. He seems to acknowledge this in *Ep.* 37, which he wrote to Marcella in approximately 385.[1] In this letter, he refuses to lend his star pupil a commentary on the Song of Songs by Reticius of Autun, on the grounds that it contains too many errors. He points in particular to the wild misinterpretations of certain Hebrew terms, and attributes them to the author's failure to consult the proper sources: 'Did he not have Origen's ten volumes [of commentary], did he not have the other translators [i.e. the *recentiores*], did he not have Jewish consultants . . . ?' (*Ep.* 37. 3). In reproaching the procedure of Reticius, Jerome outlines what he considers the most important lines of approach in interpreting the Hebrew text.

Jerome used Greek exegetical writings extensively. Indeed, he probably achieved more than anyone else in collecting as much material concerning Hebrew matters as was available in Greek exegetical works. This fact has led some to believe he was almost exclusively dependent on Greek sources in interpreting the Hebrew text.[2] But from *QHG* it would appear rather that Jerome simply exploited Greek sources as far as was possible, because they were for him the most accessible and the easiest to use. These sources, however, could take him only so far. For what is lacking in the Greek patristic corpus is a serious attempt to come to terms with the Hebrew language and a systematic procedure in dealing with the text. Indeed, it seems that one of Jerome's principal objectives in *QHG* was to demonstrate that the Greek exegetical

---

[1] For the date, see Cavallera, *Saint Jérôme*, i. 2, p. 26.

[2] See in particular Nautin, 'Hieronymus', p. 309 (cf. p. 310, and *Origène*, pp. 357–8). He is apparently relying to some degree on E. Burstein, 'La compétence en hébreu de saint Jérôme' (Diss.), Poitiers 1971.

sources were insufficient for a proper understanding of the Hebrew Bible. As he writes in the prologue, 'studii ergo nostri erit . . . eorum, qui de libris Hebraicis varia suspicantur, errores refellere.' Rather, as we have stated in Chapter 3, it was his intention to move to an approach to the Hebrew text based on the *recentiores* and rabbinic sources. Thus, while Jerome does make plentiful use of Greek exegetical writings in *QHG*, he also argues for the necessity to move beyond these sources.[3]

ORIGEN

In composing *QHG*, Jerome naturally made use of the work of Origen, although it appears to have been of less relevance for him than other Greek writings. Origen wrote homilies, a commentary, and *excerpta* on Genesis. The *Homilies* will have been of little use to Jerome in his attempt to argue for a return to the Hebrew text. For as the Latin Father himself points out in the preface to *QHG*, Origen does not concern himself with Hebrew matters in his sermons, but for the most part follows the LXX. Nor can the *Commentary* have been employed extensively. For this work, according to Origen's own statement in *Contra Celsum* 6. 49, covered only the first four chapters of Genesis.[4] It is also quite clear from Origen's description of the work in the same passage (cf. also *Cels*. 4. 37) that he was concerned primarily with the major theological and cosmological issues of the book, and not with the type of textual problems that Jerome discusses in *QHG*. This impression is in fact confirmed by the surviving fragments, some of which are quite lengthy.[5]

[3] For a more directed refutation of the view of Nautin, 'L'activité', p. 255, and 'Hieronymus', p. 306, that *QHG* is simply a derivative work based on the writings of Origen, Acacius, and Eusebius of Emesa, see my 'Studies in Jerome's *Quaestiones Hebraicae in Genesim*: The Work as Seen in the Context of Greek Scholarship', Oxford 1987 (the D.Phil. thesis on which the present book is based), pp. 84–147.

[4] For additional *testimonia*, see Devreesse, *Les anciens commentateurs*, p. 26. Cf. Nautin, *Origène*, p. 245.

[5] The main fragments may be found in *PG* 12. 45a–92a. See also the papyrus fragments published and discussed by P. Glaue, *Ein Bruchstück des Origenes über Genesis 1,28* (*MPSG* 2 = *Schriften der hessischen Hochschulen. Universität Giessen* 1928. 1), Giessen 1928, and P. Sanz, *Griechische literarische Papyri christlichen Inhaltes*, i (*Mitteilungen aus der Papyrussammlung der Nationalbibliothek in Wien* NS 4), Baden bei Wien 1946, pp. 87–104. However, there are questions of authenticity with regard to both fragments. See the bibliographical indications in *CPG*, i

The relevance of the *Excerpta*, on the other hand, cannot be denied. For as we have seen in the previous chapter, the 'mixing of genres' in *QHG* may in fact be due to the influence of this work. It is fortunate, therefore, that probably the greater part of the *Excerpta* can be recovered from *catena* fragments. For when we calculate the number of published fragments, taking into account the critical studies of Devreesse and Petit, we arrive at a figure of around 170.[6] However, a careful reading of this material reveals that Jerome did not use Origen's *Excerpta* as a major source in the composition of *QHG*.

First of all, the nature of the exegesis which Origen employs in this work prevented it from being extensively utilized by Jerome. For he is not exclusively concerned with philological issues. While it may be true that he takes more of an interest in the text and the letter than he does in his *Homilies* or *Commentary*, with regard to the Book of Genesis the general theological and ethical character of his exegesis does not undergo fundamental change when he switches to the genre of *excerpta*. For example, on many occasions he rejects the letter completely.[7] Elsewhere he simply emphasizes the Christological and spiritual lessons of the text.[8]

The point emerges with greater clarity, however, when we examine lemmata which are subject to discussion in both Origen and Jerome. In Gen. 13: 14–15, God describes to Abraham the land which he will receive. Origen, *Selecta in Genesim* ad loc. (*PG* 12. 112c–113a), draws an ethical-ascetic lesson from the passage, while Jerome explains to his readers a peculiarity in the manner in which the points of the compass are indicated in the biblical idiom.[9] With regard to Gen. 26: 19, where we read about the wells

(1983), p. 144. In addition, even if authentic, it is uncertain whether the first fragment is part of the *Commentary* or of a homily. See Glaue, pp. 27–30.

[6] Concerning the fragments of the *Excerpta in Genesim*, see above, Ch. 4 n. 64. It is not to be excluded that those fragments which relate to the first 4 chapters of Genesis (about 15 in number) have been extracted from the *Commentary* rather than the *Excerpta*. See Nautin, *Origène*, pp. 245, 373, 432 (apparently against Devreesse).

[7] *Sel. in Gen.* 2: 2; 9: 1, 2, 4–5; 18: 23; 27: 27b (*PG* 12. 97b–c, 105d, 108a, 108a–b, 116b–c, 124a–b).

[8] *Sel. in Gen.* 9: 6; 29: 31 (*PG* 12. 108b, 124c). The assessment of Heinrici, 'Scholien', p. 737, according to which textual and literal exegesis predominate in the *excerpta*, seems to be exaggerated with regard to the *Excerpta in Genesim*.

[9] *QHG* 13: 14–15. Jerome points out that in the Bible, the word *mare* is often used to designate 'west'. See Meershoek, *Le latin*, pp. 207–10, who claims to have found only one parallel for this remark in Greek scholarship: Cyril, *Comm. in Is.*

of Isaac, Origen urges his readers to 'understand the wells', and 'dig wells in themselves' (*Sel. in Gen.* 26: 19 (*PG* 12. 121c)). Jerome criticizes the use of the word 'vallis' in the LXX/*VL*. He claims that we must follow the Hebrew and render 'torrent' (*QHG* 26: 19; cf. 26: 17). In *Sel. in Gen.* 30: 37 (*PG* 12. 125a), Origen puts forward an allegory about the sticks which Jacob employs in his sheep-breeding ruse. In *QHG* 30: 32–3, 41–2, Jerome discusses the episode at length and attempts to give a detailed account of the mechanics of the ruse. Origen sees Joseph's coat of many colours as a symbol of virtue (*Sel. in Gen.* 37: 3 (*PG* 12. 128c–d)). Jerome is interested in discovering exactly what the coat looked like, employing the *recentiores* to assist him (*QHG* 37: 3). Origen applies the language of Gen. 40: 1, where we read of the sins of the chief butler and chief baker against Pharaoh, to the Christian martyrs (*Sel. in Gen.* ad loc. (*PG* 12. 129b)). Jerome explains to his readers what a chief butler actually is and how important his function was in the East (*QHG* ad loc.). In Gen. 41: 16, Joseph intimates to Pharaoh that his dream will find its proper interpretation only with God's help. Origen, *Sel. in Gen.* 41: 16 (*PG* 12. 133b–c), observes: εὔλογος Ἰωσὴφ ἐν ᾧ προοιμιάζεται ἀπὸ θεοῦ. Jerome reports the textual variants (*QHG* 41: 16). In Gen. 48: 2, we read that Israel summoned his strength, and sat up in bed to speak with Joseph and his sons. Origen comments on the deeper meaning behind the use of two names, Jacob and Israel, to designate the same person (*Sel. in Gen.* 48: 2 (*PG* 12. 144c)). In *QHG* ad loc., Jerome takes the LXX to task for their inconsistency in rendering the word מטה ('bed' or 'staff').[10]

On the other hand, in those few cases where both writers discuss the same lemmata from a textual standpoint, Jerome's remarks would appear to constitute critical responses to Origen. For example, both writers mention the fact that the words of Cain to Abel as reported in the LXX version of Gen. 4: 8, 'Let us go out into the field', are not to be found in the Hebrew text. Origen says that according to the Jews these words are found ἐν τῷ ἀποκρύφῳ.[11] Now, elsewhere he states that much legitimate ma-

2. 1 (11: 14 = *PG* 70. 336a). It is not to be excluded that Cyril is here dependent on Jerome. Cf. A. Kerrigan, *St. Cyril of Alexandria: Interpreter of the Old Testament* (AnBib 2), Rome 1952, pp. 435–9, 441–2.

[10] On this issue, see below, pp. 155–7.

[11] *Sel. in Gen.* 4: 8 (*PG* 12. 101c). Origen's exact words are difficult to interpret, and have been understood in different ways. See, e.g., N. R. M. de Lange, *Origen*

terial may be found in apocryphal books.[12] Indeed, in *Ep.* 1. 13–15,
he formulates the theory that some passages which at one time
were part of the Hebrew Bible may have been excised by the Jews
as detrimental to the interests of the Jewish authorities, and that
sometimes these are preserved in apocryphal writings. Since he
claims that this may have occurred in the case of the story of
Susanna (which is found in the version of the LXX but not in the
Hebrew), although he does not cite an apocryphal parallel for this
story specifically, it would seem logical to conclude that in his
view, when 'pluses' in the Septuagint also appear in apocrypha,
they have an extra claim to legitimacy. Such an attempt to validate
the 'pluses' in the Septuagint would be in accord with his textual
position as outlined above in Chapter 1.[13] Consequently, when in
QHG 4: 8 Jerome claims that the phrase 'Let us go out into the
field' is superfluous, on the grounds that Cain's words are 'to be
understood' from the previous verse, he may be attempting to
undermine the idea that the presence of the phrase in an apocry-
phon somehow constitutes an argument in favour of its authenticity. Indeed, the charge of superfluity is a characteristic feature
of Jerome's criticism of the LXX and the κοινή edition of that
version.[14]

In Gen. 41, it is related how Joseph rose to a very high position
in the Egyptian court. In verse 43, we read that Pharaoh honoured
him by allowing him to ride 'in his second chariot', and that the
Egyptian criers called out something as he rode along: וַיִּקְרָא
לְפָנָיו אַבְרֵךְ LXX: καὶ ἐκήρυξεν ἔμπροσθεν αὐτοῦ κῆρυξ. The word
אַבְרֵךְ, rendered by the LXX as κῆρυξ, is probably of Egyptian
origin, and posed serious problems for Jewish interpreters.[15] In
many sources, the word is interpreted as if it were a Hebrew

---

and the Jews (UCOP 25), Cambridge 1976, pp. 51–2; Hanson, *Allegory*, pp. 172–3.
Field, i, pp. 18–19, cites two parallel scholia which shed some light on the meaning
of Origen's note as it is printed in *PG* 12. For additional information on these
scholia, see Petit, 'Le dossier', p. 80 (no. 512).

[12] *Comm. ser. in Mt.* 28 (23: 37–9 = GCS 38, p. 51). Cf. the passages cited by
de Lange in the introduction to his edition of *Ep.* 1 (Paris 1983 = SC 302), p. 497;
to which references add *Comm. ser. in Mt.* 117 (27: 3–10 = GCS 38, pp. 249–50).

[13] See above, pp. 6, 13.

[14] See *QHG* 13: 13; *Ep.* 106. 11, 14, 15, 26, 34, 40, 42, 43, 44. Cf. A. Thibaut,
'La revision hexaplaire de saint Jérôme', *Richesses et déficiences des anciens Psautiers
latins* (CBLa 13), Rome 1959, p. 114.

[15] See Rashi, *Comm. in Pent.* ad loc.; Geiger, op. cit. (Ch. 2 n. 102), pp. 463–4;
G. Vermes, *CHB*, i (1970), pp. 203–4.

compound, 'tender father'.[16] Jerome explains this interpretation, prefixing an account of the renderings of the *recentiores*:

Aquila transtulit: 'et clamavit in conspectu eius adgeniculationem'. Symmachus ipsum Hebraicum sermonem interpretans ait: 'et clamavit ante eum abrech'. unde mihi videtur non tam praeco sive adgeniculatio, quae in salutando vel adorando Joseph accipi potest, intellegenda, quam illud, quod Hebraei tradunt, dicentes patrem tenerum ex hoc sermone transferri. ab quippe dicitur pater, rech delicatus sive tenerrimus, significante scriptura quod iuxta prudentiam quidem pater omnium fuerit, sed iuxta aetatem tenerrimus adolescens et puer. (*QHG* 41: 43)

In this passage we have a clear explanation of different interpretations of the verse.[17] When we turn to Origen, however, we find a different approach:

τὸ Ἑβραϊκὸν ἔχει Ἀβρήχ, ὃ κυρίως σημαίνει, πατὴρ ἁπαλός. εἰκότως πατέρα ἁπαλὸν ἐκάλεσε τὸν Ἰωσήφ, ἐπειδήπερ ἁπαλὸς ὢν κατὰ τὴν ἡλικίαν, ὡς πατὴρ σωτήριον ἀρχὴν Αἰγυπτίοις ἐνεδείξατο. δηλοῖ δὲ οὐδὲν ἡ λέξις ἢ τὸ γονατίζειν. φανερὰ γάρ ἐστιν ἡ φωνὴ τοῦ κήρυκος. (*Sel. in. Gen.* 41: 43 (*PG* 12. 133d–136a)

This passage is characteristic of Origen's use of the Hebrew text and the *recentiores* as described above.[18] For he cites both the rendering of Aquila and the Jewish interpretation as the correct literal translation of the word 'avrech', rather than presenting them as alternative translations of a difficult word. Nor does he distinguish these interpretations from that of the LXX, which he sews on as the conclusion of his comment. It is therefore difficult to accept the view of B. de Montfaucon and others, who believe that Jerome is here dependent on Origen.[19] In the first place,

---

[16] *Sif. Dev.* 1 (ed. Horovitz and Finkelstein, p. 8); *Ber. R.* 90. 3. In *T. Frag.*, *CN, T. Ps.-J.*, ad loc., the rendering appears together with an additional interpretation, 'father of the king'.

[17] While in his discussion of the name Zaphenath-paneah in the immediately following lemma (*QHG* 41: 45) Jerome shows his awareness that one must interpret Egyptian words by means of the Egyptian language, he does not consider the possibility that אברך is an Egyptian word. This may be because there is nothing in the context which points in this direction, and perhaps also because he was willing to accept the existence of such a Hebrew compound on the basis of a Greek parallel. For there was a current tradition that one of the great figures of 4th-cent. monasticism, Macarius the Egyptian, was called παιδαριογέρων in his youth for reasons similar to those for which Joseph was (according to the Jewish interpretation) called אברך. See Palladius, *H. Laus.* 17. 2; Sozomen, *HE* 3. 14. 2.

[18] See above, p. 25.

[19] See *PG* 15. 301. The same view is expressed by L. Ginzberg, 'Die Haggada bei den Kirchenvätern und in der apokryphischen Litteratur', *MGWJ* 43 (1899), p. 546, and Bardy, *RB* 34 (1925), p. 230.

Origen does not even say that the first interpretation which he cites is of Jewish origin, so from what source did Jerome obtain this information? In fact, we should probably see Jerome's comment as an indirect critique of the methods of his predecessor. For the Latin Father generally attempts to interpret the Hebrew text itself by critically employing the *recentiores* and Jewish teachers, not by simply sewing them together.[20]

THE *LIBER NOMINUM*

Much of *QHG* is devoted to etymological discussions. In these discussions, Jerome has a definite objective. His main intention, as he himself says in the preface, is to explain etymologies 'quae in nostro sermone non resonant'. Hebrew names and their meanings, even when accompanied by etymological explanations in the biblical text, are of course not fully comprehensible in the Greek and Latin versions. In a literal rendering the translator must either transliterate the proper name or translate it. It is impossible in the former case to appreciate the meaning of the name, in the latter to recognize the name itself, which may be known to the reader from other passages.[21] Yet etymology had always aroused considerable interest in Christian circles. For as scholars have often pointed out, it was widely believed that names were not haphazard, but contained mysteries and theological truths.[22]

---

[20] That Jerome allowed himself the freedom to employ both the rendering of the LXX and that of Aquila in his translation of Gen. 41: 43 in *IH* simply indicates that in the latter work he not only had a scholarly agenda, but also attempted to maintain the traditional LXX/*VL* version to a certain degree, and to provide a readable, readily comprehensible text. See above, pp. 69–70, 81. It is not necessary to follow M. Rahmer, *Die hebräischen Traditionen in den Werken des Hieronymus*, i. *Die 'Quaestiones in Genesin'*, Breslau 1861, p. 50, who thinks that the text of the Vulgate does not represent the version of Jerome, nor C. Gordon, *JBL* 49 (1930), p. 385 (cf. A. Condamin, 'L'influence de la tradition juive dans la version de saint Jérôme', *RSR* 5 (1914), p. 7), who suggests that Jerome could have changed his mind concerning the correct interpretation of the verse after the completion of *QHG*.

[21] Cf. B. and J. Kramer, 'Les éléments linguistiques hébreux chez Didyme l'Aveugle', *ΑΛΕΞΑΝΔΡΙΝΑ* (cited above, Ch. 2 n. 15), p. 314.

[22] See, e.g., de Lange, *Origen*, pp. 117–18. Among the texts he quotes are Origen, *Cels.* 1. 24; *Hom. in Num.* 25. 3; *Hom. in Jos.* 23. 4; a *catena* fragment variously attributed to Origen and Cyril (= *CS* G 61). Note also Jerome, *Praef. in Par.* (*iuxta LXX*); *Comm. in Jer.* 4. 63. 6. Cf. *Comm. in Dan.* 1 (1: 7); Augustine, *Doct. Chr.* 2. 23.

Accordingly, by demonstrating the extent to which this aspect of revelation was closed to Greek and Latin readers, Jerome shows that a return to the Hebrew text was necessary.

The chief source which Jerome employed in his attempt to achieve this objective was the so-called *Liber nominum*. This work, now lost, was a list of Hebrew names (in Greek transliteration) along with their meanings in Greek, which is attributed by Jerome on the basis of Origen's authority to Philo of Alexandria.[23] It is this list that Jerome claims to have translated, and his version is known as the *De nominibus Hebraicis*, a work which we have already mentioned.[24] Other related lists were also in circulation, and the remains of these have been published by P. de Lagarde and F. X. Wutz.[25] In addition to such works, Jerome will have had at his disposal the etymological information which is contained in the writings of the Greek Fathers. This material is considerable, and one has access to much of it via the references collected by Wutz.[26]

In *QHG*, Jerome concentrates much of his attention on names for which etymological explanations are given in the biblical text itself. As stated, however, such explanations are not fully comprehensible in the versions, if the actual name is given only in translation or transliteration. It is the job of the commentator to provide the 'missing link', i.e. the transliteration or the translation, whichever is not present in the version. This is a fairly straightforward matter, and Jerome was not the first exegete to undertake such a task. Some of his explanations have parallels in Greek comment-

[23] See *Nom. Hebr.* prol. F. X. Wutz, *Onomastica sacra: Untersuchungen zum Liber interpretationis nominum Hebraicorum des hl. Hieronymus* (TU 41. 1–2), Leipzig 1914–15, p. 24, points out that nowhere in his extant works does Origen refer to Philo as the author. On the other hand, Eusebius, *HE* 2. 18. 7, says that the work is attributed to Philo. The Philonic authorship of the *Liber nominum* is not accepted in modern times. See Wutz, pp. 14–24. However, it may go back to Jewish Alexandrian sources. See de Lange, *Origen*, p. 118.

[24] The work is also known as the *Liber interpretationis Hebraicorum nominum*. In this book, however, the title *De nominibus Hebraicis* (= *Nom. Hebr.*) will be employed. The title *Liber nominum* will designate Jerome's (lost) Greek *Vorlage*.

[25] De Lagarde, *Onomastica Graeca minora*, in his *Onomastica sacra²*, Göttingen 1887; Wutz, *Onomastica*. The work of Wutz is fundamental for the study of this subject, and the reader is referred to it for questions concerning the interrelationships between the original *Liber nominum*, Jerome's translation, and the later Greek lists. For a shorter treatment of the subject (based largely on Wutz), see I. Opelt, 'Etymologie', *RAC* 6. 46 (1965), cols. 826–44.

[26] For the most important of these, see *Onomastica*, pp. 733–48, 764–71, 1057–69.

ators. However, there is a tendency noticeable particularly in Alexandrian exegesis whereby this task is neglected. This failure to explain the biblical data may have been due to the perception that once the name appeared in transliterated form together with the translation, such data would be self-explanatory even without an explicit comment. Generally, however, it appears that the Alexandrians had less interest in explaining etymological information in the Bible than in employing the 'ready made' etymologies from the lists in formulating deeper conclusions concerning the meaning of the text.[27] Jerome, on the other hand, at least in *QHG*, attempts to use the *Liber nominum* as a tool for understanding the origins of Hebrew names as related in the biblical text.

On many occasions Jerome simply reports an etymology in a few words with no further discussion. In these cases it is unnecessary to look beyond a fairly simple application of material in the *Liber nominum* to the context in question. Note the following examples:

1. We find three translations for the name 'Eve' in *Nom. Hebr.*, viz. 'vita', 'calamitas', and 'vae' (5. 16–17; 75. 19–20; 76. 7; 78. 20; 81. 12). The origin of the name, however, is given in Gen. 3: 20: 'The man called his wife's name Eve [Hebrew חוה, Greek ζωή], because she was the mother of all living [Hebrew כל חי, Greek πάντων τῶν ζώντων].' On the basis of the biblical evidence, it is a fairly simple matter to select the appropriate etymology, and to indicate that underneath the *pro re* rendering in the LXX version lies the proper name Eve. It is not surprising, therefore, that Jerome's brief explanation in *QHG* 3: 20 is similar to those of Josephus, *Antiquitates Judaicae* 1. 36, and Apollinaris of Laodicea.[28]

2. Only one etymology for Ishmael appears in *Nom. Hebr.*, 'auditio Dei'.[29] The same rendering appears in Philo, *Fug.* 208; *Quaest. in Gn.* 3. 32 (cf. *Mut.* 202). Philo, however, is more interested in a 'spiritual' explanation of the name than its origin

---

[27] Cf. Kramer and Kramer, 'Les éléments', p. 316.

[28] See the *catena* fragment in Devreesse, *Les anciens commentateurs*, p. 130. Cf. the expansion of the LXX version of Gen. 3: 20 as reported by J. W. Wevers in the apparatus of his edition (Göttingen 1974 = *Septuaginta*, i), p. 94. The rendering of the name Eve with ζωή is also found in Philo, *Agr.* 95.

[29] 7. 15. Cf. *OGM* 170. 88–9; 193. 6; and the *catena* fragment printed in *PG* 12. 121a. On this fragment, see Petit, 'Le dossier', p. 89 (ad nos. 1140, 1145).

as described in Gen. 16: 11. A simpler approach is found in
Josephus, *Ant.* 1. 190, and Jerome, *QHG* 16: 11.[30]

3. Cain is translated 'possessio vel adquisitio' in *Nom. Hebr.*
4. 2 (cf. 73. 16; 77. 28). Jerome uses this etymology in his explanation of Gen. 4: 1: 'Cain adquisitio sive possessio interpretatur, id
est κτῆσις, unde etymologiam ipsius exprimens ait [sc. Eve]: "cani-
thi", id est, "possedi hominem per Deum"' (*QHG* 4: 1). We find
analogous explanations in Theodoret, *Qu. in Gen.* 60, Epiphanius,
Pan. 39. 5. 5, and Augustine, *Civ.* 15. 17, and one may deduce a
similar reasoning in Philo, *Cher.* 52, 65, 124. Ambrose, on the
other hand, is more interested in elucidating the etymology on the
basis of Cain's character: 'Cain . . . dictus est adquisitio, quod
omnia sibi adquireret' (*Cain* 1. 3; cf. *Exh. virg.* 36; Philo, *Cher.*
65, 124; Didymus, *Comm. in Gen.* 4: 25 (144. 15–16)). Eusebius
gives the non-biblical etymology ζῆλος, and says that Cain was
given the name because of his jealousy towards his brother.[31]

4. The name Dan is translated as 'iudicium aut iudicans' in
Nom. Hebr. 5. 7–8 (cf. 12. 22 and *OGM* 172. 52; 177. 81; 202. 65).
Similar renderings are found in Josephus, *Ant.* 1. 305; Philo, *All.*
2. 96; *Agr.* 95; Ambrose, *Patr.* 34; *Psal.* 40. 25; Cyril, *Glaph. Gen.*
4 (*PG* 69. 216b, d); 7 (*PG* 69. 361d); Procopius of Gaza, *Comm.
in Gen.* 30 (*PG* 87. 437–8); 49: 16–18 (*PG* 87. 503–4). On the
other hand, in none of these sources, including those in which the
focus is on Gen. 30, the chapter in which the names of the sons
of Jacob are explained, do we find an explanation of the origin of
the name as given in the Bible. Jerome executes this task briefly
in *QHG* 30: 5–6.

In other cases the application of the material in the *Liber nominum*
to the etymologies given in the biblical text is not such an easy
task. In such cases we find Jerome making a serious attempt to
evaluate the material contained in it in light of the biblical evidence
in the Hebrew text. Sometimes it is a matter of explanatory

---

[30] The remnants of a similar explanation based on the version of Aquila are
perhaps to be found in an anonymous *catena* fragment concerning Gen. 16: 11
cited by Field, i, p. 33, and Wevers, p. 175.

[31] *PE* 11. 6. 23. We find a similar comment in *Hom. Clem.* 3. 42. 7. In the same
text, 3. 25. 1, both the renderings ζῆλος and κτῆσις are mentioned. The origin of
the former etymology will have been the root קָנָא rather than the biblical קָנָה.
Cf. Wutz, *Onomastica*, p. 397. Both of these etymologies (or variations of them)
occur in the other lists. See *OGM* 172. 47–8; 177. 68 (cf. Wutz, p. 685); 193. 25;
203. 3; and Wutz, pp. 714, 725.

reconciliation, or choosing judiciously among etymologies contained in the list. On other occasions Jerome finds that the *Liber nominum* is wholly unsatisfactory. In short, *QHG* must be seen as a sort of corrective appendix to *Nom. Hebr.*

Furthermore, it is this aspect of the work that allows us to appreciate Jerome's critical stance *vis-à-vis* his Greek contemporaries and predecessors. For the discriminating manner with which Jerome approaches the *Liber nominum* is generally absent from Greek writings. Among the Greeks we find a rather arbitrary use of the list, which often results in imprecision in the citation of biblical etymologies and extensive utilization of non-biblical etymologies. The latter may be described as simple renderings of names in which no regard is given to the biblical explanations. One finds many such etymologies in the various remnants of the *Liber nominum*, and it is clear from the writings of Philo that they were in circulation from an early date. It would seem, therefore, that Jerome's intention is to demonstrate that the common method of Greek exegesis, namely, the use of the LXX together with the *Liber nominum*, is not always satisfactory for an understanding of biblical etymology. Rather, it could lead to an aggravation of the obscurity already present in biblical etymological explanations as preserved in the Greek and Latin versions.[32] For Jerome, a proper understanding of the biblical material was to be obtained by paying closer attention to the Hebrew text, and by moving beyond the *Liber nominum* where necessary. This could be achieved by turning to the *recentiores* and contemporary rabbinic informants. The following examples should serve as evidence for these assertions.[33]

1. The etymology of the name Seth is to be found in Gen. 4: 25:

And Adam knew his wife again, and she bore a son and called his name Seth [Hebrew שֵׁת, Greek Σήθ], for she said, 'God has appointed [Hebrew שָׁת, Greek ἐξανέστησεν] for me another child instead of Abel, for Cain slew him.'

---

[32] Wutz, *Onomastica*, pp. 21–2, believes that the criticisms present in certain passages of *QHG* are directed against Philo himself. It is probable, however, as should be evident from a discussion of these same passages below, that the criticisms are more broadly aimed.

[33] That in works other than *QHG* Jerome does not always maintain a critical approach in using the *Liber nominum*, but employs it in the same arbitrary fashion as do the Greek Fathers, may be freely acknowledged. For a discussion of the problems raised by this phenomenon, see Jay, *L'exégèse*, pp. 295–7.

In *Nom. Hebr.* 10. 12–13; 20. 17; 65. 28–30, however, we find the following among other renderings: 'positio', 'posuit', 'poculum', 'gramen', 'semen', and 'resurrectio'.[34] Jerome indicates his preference in his comment on Gen. 4: 25, citing Aquila's translation:

Seth proprie θέσις, id est positio, dicitur. quia igitur posuerit eum Deus pro Abel, propterea Seth, id est positio, appellatur. denique Aquila, 'et vocavit' inquit, 'nomen eius Seth dicens: Quia posuit mihi Dominus semen alterum'. (*QHG* 4: 25)

It is interesting to contrast this comment with those of other Greek and Latin writers. Philo and Didymus, for example, disregard the biblical etymology. The former renders the name as 'one who drinks water' in *Quaest. in Gn.* 1. 78, and as ποτισμός in *Post.* 10, 124, 170. Didymus employs this second interpretation in *Comm. in Gen.* 4: 25 (144. 8–9).[35] Epiphanius and Augustine, on the other hand, prefer etymologies which have been imposed on the Hebrew via the Greek translation. Epiphanius translates the name as ἀνταλλαγή, and explains by citing the text, ἀνέστησεν γάρ μοι ὁ θεὸς σπέρμα ἀντὶ Ἄβελ (*Pan.* 39. 5. 7). The rendering cited by Augustine in *Civ.* 15. 17, 'resurrectio', derives no doubt from the Greek ἐξανέστησε.[36] This etymology had its origins in Christian doctrinal considerations. The interpretation given by Hilary in *Myst.* 1. 11, 'fundamentum fidei', seems to be based on the Greek θέσις, which probably underlies 'positio' in *Nom. Hebr.*[37] However, Hilary adds the extraneous element 'fides', and indeed bases his explanation of the name on this word in a manner completely unrelated to the biblical statement.[38]

2. Asher is rendered by 'beatitudo' and 'beatus' in *Nom. Hebr.* 3. 7–8; 12. 6; 24. 16–17; 56. 27; 80. 10–11; (cf. 64. 4 and *OGM*

---

[34] Some of these have parallels in the Greek lists. Ἀνάστασις is mentioned as a possible rendering in *OGM* 177. 68, as is θέμενος in 204. 39.

[35] For an explanation of the origin of these etymologies see Wutz, *Onomastica*, p. 372. Cf. A. F. J. Klijn, *Seth in Jewish, Christian and Gnostic Literature* (NT.S 46), Leiden 1977, p. 34.

[36] Cf. Klijn, op. cit., pp. 34–5.

[37] See J.-P. Brisson in his edition of *Myst.* (Paris 1967² = SC 19), p. 96 n. 2. Cf. J. Daniélou, 'Hilaire et ses sources juives', *Hilaire et son temps*, Paris 1969, p. 146.

[38] The etymology 'foundation' is also employed by Ishodad of Merv in his *Comm. in Gen.* 4: 25. However, his interpretation seems to have more in common with *Bem. R.* 14. 12 than with any Greek source. Cf. T. Jansma, *OTS* 12 (1958), pp. 176–7.

177. 82; 178. 5). This is the biblical etymology, as is clear from Gen. 30: 13: 'And Leah said, "Happy am I! For the women will call me happy"; so she called his name Asher.' This etymology is explained by Josephus, *Ant.* 1. 306. On the other hand, some LXX manuscripts contain the gloss (ὅ ἐστι) πλοῦτος after the word 'Asher' in the verse in question.[39] Some Fathers, notably Ambrose and Cyril, present rather elaborate interpretations based on this etymology.[40] Jerome objects to the gloss/etymology on biblical grounds:

Male additae sunt divitiae, id est πλοῦτος, cum etymologia nominis Aser scripturae auctoritate pandatur dicentis: 'beata sum ego, et beatificant me mulieres'. et ab eo, quod beata dicatur ab hominibus, filium suum beatum vocaverit. Aser ergo non divitiae, sed beatus dicitur, dumtaxat in praesenti loco. nam in aliis secundum ambiguitatem verbi possunt et divitiae sic vocari.[41]

3. In *Nom. Hebr.* 11. 29–12. 2; 15. 6; 63. 14–15; 81. 7, we find a number of etymologies for Zebulun, 'iusiurandum eius', 'fluxus noctis', 'habitaculum', and 'habitaculum pulchritudinis' among them. In Gen. 30: 20, the etymology is related as follows:

ותאמר לאה זבדני אלהים אתי זבד טוב הפעם יִזְבְּלֵנִי אישי כי ילדתי לו
ששה בנים ותקרא את שמו זְבֻלוּן:

καὶ εἶπεν Λεία Δεδώρηταί μοι ὁ θεὸς δῶρον καλόν· ἐν τῷ νῦν καιρῷ αἱρετιεῖ με ὁ ἀνήρ μου, ἔτεκον γὰρ αὐτῷ υἱοὺς ἕξ· καὶ ἐκάλεσεν τὸ ὄνομα αὐτοῦ Ζαβουλών.

---

[39] See the apparatus criticus of Wevers, ad loc. Cf. *OGM* 200. 18: Ἀσὴρ πλοῦτος. The origin of this rendering may be connected with Gen. 49: 20. See Epiphanius, *De gemmis*, ed. R. P. Blake, London 1934 (= StD 2), p. 148.

[40] Ambrose, *Patr.* 38–9; Cyril, *Glaph. Gen.* 4 (*PG* 69. 216d–217b); 7 (*PG* 69. 368c–369c). Cf. Procopius of Gaza, *Comm. in Gen.* 30 (*PG* 87. 437–40); 49 (*PG* 87. 505–8). In Philo, *Som.* 2. 35, 40; *Migr.* 95, on the other hand, the renderings πλοῦτος and μακάρι-ος/σμός seem to be assimilated. They are both given as alternative etymologies of Asher in a variant reading of the title of the *Testament of Asher* (see the edition of M. de Jonge (Leiden 1978 = PVTG 1. 2), p. 135), and in *OGM* 173. 53; 187. 40.

[41] *QHG* 30. 12–13. The 'ambiguity' to which Jerome is alluding actually concerns two roots, עשר and אשר. However, since he shows clear awareness of the difference between the spelling of אשר and חצר in *Nom. Hebr.* 24. 16–18, it is unnecessary to assume that he was unaware of the similar difference between עשר and אשר. Rather, he is speaking in shorthand, and is referring to the ambiguity which is present in the Greek or Latin transcription of the words. Note the similar procedure which he employs when listing under the letter *A* names which begin with different letters in the Hebrew alphabet: 'quia apud nos non est vocum tanta diversitas, simplici sumus elatione contenti' (*Nom. Hebr.* 2. 11–12). Cf. the note of Martianay, *PL* 23. 1601a–b9.

There is in this verse a word play with the root זבד (Greek δωρέω), and reliance on the Greek text alone could lead one to think that the biblical etymology of the name Zebulun is based on this root.[42] Yet Jerome seems to have made a closer reading of the Hebrew text, for he connects the biblical etymology with the word יִזְבְּלֵנִי. He renders this word 'habitabit mecum', most probably following Aquila, who translates συνοικήσει μοι.[43] Accordingly, he states that the proper name means 'habitaculum', and concludes his comments polemically: 'male igitur et violenter in libro nominum Zabulon fluxus noctis interpretatur' (*QHG* 30: 19–20).

Jerome has attempted to employ the *Liber nominum* critically, selecting the etymology which seems to receive corroboration from the biblical text. But why does he single out only one of the non-biblical etymologies in the *Liber nominum*, 'fluxus noctis', for reproach? Probably because it was the one which was most popular among exegetes. We find it in Philo, *Som.* 2. 34; Ambrose, *Ep.* 12(30). 10; 19(71). 5; (cf. *Patr.* 26), and in a *catena* fragment printed in the old edition of Theodoret, *Comm. in Is.* 9: 2 (*PG* 81. 292c).[44] Josephus puts forward an etymology which seems to be based on the word חֶבֶל.[45] Cyril on the other hand offers such etymologies as εὐλογία and εὐόδωμα.[46]

4. The episode concerning the naming of Benjamin is related in Gen. 35: 18:

ויהי בצאת נפשה כי מתה [sc. Rachel] ותקרא שמו בן־אוני ואביו קרא
לו בנימין:

[42] Note the rendering δῶρον in *OGM* 172. 51–2; 177. 81; and Wutz, *Onomastica*, p. 715. Cf. also *Testament of Zebulon* 1. 3; Hippolytus, *De benedictionibus* 2 (*PO* 27. 1–2, p. 178).

[43] This version is probably based on Gen. 49: 13 (זְבוּלֻן . . . ישׁכֹּן), and on the normal interpretation of the word זְבֻל as 'dwelling'. See the LXX version of II Chr. 6: 2 and Is. 63: 15, and Aquila's translation of III Reg. 8: 13 and Is. 63: 15. Cf. *Shem. R.* 1. 5; *Leq. T.* ad Gen. 30: 20.

[44] Note also *OGM* 164. 72–3. For the origin of the etymology, see Wutz, *Onomastica*, p. 481.

[45] *Ant.* 1. 308. See the note of H. St John Thackeray in his edition of the text (Cambridge, Mass. 1930 = LCL Josephus, iv), p. 149. The rendering 'iusiurandum eius', on the other hand, may be connected with the word שְׁבוּעָה. See Wutz, *Onomastica*, p. 378.

[46] *Glaph. Gen.* 4 (*PG* 69. 220d–221a). Cf. Procopius of Gaza, *Comm. in Gen.* 30 (*PG* 87. 439–40). The rendering εὐόδωμα also appears in *OGM* 178. 96. Regardless of its origin (see Wutz, *Onomastica*, p. 482), Cyril seems to have understood the word in the sense of εὐοδία. See *Glaph. Gen.* 4 (*PG* 69. 213b); *Fr. Mt.* 4: 24–5 (*PG* 72. 373b); and cf. *PGL*, s.v. εὐόδωμα.

ἐγένετο δὲ ἐν τῷ ἀφιέναι αὐτὴν τὴν ψυχήν, ἀπέθνῃσκεν γάρ, ἐκάλεσεν τὸ ὄνομα αὐτοῦ υἱὸς ὀδύνης μου· ὁ δὲ πατὴρ ἐκάλεσεν αὐτὸν Βενιαμίν.

It is extremely difficult to grasp the word-play in the Greek version, since the first name is rendered *pro re* and the second is transliterated. Jerome explains to his readers: 'in Hebraeo similitudo nominis resonat: filius enim doloris mei, quod nomen moriens mater inposuit, dicitur Benoni, filius vero dexterae, hoc est virtutis, quod Jacob mutavit, appellatur Beniamin' (*QHG* 35: 18; cf. *Tract. Psal. I* 7: 1). Such a distinction is preserved in *Nom. Hebr.*, where Benoni is rendered as 'filius doloris mei' (3. 23–4), and Beniamin as 'filius dext(e)rae' (3. 24; 16. 17; 74. 1; 76. 24; 80. 14–15).

We hardly find similar clarity when we turn to the Greek sources. In Procopius of Gaza, *Comm. in Gen.* 35: 18 (*PG* 87. 463–4b), the etymology of Benjamin is indeed correctly given as υἱὸς δυνάμεων and is correctly applied to the biblical text, but there is no attempt to explain the word-play with Benoni. Most Greek writers, however, did not even reach this level of coherence. Josephus, *Ant.* 1. 343, not only neglects to mention Benoni, he also refers the etymology of his name to Benjamin. Similarly in another passage of Procopius, we find Benjamin translated as 'doloris filius' (*Comm. in Gen.* 30 (*PG* 87. 439–40)). Cyril, on the other hand, renders both Benoni and Benjamin as υἱὸς ὀδύνης (*Glaph. Gen.* 4 (*PG* 69. 213b, 224a–b)). This muddling of the biblical data is reflected in the Greek *onomastica*. For the name Benjamin is rendered indiscriminately as both υἱὸς δεξιᾶς and τέκνον ὀδύνης.[47] The name Benoni does not seem to appear in the Greek lists.[48] One may conclude from this state of affairs that the entries in *Nom. Hebr.* have been adjusted by Jerome himself.

Philo prefers the non-biblical etymology υἱὸς ἡμερῶν (*Mut.* 92–3; *Som.* 2. 36). This interpretation is also found in *Testament of Benjamin* 1. 5–6 and is reflected in a late rabbinic source.[49] It is probably based on Gen. 44: 20, where Benjamin is called a child of Jacob's old age, and perhaps on the attribution of an Aramaic

---

[47] In *OGM* 177. 83–178. 84 and 201. 52, both renderings are given (cf. Wutz, *Onomastica*, p. 719); in 173. 54, only τέκνον ὀδύνης (cf. 184. 69–70; Wutz, pp. 714, 722); in 179. 10, only υἱὸς δεξιός. Origen, *Hom. in Jer.* 19. 13; *Fr. in Jer.* 11 (GCS 6, p. 202), employs υἱὸς δεξιᾶς.

[48] See the indices to *OGM*, and in Wutz, *Onomastica*, s.v.

[49] *Leq. T.* ad Gen. 35: 18. See Ginzberg, 'Die Haggada' (*MGWJ* 43), p. 537. The etymology is also given as an alternative to τέκνον ὀδύνης in *OGM* 188. 70–1.

rather than a Hebrew etymology to the name.[50] Jerome, however, reacts against this interpretation: 'errant qui putant Beniamin filium dierum interpretari. cum enim dextera appelletur iamin et finiatur in N literam, dies quidem appellantur et ipsi iamim, sed in M literam terminantur.'[51]

5–6. In Gen. 17, two important name changes are related. According to the Greek text, in verse 5 Ἀβράμ becomes Ἀβραάμ, and in verse 15 Σάρα becomes Σάρρα. Greek exegetes, following the LXX, naturally discuss the changes in Greek terms. Philo speaks of doublings of the letters *alpha* and *rho* (*Mut.* 61, 77; *Abr.* 81; *Quaest. in Gn.* 3. 43, 53). Christian writers such as Justin, *Dial.* 113, Ambrose, *Abr.* 2. 85, and Didymus, *Comm. in Gen.* 3: 24 (114. 3), follow in his footsteps. This view of the changes is reflected in the Greek *onomastica*.[52]

In *QHG* 17: 3–5, 15–16, Jerome reacts against this Greek perspective, reporting an interesting Jewish tradition: 'dicunt autem Hebraei, quod ex nomine suo Deus, quod apud illos tetragrammum est [i.e. יהוה], he literam [i.e. ה] Abrahae et Sarae addiderit.'[53] He goes on to point out that in Abraham's name the letter *he* [ה] has been added, and explains that it is sometimes pronounced as an *a* in Hebrew (an accurate statement when we remember that in his day written vocalization was not yet in existence). He makes clear in this manner why in Greek it appears that an *alpha* has been added to the name Ἀβράμ.[54]

With regard to Sarah, on the other hand, he lashes out with

---

[50] Cf. the note of D. Vallarsi, *PL* 23. 1042d–43c.

[51] *QHG* 35: 18. Cf. *Ep.* 140. 16. According to Wutz, *Onomastica*, p. 21, Jerome's critical remark is aimed at Philo.

[52] *OGM* 173. 59; 204. 41–2; Wutz, *Onomastica*, p. 728.

[53] This tradition, according to which God employed a *he* from his own name in instituting the name changes of Abraham and Sarah, is clearly distinct from the tradition preserved in *Ber. R.* 47. 1. In this latter text it is reported in the name of Joshua ben Karha (*fl. c.*135–60) that from the *yod* taken from Sarai's name (which has a numerical value of 10) half was given to Abraham and half was returned to Sarah (i.e. the *yod* became two *hes*, each of which has a numerical value of 5). Accordingly, the statement of Rahmer, *Die hebräischen Traditionen*, p. 28, that Jerome is giving an 'inexact' version of a [single] tradition is misleading. Indeed, after Rahmer's work appeared, S. Buber published an edition of the so-called *Midrash Aggada* (Vienna 1894), a late compilation relating to the Pentateuch. In a comment on Num. 2: 2 preserved in this text (vol. ii, p. 79), we find an allusion to the tradition cited by Jerome.

[54] On the manner in which Jerome expresses himself in this passage, see Barr, *JSSt* 12 (1967), pp. 28–9.

venom against those who interpret the change in her name from
the perspective of the version of the LXX, namely, as a doubling
of the letter *rho*, and who, on the basis of the fact that this letter
is the symbol for the number 100 in Greek, 'multas super nomine
eius ineptias suspicantur'. He affirms the principle that one must
explain etymologies via the language of the names themselves, not
via the logic of a foreign language, and explains, 'Sarai igitur
primum vocata est per sin res ioth [i.e. שְׂרִי]: sublato ergo ioth, id
est I elemento, addita est he litera, quae per A legitur, et vocata
est Saraa.' When we see Jerome's transcriptions of the names, it
is clear why he objects so much more forcefully to the Greek
description of Sarah's name change than to that of Abraham's:
with regard to Abraham, the Greek transcriptions reflect at least
as far as possible the phonetic change. In the case of Sarah, the
Greek spellings are completely misleading.[55] Again we see how
Jerome attempts to impress upon his readers the fact that there
were serious flaws in the LXX-based philology of the Greeks. He
also replaces, as it were, the 'ineptiae' of the Greeks with a Jewish
aggada which, if no less fanciful, at least corresponds to the philological reality.

Jerome's discussions of the name changes themselves are equally
instructive. The relevant passage for the case of Sarah is Gen.
17: 15–16:

ויאמר אלהים אל אברהם שרי אשתך לא תקרא את שמה שרי כי שרה
שמה: (16) וברכתי אתה וגם נתתי ממנה לך בן וברכתיה והיתה לגוים
מלכי עמים ממנה יהיו:

καὶ εἶπεν ὁ θεὸς τῷ Ἀβραάμ Σάρα ἡ γυνή σου, οὐ κληθήσεται τὸ ὄνομα αὐτῆς
Σάρα, ἀλλὰ Σάρρα ἔσται τὸ ὄνομα αὐτῆς. (16) εὐλογήσω δὲ αὐτὴν καὶ δώσω σοι
ἐξ αὐτῆς τέκνον· καὶ εὐλογήσω αὐτόν [v.l. αὐτήν], καὶ ἔσται εἰς ἔθνη, καὶ
βασιλεῖς ἐθνῶν ἐξ αὐτοῦ [v.l. αὐτῆς] ἔσονται.

[55] In view of this evidence, there can be no doubt that the spellings in *Nom.
Hebr.* have been revised by Jerome. For Sarai appears as Sarai (10. 22) and Sarah
as Saraa (10. 28). By contrast, the form Σάραι or a similar form does not appear
in the Greek or Latin onomastical lists (see the indices to *OGM* and in Wutz,
Onomastica, s.v.). The form Σαραά does occur to *OGM* 179. 30 (cf. Wutz, p. 691)
and Σαρόα (*legendum Σαραα?* see Wutz, p. 181) occurs in 198. 54. However, in both
cases the etymology given is that of Σάρα, viz. ἀρχή μου (ἀρχὴ ἐμή should be read
for ἐρχομένη in *OGM* 179. 30, see Wutz, p. 91), not that of Σάρρα, i.e. Jerome's
Saraa. Accordingly, this spelling could reflect error rather than design. The fact
that Jerome is not always consistent, and appears to employ different spellings of
both forms of the name in his various writings, need hardly cause concern. He
may be making concessions to established custom or following sources closely.

Philo translates Σάρα as ἀρχή μου (*Cher.* 5; *Congr.* 2) and Σάρρα as
ἄρχουσα (*Cher.* 7, 41; *Abr.* 99). These renderings are found in
Jerome's *Nom. Hebr.* 10. 22, 28, and other patristic sources.[56]
Philo discusses the reasons for the name change in *Cher.* 5, 7,
Mut. 77–8, and *Quaest. in Gn.* 3. 53, and explains it in terms of
an elevation to a higher level of virtue.[57] Both Ambrose, *Abr.*
2. 85, and Didymus, *Comm. in Gen.* 3: 24 (114. 3–6), follow his
lead.[58] For his part, Augustine says explicitly that no reason for
the name change is given in the biblical text (*Civ.* 16. 28).

Jerome also follows the Philonic–*Liber nominum* renderings, but
he explains the name change in terms of the biblical data:

> Causa autem ita nominis immutati haec est, quod antea dicebatur princeps
> mea, unius tantum modo domus mater familiae, postea vero dicitur
> absolute princeps, id est ἄρχουσα. sequitur enim, 'dabo tibi ex ea filium
> et benedicam ei: et erit in gentes, et reges populorum erunt ex ea [v.l.
> eo]'. signanterque non, ut in Graeco legimus: 'dixit Deus ad Abraham:
> Sarai uxor tua, non vocabitur nomen eius Sarai', in Hebraeo habetur:
> 'non vocabis nomen eius Sarai', id est, non dices ei, 'princeps mea es':
> omnium quippe gentium futura iam princeps est. (*QHG* 17: 15–16)

Jerome emphasizes the connection between one verse and the
next, noting that in verse 16 we find the explanation of why Sarah
can be called 'absolute princeps': she will rule many peoples
through her posterity.[59] Previously she was called 'my princess',
i.e. Abraham's princess, because she was the head of his household. This latter point is clearer in the Hebrew text since the
command of verse 15 is addressed to Abraham, whereas in Greek
it is impersonal. However, it is Abraham that will no longer be
able to address his wife as 'my princess'.

---

[56] Clement, *Str.* 1. 31. 1 (Σάρα = ἀρχή μου); Cyril, *Glaph. Gen.* 3 (*PG* 69. 116b–c,
125d: Σάρρα = ἄρχουσα); Augustine, *Civ.* 16. 28 (Sara = 'princeps mea'); Ambrose,
Abr. 2. 85 (both names rendered as in Philo). Cf. *OGM* 173. 59 (where ἀρχὴ ἐμή
should be read for ἀρχομένη, see previous note).

[57] This may explain why we find Sarra actually rendered as 'virtus' by Augustine, *Civ.* 16. 28. Perhaps Origen, *Hom. in Gen.* 6. 1, played an intermediating
role. In this text we read, 'puto ergo Sarram, quae interpretatur princeps vel
principatum agens, formam tenere ἀρετῆς, quod est animi virtus. . . . donec enim
uxor *appellatur* virtus, . . .' (GCS 29, pp. 66–7). Cf. Wutz, *Onomastica*, p. 22 n. 1.

[58] Didymus, however, translates Σάρα as μικρότης. This seems to be based on
the root צער. Cf. Wutz, *Onomastica*, p. 237.

[59] The layout of this passage in de Lagarde's edition, p. 27 (= CChr.SL 72,
p. 21), is misleading. For the words 'sequitur enim' mark the beginning of a new
lemma. The link between these words and the previous sentence is therefore
slightly obfuscated. The text is printed correctly by Vallarsi. See *PL* 23. 1013a–14a.

Another reason for the fact that the link between verses 15 and 16, and, accordingly, the explanation for the name change, is more clearly manifest in the Hebrew text is the formulation of verse 16 in that text. For Sarah, rather than her son, is not only the object of the second blessing of God, but also the subject of the phrase 'shall be [sc. a ruler?] unto nations' or 'shall [become many] nations', and the person from whom the kings shall spring. And although it could be said that according to the standard Septuagint text as well Sarah obtains the status of 'princeps' through her son, that status is much more clearly visible in the Hebrew text.

In fact, that Jerome himself may be alluding to this Hebrew form of verse 16 as well seems evident from his use of the pronoun 'ea' rather than 'eo' in his citation of the phrase, 'et reges populorum erunt ex ea.'[60] In addition, the final sentence of his comment as cited above, 'omnium quippe gentium futura iam princeps est', appears to represent a paraphrase of verse 16 in its Hebrew form, in which Sarah is the subject of the phrase, 'et erit in gentes' (note the use of the word 'gentes' and the fact that 'futura est' probably reflects 'erit').[61]

It is of course not to be excluded that these two features of

[60] The reading 'ea' is relegated to the apparatus criticus by de Lagarde, p. 27 (= CChr.SL 72, p. 21), who prints 'eo'. Yet the reading 'ea' is guaranteed here not so much by its presence in φ, de Lagarde's oldest MS (which contains some trivial errors), but by the fact that it is employed by Isidore, *Origines* 7. 6. 29, in his adaptation of this passage of *QHG*. For since the reading 'ea' is attested in the Latin versions apparently only in these two passages (see B. Fischer's edition of the Old Latin version of Genesis (Freiburg (im Breisgau) 1951–4 = *Vetus Latina: Die Reste der altlateinischen Bibel*, ii), p. 191), whereas 'eo' represents the standard text of the *VL* as well as of *IH* ('ea' is not even listed as a variant in the edition of H. Quentin (Rome 1926 = *Biblia Sacra iuxta Latinam vulgatam versionem*, i), p. 206), it is easier to believe that the reading in Isidore is derived from *QHG* than from some other source. On the other hand, the reading 'eo' in some MSS of *QHG* should be seen as the result of a tendency to accommodate the biblical citations to more standard texts.

[61] As stated in the previous paragraph, another feature of the Hebrew text of Gen. 17: 16 over against the standard Greek text, is the fact that Sarah, rather than her child, is the object of the second as well as the first occurrence of the verb 'bless'. One cannot prove that Jerome's citation follows the Hebrew rather than the LXX/*VL* with regard to this matter, however, since he employs the ambiguous Latin version 'benedicam ei'. And even the fact that he uses this phrase instead of the normal *VL* reading 'benedicam illum' (see Fischer, pp. 190–1) does not constitute sufficient evidence for the assumption that he is following the Hebrew and wishes to refer the pronoun to Sarah rather than to her child. For the construction of 'benedico' with the accusative is simply a feature of translation literalism that offended him. He normally replaces it with the dative construction in *IH*. See *Thesaurus linguae Latinae*, ii, col. 1867, ll. 20–4.

Jerome's discussion simply reflect an incidental use of a form of the LXX in which the pronouns αὐτήν and αὐτῆς were read. For even in the Greek text, if the gender of both of these pronouns is feminine, the natural subject of ἔσται εἰς ἔθνη is Sarah.[62] Nevertheless, incidental use of such a text-form seems unlikely. It is true that the readings αὐτήν and αὐτῆς are attested early and are even regarded as original by J. W. Wevers.[63] However, they were not the standard readings in the time of Jerome. The forms αὐτόν and αὐτοῦ are employed in the major Greek uncial manuscripts, in the *VL*, and by the Greek Fathers.[64] And in fact, Jerome himself, in his use of this verse elsewhere, seems to have known the LXX/ *VL* in the form ἐξ αὐτοῦ.[65] Accordingly, it seems that Jerome is relying on a Hebrew text in his treatment of Gen. 17: 16 in *QHG*. Indeed, it seems logical to conclude that he viewed the greater clarity of the explanation of the name change of Sarah in the Hebrew text as dependent on this verse as well as verse 15. That he fails to communicate this fact explicitly to his readers may be inadvertent.

In the present case Jerome was able to accept the etymologies found in the *Liber nominum*. This acceptance, however, was based on a critical reading of the text in its Hebrew form.[66] Indeed, in the eyes of Jerome, it is the Hebrew rather than the Greek text that allows one to come to this judgement. For use of the Greek or Latin text alone together with the *Liber nominum* was clearly

---

[62] See Philo's interpretation of the text in *Mut.* 148–50.

[63] See his edition, ad loc. He seems to have based his decision primarily on the evidence of Philo, loc. cit., and an early papyrus.

[64] See the edition of Wevers as well as the manual edition of Rahlfs (Stuttgart 1935), ad loc. For the *VL*, see Fischer, pp. 190–1. For the Greek Fathers, in addition to Chrysostom, *Hom. in Gen.* 40. 1 (*PG* 53. 369–70, cited by Wevers), see Procopius of Gaza, *Comm. in Gen.* 17: 16 (Greek text in *CS*, p. 71).

[65] *Pelag.* 3. 12 (*PL* 23. 609c). The use of the pronoun 'ipse' in the translation 'ex ipso' points to a Greek rather than a Hebrew *Vorlage*. The fact that Jerome employs 'ex eo' in *IH* would also indicate that his MSS of the LXX/*VL* text contained this reading. For his use of 'eo' and not 'ea' in *IH* is easier to explain by the hypothesis that he is simply following the LXX/*VL* than by the idea that he is relying on a Hebrew text which was different from our own.

[66] The assumption of Rahmer, *Die hebräischen Traditionen*, p. 28, that Jerome's interpretation of the name change of Sarah is based on a rabbinic source similar to *b. Ber.* 13a (note also the parallel passages in *Ber. R.* 47. 1 and *t. Ber.* 1. 13), where we read, 'At first she [sc. Sarah] became a princess to her own people, but later she became a princess to all the world,' is unnecessary. For Jerome's formulation does not allow us to conclude that he did anything more than interpret the renderings in the *Liber nominum* in the light of the Hebrew text.

insufficient. Such a procedure seems to have led Augustine (and perhaps other Fathers) to believe that there was no biblical explanation for the change in Sarah's name.

With regard to the case of Abraham, on the other hand, Jerome is forced to abandon the material in the *Liber nominum* as incompatible with the biblical text. The name Abraham is rendered in *Nom. Hebr.* as 'pater videns populum' (3. 3–4; 60. 8; 73. 23; 81. 9) and 'pater videns multitudinem' (76. 2–3, 14; 77. 25; cf. 72. 13).[67] In Gen. 17: 4–5, however, God addresses the patriarch as follows:

'Behold, my covenant is with you, and you shall be the father of a multitude of nations. No longer shall your name be Abram [Hebrew אברם, Greek Ἀβράμ], but your name shall be Abraham [Hebrew אברהם, Greek, Ἀβραάμ]; for I have made you the father of a multitude of nations [Hebrew, כי אב המון גוים נתתיך, Greek, ὅτι πατέρα πολλῶν ἐθνῶν τέθεικά σε].'

Jerome makes an effort to understand in exactly what sense the different components of the etymology correspond to the components of the name itself.[68] He writes, 'vocatus est Abraham, quod transfertur pater multarum: nam quod sequitur, gentium, non habetur in nomine, sed subauditur' (*QHG* 17: 3–5). It is clear that he ascribes to the biblical text supreme authority, seeing in the last two letters of the name a reference to the word המון in the sentence that follows. It is probably not necessary to assume that in coming to such a conclusion he was consciously applying the rabbinic principle of *notarikon*, according to which words are given in an abbreviated form.[69] For in this passage, a close reading of the text together with a minimum knowledge of Hebrew will have been sufficient.

We find a different picture when we turn to other Greek and Latin writers. It is true that Origen, *Hom. in Gen.* 8. 1, and Augustine, *Civ.* 16. 28, do pay attention to the biblical explanation of the name change, but they are unable to do more than quote the passage in question.[70] It was no doubt this uncritical approach that led to the inclusion of the rendering πατὴρ ἐθνῶν in the

[67] For an explanation of these etymologies, see Wutz, *Onomastica*, p. 159.

[68] Jerome makes similar efforts in his discussions of the etymologies of Ammon and Issachar. See *QHG* 19: 36–8; 30: 17–18.

[69] For the rabbinic *notarikon*, see Bacher, *Die exegetische Terminologie*, pp. 125–6. For the application of the principle to Gen. 17: 5, see *Ber. R.* 46. 7.

[70] Cf. Ps.-Cyprian, *Mont.* 5; Chrysostom, *Hom. in Gen.* 39. 3 (*PG* 53. 364–5); *De inani gloria* 49.

onomastica.[71] By contrast, Jerome attempts to correct the impression that the word 'gentium' was part of the etymology.

Philo prefers a non-biblical etymology, πατὴρ ἐκλεκτὸς ἠχοῦς (*Cher.* 7; *Abr.* 82), a rendering also found in patristic sources.[72] Moreover, he does not follow the biblical explanation of the name change, but describes the adoption of the new name as a symbol of Abraham's passage from the world of the perceptible to the world of the intelligible (*Quaest. in Gn.* 3. 43; cf. *Gig.* 62–4; *Mut.* 66–76). Didymus, on the other hand, translates Abraham as πατὴρ υἱῶν, but seems to have been influenced by the Philonic explanation of the name change.[73] For his part, Ambrose, *Abr.* 1. 27, would have us believe that Abraham means 'pater sublimis' (actually the etymology for Abram as reported in the *Liber nominum*; see *Nom. Hebr.* 2. 28–9; *OGM* 177. 75–6; Philo, *Cher.* 4; *All.* 3. 83) or 'pater filii'.[74] The explanations he provides for the change have nothing to do with Gen. 17: 4–5.

Finally, Eusebius, *PE* 11. 6. 25–6, explains the name change in a manner similar to that of Philo, but then cites Gen. 17: 5 as if in support of his explanation. In other words, his reliance on the LXX seems to have prevented him from perceiving the reason for the new name as given in the biblical text.[75] It is clearly against this type of approach that Jerome is arguing.

7. The story of how Jacob received the name Israel is related in Gen. 32: 23–33. In this passage we read that a 'man' who wrestled with him gave him that name after their encounter. In *Nom. Hebr.*, the meaning of the name is given as follows: 'videre Deum sive vir aut mens videns Deum' (13. 21; cf. 63. 22; 74. 15–16; 76. 20). We read similar renderings in the Greek lists.[76] The formation of

---

[71] *OGM* 200. 13–14. Cf. the etymology in the Latin fragment printed in Wutz, *Onomastica*, p. 752: 'pater gentium'; and also *OGM* 177. 76–7.

[72] Origen, *Cels.* 5. 45; Ambrose, *Abr.* 2. 77.

[73] *Comm. in Gen.* 3: 24 (113. 25–114. 3). The rendering πατὴρ υἱῶν also occurs in *OGM* 185. 94.

[74] Didymus, loc. cit., ascribes this etymology to the name Ἀβράμ. However, it is ascribed to the name Ἀβραάμ in *OGM* 185. 88

[75] Eusebius' claim that a full explanation of the name change would require excessive length hardly allows us to conclude that he would have somehow reconciled the Philonic explanation with the biblical one. Rather, one must agree with Wutz, *Onomastica*, p. 160, who writes of Eusebius, 'er ist ratlos der Etym. gegenüber'.

[76] *OGM* 170. 90–1; 176. 36–7 (cf. Wutz, *Onomastica*, p. 709); 181. 82; 193. 15–16; 203. 92; Wutz, pp. 700, 706, 725. For a discussion of these renderings, see Wutz, pp. 88–9, 526–7 (cf. p. 583).

such etymologies was due not only to the possible interpretations of the name itself, but probably also to Gen. 32: 31(30), where Jacob says, 'I have seen God face to face'.[77] However, in the biblical narrative, this statement is actually given as the explanation of the naming of a place, Peniel, i.e. 'the face of God'. This is where Jacob had had his encounter with the 'man'. The etymology of the name Israel is actually related two verses previously, in Gen. 32: 29(28):

וַיֹּאמֶר [sc. the 'man'] לֹא יַעֲקֹב יֵאָמֵר עוֹד שִׁמְךָ כִּי אִם יִשְׂרָאֵל כִּי שָׂרִיתָ
עִם אֱלֹהִים וְעִם אֲנָשִׁים וַתּוּכָל:

εἶπεν δὲ αὐτῷ Οὐ κληθήσεται ἔτι τὸ ὄνομά σου Ἰακώβ, ἀλλὰ Ἰσραὴλ ἔσται τὸ ὄνομά σου, ὅτι ἐνίσχυσας μετὰ θεοῦ καὶ μετὰ ἀνθρώπων δυνατός.

The biblical etymology of the name is clearly based on the verb שָׂרִיתָ, here rendered in the LXX by the verb ἐνίσχυσας. We do find awareness of this fact on the part of some Fathers. Origen recognizes that the name could be translated on the basis of Gen. 32: 29(28)b, and Tertullian even mentions a rendering.[78] However, such efforts do not represent more than attempts to interpret the meaning of the name on the basis of the LXX.

In fact, it was the etymology of the *Liber nominum* that came to be preferred in Christian circles. As Jerome puts it in his discussion of the origin of the name Israel, which occurs in *QHG* 32: 28–9, this rendering was 'omnium paene sermone detritum'. This statement is no exaggeration. The translations in the *Liber nominum*, or minor variations of them, were adopted almost universally among Greek and Latin exegetes.[79] The following list constitutes a representative selection:

  1. Philo, *Abr.* 57; *Ebr.* 82; *Mut.* 81; *Migr.* 201; *Leg. Gai.* 4; *Her.* 78; *Quaest. in Gn.* 3. 49.

---

[77] Cf. Origen, *Comm. in Rom.* 7. 14 (*PG* 14. 1141c).

[78] Origen, *Fr. in Jer.* 25 (GCS 6, p. 210); Tertullian, *Marc.* 4. 39. 7. Cf. the very vague words of Epiphanius, *Pan.* 4. 1. 13–14. According to Crouzel and Simonetti, Origen is also referring to the biblical etymology of Gen. 32: 29(28) in *Princ.* 3. 2. 5 and *Sel. in Gen.* 32: 24–30 (a *catena* fragment). See vol. iv of their edition and commentary of *Princ.* (Paris 1980 = SC 269), pp. 66–7. However, in *Princ.* 3. 2. 5 Origen does not manifestly elicit an etymology from Gen. 32: 29(28), and his words are open to another interpretation. See below, n. 83. The second passage, *Sel. in Gen.* 32: 24–30 (*PG* 12. 128b–c; cf. Devreesse, *Les anciens commentateurs*, p. 37), is in fact an extract from Eusebius, *Ecl.* 1. 7. See below, n. 82.

[79] An exception is Justin, who in *Dial.* 125 renders ἄνθρωπος νικῶν δύναμιν. For this etymology, see Wutz, *Onomastica*, p. 527.

2. *Prayer of Joseph, apud* Origen, *Comm. in Jo.* 2. 189.
3. Clement, *Str.* 2. 20. 2.
4. Origen, *Fr. in Lc.* 45 (GCS 49, p. 245); *Comm. in Rom.* 7. 14 (*PG* 14. 1141c); *Comm. in Cant.* prol. (GCS 33, pp. 78–9); *Hom. in Gen.* 15. 3; *Hom. in Num.* 11. 4, 7; 12. 2; 16. 7; 17. 4.
5. Eusebius, *PE* 11. 6. 31; *DE* 7. 2. 36.
6. Didymus, *De spiritu sancto* 44; *Comm. in Gen.* 3: 24 (114. 8–12); *Comm. in Zach.* 1. 88.
7. Chrysostom, *Hom. in Gen.* 58. 2 (*PG* 54. 509); *De inani gloria* 49.
8. *Constitutiones apostolorum* 7. 36. 2; cf. 8. 15. 7.
9. Ambrosiaster, *Comm. in Col.* 1: 15. 3.
10. Gregory of Elvira, *Fid. orth.* 81.
11. Augustine, *Civ.* 16. 39; 17. 13.[80]

This etymology of the *Liber nominum* became so popular that some Fathers actually graft it on to the biblical text of Gen. 32: 29(28). In a fragment attributed to Diodore of Tarsus, the words spoken by the 'man', ἐνίσχυσας μετὰ θεοῦ, a clear reference to Jacob's encounter with the divine, are understood as evidence that Jacob 'saw God', rather than as a different etymology.[81] Eusebius of Caesarea seems to put forward a similar view.[82] In what is apparently his comment on Gen. 32: 25–9, Eusebius of Emesa also justifies the rendering in the *Liber nominum* on the basis of the faith which Jacob shows in his battle with the 'man', without, however, at least in the transmitted Greek fragment, citing the testimony of Gen. 32: 29(28).[83]

Most probably, it was this unsatisfactory treatment of the testimony of Scripture on the part of Greek Christian exegetes that induced Jerome to turn to Josephus, *Ant.* 1. 333, where the name Israel is translated as ὁ ἀντιστάτης ἀγγέλῳ θεοῦ. Although he rejects this rendering, Jerome claims that he made diligent efforts to discover the justification for such an etymology in Hebrew (*QHG*

---

[80] For additional references in [Basil?], Cyril, and Theodoret, see Wutz, *Onomastica*, pp. 1058, 1060, 1062.
[81] *C. Cois.* 252 (p. 234). For the attribution problem, see Petit's note, ad loc.
[82] *PE* 7. 8. 27–8. Cf. *Ecl.* 1. 7 (*PG* 22. 1041d–1044a); *Comm. in Is.* 1. 41 (6: 1); 2. 45 (56: 5); *HE* 1. 2. 9.
[83] See Devreesse, *Les anciens commentateurs*, p. 78. The words of Origen in *Princ.* 3. 2. 5, 'qui [sc. the 'man'] et cognitis profectibus eius [sc. Jacob] etiam nomen ei Israhel dedit', could reflect a similar interpretation.

32: 28–9). The most likely reason for such efforts is the fact that
the Josephan interpretation seemed to him to have emanated from
Gen. 32: 29(28). On the other hand, he has nothing but scorn for
the etymology in the *Liber nominum*, which he regards as 'non tam
vere quam violenter interpretatum'. He refutes this etymology by
explaining exactly how the name Israel would have to be written
for it to mean 'vir videns Deum' (ibid.).[84]

In his own attempt to come to grips with the testimony of Gen.
32: 29(28), Jerome proceeds to the heart of the problem: the
meaning of the Hebrew word שָׂרִיתָ. He turns to the *recentiores*
for help in understanding a difficult word which appears only here
and in Hos. 12: 4(3) and 5(4), citing the translations of all three
of them as well as that of the LXX. Immediately after rejecting
the Josephan interpretation, he writes:

Et quid me necesse est opiniones quaerere singulorum, cum etymologiam
nominis exponat ipse, qui posuit: 'non vocabitur' inquit, 'nomen tuum
Jacob, sed Israhel erit nomen tuum'. quare interpretatur Aquila, ὅτι ἦρξας
μετὰ θεοῦ, Symmachus, ὅτι ἦρξω πρὸς θεόν, LXX et Theodotion, ὅτι
ἐνίσχυσας μετὰ θεοῦ. sarith enim, quod ab Israhel vocabulo derivatur,
principem [sc. esse?] sonat. sensus itaque hic est: non vocabitur nomen
tuum subplantator, hoc est Jacob, sed vocabitur nomen tuum princeps
cum Deo, hoc est Israhel. quomodo enim ego princeps sum, sic et tu,
qui mecum luctari potuisti, princeps vocaberis.[85]

Aquila at least seems to have thought that שׂרה was an alternative
form of the verb שׂרר, 'rule'. For he (and Symmachus) use the
active form of ἄρχω primarily for rendering that verb.[86] Whether
the middle form of ἄρχω in the version of Symmachus indicates
a similar concept is not certain, although it may have been understood to do so by Jerome.[87] In any case, it seems to have been the

---

[84] It is true that on other occasions Jerome does use the etymology from the
Liber nominum. For a discussion of this apparently contradictory approach, see
Jay, loc. cit. (n. 33 above). Cf. the remarks of Martianay, *PL* 23. 1580a–81d.

[85] *QHG* 32: 28–9. Even if his meaning is clear, Jerome expresses himself
somewhat awkwardly when he says, 'sarith enim, quod ab Israhel vocabulo derivatur, principem sonat.' There may be textual corruption here. See the notes of
Martianay and Vallarsi, ad loc. (*PL* 23. 1038d).

[86] This can be determined on the basis of E. Hatch and H. A. Redpath, *A
Concordance to the Septuagint and the Other Greek Versions of the Old Testament*,
i, Oxford 1897, and J. Reider and N. Turner, *An Index to Aquila* (VT.S 12),
Leiden 1966.

[87] The middle form of ἄρχω does not appear to be attested elsewhere in the
extant remains of the version of Symmachus. On the other hand, Aquila uses
the passive or middle forms of that verb on two or perhaps three occasions in the

use of this Greek verb on the part of Aquila and Symmachus that influenced Jerome's understanding of the Hebrew verb שׂרה. For the participle ἄρχων is often used in the Greek versions as a translation for the Hebrew noun שַׂר, and the word which Jerome employs in translating שׂרה, i.e. 'princeps' (probably sc. 'esse'; cf. 'quomodo ego princeps sum'), is a common rendering for the same Hebrew noun in *IH*.[88] In other words, the versions of Aquila and Symmachus seem to have led Jerome to connect the verb שׂרה with the noun שַׂר. But why does he elect to make use of a circumlocution with a noun in his rendering, when Aquila and Symmachus employ verbs? He may have been influenced by certain rabbinic views, according to which the verb שׂרה is interpreted as נעשׂה שׂר.[89] Indeed, Jerome appears to explain the Greek versions by means of this rabbinic interpretation ('sarith *enim* . . .'). If so, in formulating his own rendering, he will have used contemporary rabbinic sources in an attempt to elaborate on the versions of Aquila and Symmachus.[90]

---

sense of 'begin' to render the root חלל. This fact may lend additional support to the contention of Field, i, p. 48, that Symmachus' rendering of the phrase שׂרית עם אלהים, namely, ἤρξω πρὸς θεόν, must mean 'incepisti ad Deum' and not 'princeps fuisti ad Deum'. However, since Jerome seems to think that he is citing a phrase which is complete in itself, it is hard to believe that he at any rate did not understand Symmachus in the latter sense. Although such a middle usage of the verb ἄρχω would be highly unusual, it may be present or at least has been understood to be present in Jdc. 5: 2 as rendered by the LXX (*Codex Alexandrinus*, etc.) and Theodotion. See J. F. Schleusner, *Novus thesaurus philologico-criticus sive lexicon in LXX et reliquos interpretes Graecos ac scriptores apocryphos Veteris Testamenti*[2], i, London 1829, p. 369, and de Montfaucon's edition of the *Hexapla*, *PG* 15. 1081-2. On the other hand, it is also possible that this fragment of Symmachus has come down to us in a corrupt form. See Field, loc. cit.

[88] For the Greek versions, see the works cited in n. 86 above. For *IH*, see, e.g., Gen. 12: 15; Num. 22: 13, 14, 35; Jdc. 8: 6; Is. 1: 23; 10:(8)-9; 19: 11; 23: 8; 34: 12; 49: 7; Jer. 1: 18; 2: 26; Est. 1: 3.

[89] See *b. Hul.* 92a, and cf. *Ber. R.* 78. 3 with the note in the edition of J. Theodor and Ch. Albeck (Berlin 1903–29), p. 921. Cf. also A. Butterweck, *Jakobs Ringkampf am Jabbok* (Judentum und Umwelt 3), Frankfurt am Main 1981, pp. 29, 186, who cites further *TO* Gen. 32: 29: רב את קדם יי. On the other hand, her suggestion that the rendering λαὸς ἰσχυρός, which we read in *OGM* 181. 82–3 and Wutz, *Onomastica*, p. 723 [and cf. *OGM* 193. 15–16], is based on a view similar to that of Jerome, seems wide of the mark. For the adjective ἰσχυρός is related to the אל of ישׂראל and not the שַׂר. See Wutz, p. 527; Eusebius, *PE* 11. 6. 20.

[90] Butterweck, *Jakobs Ringkampf*, pp. 185–6, seems to think that Jerome is putting forth a view unrelated to the versions of the *recentiores*, and W. T. Miller, *Mysterious Encounters at Mamre and Jabbok* (Brown Judaic Studies 50), Chico, Calif. 1984, p. 215 n. 66, even states that he is criticizing them. Such views can hardly be reconciled with the text of *QHG* 32: 28–9.

On the other hand, Jerome also mentions the alternative rendering "directus Dei, hoc est εὐθύτατος θεοῦ", an etymology which he puts forward on other occasions in the forms 'rectissimus' or 'rectus Domini'.[91] He explains the origin of this etymology in his comment on Hos. 12: 4(3), a verse in which Jacob is again the subject of the phrase שָׂרָה אֶת אֱלֹהִים, the same expression which appears in Gen. 32: 29(28): 'quia directus est [sc. Jacob] cum angelo, propterea εὐθυτάτου, quod Hebraice dicitur isar, hoc est dirigentis sive directi, nomen accepit' (*Comm. in Os.* 3 (12: 2–6)). Jerome's translation of the Hebrew verb שָׂרָה with 'directus est', which also appears in *IH*, may be traced to Aquila. For on the basis of material in the Syro-Hexaplar version, it has been conjectured that the rendering of the Greek translator was κατώρθωσε πρὸς ἄγγελον.[92]

This Greek phrase by itself, as well as Jerome's corresponding version, could be taken to indicate either tangible success or moral rectitude.[93] In view of the full context of the passage, however, it is no doubt to be understood in the former sense. That this was the view of Jerome is clear from his own translation of Hos. 12: 5(4), where the words from the preceding verse are repeated in fuller form: וַיָּשַׂר אֶל מַלְאָךְ וַיֻּכָל. Jerome translates these words: 'invaluit ad angelum et confortatus est'.[94] However, in deriving an etymology from the phrase as rendered by Aquila, Jerome puts the emphasis on moral rectitude. So much may be seen from the

---

[91] *Pelag.* 3. 8; *Comm. in Mal.* 1: 2 5 (CChr.SL 76A, p. 905). On the basis of the latter passage, it can be determined that the words, 'sed melius rectus Domini', which follow the traditional etymology in *Nom. Hebr.* 63. 22–3, represent a Hieronymian intervention. See also *Nom. Hebr.* 13. 21–2.

[92] See Field, ii, p. 959. The words 'cum angelo' in the translation of Jerome also seem to reflect the version of Aquila or a Hebrew *Vorlage* identical to the one used by him. We read אֶת אֱלֹהִים in the Masoretic Text and πρὸς θεόν in the LXX.

[93] In classical Greek, when κατορθόω is used intransitively, it may be translated as 'succeed' or 'prosper'. In the LXX, however, the intransitive use can also indicate correct moral behaviour. See, e.g., Prov. 14: 11; Mi. 7: 2. This usage becomes common in patristic Greek. See *PGL*, s.v., B1. For a similar range of meanings in the later Latin usage of 'dirigi', see *Thesaurus linguae Latinae*, v. 1, col. 1243, ll. 49–52, col. 1245, ll. 58–64.

[94] In translating the phrase וַיָּשַׂר אֶל מַלְאָךְ in Hos. 12: 5(4), Aquila and Theodotion employ the same verb as Aquila does in 12: 4(3), viz. κατορθόω. Symmachus appears to have rendered κατεδυνάστευσε τὸν ἄγγελον. See Field, ii, p. 960. The LXX use the words ἐνίσχυσεν μετὰ ἀγγέλου. It would seem therefore that in his understanding of this passage, Jerome was influenced by the latter two versions. No doubt he was also aiming at *varietas*, a principle known to be operative in *IH*. See Stummer, *Einführung*, pp. 114–15.

fact that elsewhere he gives the etymology in the forms 'rectissimus' or 'rectus Domini'. The reason for this, as is evident from his comment cited above, is that Jerome was aware that Aquila's translation of Hos. 12: 4–5(3–4) had an etymological basis different from that underlying his rendering of Gen. 32: 29(28), namely, an assumed connection between the verb שרה and the root ישר, not שרר. For he correctly applied this understanding of the verb to the text of Gen. 32: 29(28), and derived from it the appropriate etymology for the name 'Israel' based on that root. Indeed, the word 'rectus' is simply a faithful rendering of the Hebrew adjective יָשָׁר as it is used in the Hebrew Bible.[95]

However, Jerome's use of the superlative form of the same adjective in Greek, εὐθύτατος, and in Latin, 'rectissimus', allows us to determine that he derived the actual form of these renderings of the name Israel from the *recentiores'* versions of another word, namely, יְשֻׁרוּן. For the word εὐθύτατος, which Jerome employs in rendering the name Israel in *QHG* and in the passage of *Comm. in Hos.* cited above (cf. *Comm. in Mal.* 1: 2–5), appears to be attested in the Greek versions of the Bible only as Aquila's translation of יְשֻׁרוּן.[96] And, in fact, Jerome explicitly refers to this rendering in his comment on Is. 44: 1–2, verses in which the words 'Israel' and יְשֻׁרוּן are used in parallel constructions:

Alio nomine Israelem vocat. isurun enim verbum Hebraicum, ceteri εὐθύτατον sive εὐθῆ, id est rectissimum et rectum interpretati sunt; soli LXX dilectissimum, iungentes de suo, Israel. proprie enim iuxta Hebraeos et litterarum fidem Israel rectus Dei dicitur. vir autem videns Deum non in elementis, sed in sono vocis est. (*Comm. in Is.* 12 (44: 1–5))

We know from elsewhere that εὐθής is the rendering of Symmachus and Theodotion.[97] Therefore, it is from the *recentiores'* versions of יְשֻׁרוּן that Jerome derives his actual renderings of the name Israel. That is, he thought that יְשֻׁרוּן was in fact an etymological variation of that name. Why? First of all, as he himself notes, יְשֻׁרוּן is employed as an alternative designation for Israel/Jacob.[98]

[95] If Didymus' use of the word κατόρθωσις in *Comm. in Gen.* 3: 24 (114. 8–12) reflects a reading of Aquila's version of Hos. 12: 4–5(3–4), there is nevertheless no awareness on his part of the implications of that version for the etymology of the name Israel.

[96] See the LXX version of Dtn. edited by Wevers (Göttingen 1977 = *Septuaginta*, iii. 2) ad 32: 15.

[97] See Wevers' edition of Dtn. ad 32: 15 and 33: 5.

[98] Cf. the LXX version of Dtn. 32: 15, and *TO* Dtn. 32: 15; 33: 5, 26.

In addition, the two words could be translated in a similar manner. On the one hand, the word יְשֻׁרוּן was rendered by the *recentiores* as εὐθύτατος or εὐθής. On the other hand, it was no doubt his understanding of the etymological basis of Aquila's version of Hos. 12: 4–5(3–4) that allowed Jerome to assert that 'iuxta fidem litterarum' the name 'Israel' could be translated 'rectus Dei'.[99] Finally, as seems clear from his transcriptions of the Hebrew forms, he also considered the orthographic similarity between ישראל and יְשֻׁרוּן.[100] Thus, it was logical to conclude that the two words were related etymologically.[101]

In short, on the basis of Aquila's version of Hos. 12: 4–5(3–4), Jerome understood that there was an alternative manner in which one could interpret the verb שׂרה in Gen. 32: 29(28). However, in putting forward a corresponding alternative etymology of the name 'Israel', Jerome employed Aquila's rendering of another word, יְשֻׁרוּן. Whether Aquila himself regarded the name Israel (as it could be understood on the basis of his version of Hos. 12: 4–5(3–4)) as etymologically related to יְשֻׁרוּן is difficult to determine. For he translates the verb שׂרה in Hos. 12: 4–5(3–4) with a Greek root different from the one he employs in translating יְשֻׁרוּן. However, he uses roots kindred in meaning. Because of this, because of the fact that the two words are used to indicate the same person/nation, and no doubt also because of the similarity of the Hebrew forms of the names, Jerome concludes that the two words are etymologically related. Thus, we probably have a case of Ἀκύλαν ἐξ Ἀκύλα σαφηνίζειν, in conjunction with the use of the Hebrew text.

---

[99] In making this assertion, Jerome may also have consulted rabbinic informants. Indeed, this could be the meaning of the phrase 'iuxta Hebraeos' in this passage of *Comm. in Is.* (cf. the translation of these words in Jay, *L'exégèse*, p. 296). Such an interpretation is supported by the fact that in *M. Teh.* 4. 3 (ed. Buber, Vilna 1891, p. 21b), the etymology of Israel (understood as a collective) is given as יְשָׁרִי אל. On the other hand, Butterweck, *Jakobs Ringkampf*, p. 30, states that the view of the etymology of Israel which seems to be present in Aquila's version of Hos. 12: 4–5(3–4) had no reverberations in later times. This statement needs to be corrected in the light of Jerome's discussions as well as this rabbinic parallel.

[100] A similarity in pronunciation may also have been involved if the distinction between *shin* and *sin* was not in every instance known to Jerome. On this question, see Barr, *JSSt* 12 (1967), pp. 23–8.

[101] The idea of an etymological connection between ישראל and יְשֻׁרוּן, according to which both are connected with the root יָשַׁר, is advocated by some modern scholars. For a recent example, see L. Wächter, 'Israel und Jeschurun', *Schalom* (*FS* A. Jepsen = AzTh 1. 46), Stuttgart 1971, pp. 58–64.

That Jerome put forward two possible etymologies of the name Israel is understandable. He was faced with different renderings of the key verb on the part of the *recentiores*. However, since that verb occurs only three times in the Hebrew Bible, it will have been difficult for him to find new criteria from which to judge between them. In fact, his efforts to understand the etymology on the basis of the verb שׂרה stand in considerable contrast to the manner in which the problem was handled by the Greek Fathers.

THE ANTIOCHENE FATHERS

The most relevant of all Greek exegetical sources which Jerome consulted when composing *QHG* seem to have been the writings of Antiochene scholars. The Antiochenes had a keen awareness of the linguistic problems involved in the interpretation of the Bible. This awareness led to an interest on their part in non-LXX forms of the biblical text. Jerome clearly exploited this feature of Antiochene exegesis in advocating a return to the original Hebrew text, and the use of Antiochene sources is easily visible in *QHG*.

In particular, Jerome employed the work of Eusebius of Emesa and probably that of Diodore of Tarsus as well. As we have seen in Chapter 4, both of these writers seem to have composed *quaestiones* commentaries on the Octateuch. That Jerome knew of the work of Eusebius is clear from the fact that he explicitly cites an interpretation of his in *QHG* 22: 13. Although a similar explicit reference to Diodore is lacking, we know that at the time when Jerome composed *QHG*, he was generally familiar with his writings. For he devotes a chapter to him in his *De viris illustribus*, written in 393, and refers to his various works on different occasions.[102] However, both Jerome and modern scholars have noted that Diodore often follows the exegesis of his teacher and predecessor Eusebius.[103] Therefore, even if Jerome sometimes appears to be drawing on Diodore, it is not to be excluded that both writers are drawing on Eusebius.

Nevertheless, the primary focus in this section will be the con-

---

[102] *Vir. ill.* 119. For other references to Diodore in Jerome's works, see Courcelle, *Les lettres grecques*, p. 107.

[103] Jerome, *Vir. ill.* 119; E. Schweizer, *ZNW* 40 (1941), p. 68; Devreesse, *Les anciens commentateurs*, p. 155; Petit, *Muséon* 92 (1979), p. 284.

trast between Jerome and certain basic tendencies among Antiochene exegetes. Accordingly, the ultimate source of the Antiochene material which was available to Jerome need not be a chief concern. Indeed, for this reason, the commentaries of later Antiochene writers such as Theodore of Mopsuestia, Theodoret, and Gennadius of Constantinople, are also relevant here. For not only do they probably preserve material from the lost works of Eusebius and Diodore, but they also provide additional samples of the Antiochene exegetical approach as applied to the Book of Genesis.

Of these Antiochene writings, only the *Quaestiones in Octateuchum* of Theodoret has come down to us in direct tradition in Greek. None the less, we can form a fairly clear picture of the Antiochene exegetical tradition as it existed in the days of Jerome, because extensive remains of that tradition have reached us via other means of transmission. First and foremost, we have the fragments preserved in the *catenae* and in the Ἐπιτομὴ ἐκλογῶν of Procopius of Gaza. Fortunately, much of this material is now available in the critical editions of J. Deconinck, Devreesse, and Petit.[104] In addition, there is an Armenian translation of a commentary on the Octateuch which, although ascribed to Cyril of Alexandria in the manuscripts, is believed by scholars to be the work of Eusebius of Emesa, since much of the material in it corresponds with the *catena* fragments handed down in his name.[105] The text has been known for a long time, but has only recently been edited by V. Hovhanessian under the title *Commentaire de l'Octateuque*.[106] J.-P. Mahé has translated the introduction to the *Commentary* and various other passages, and has kindly made available to me this translation, which remains as yet unpublished.[107]

[104] Deconinck, *Essai sur la chaîne de l'Octateuque* (BEHE.H 195), Paris 1912; Devreesse, *Les anciens commentateurs*. For the editions of *catenae* edited by Petit, see the Abbreviations above.

[105] For a history of the question, see Buytaert, *L'héritage*, pp. 186–8, and H. J. Lehmann, 'An Important Text Preserved in MS Ven. Mekh. No. 873, Dated A.D. 1299', *Medieval Armenian Culture: Proceedings of the Third Dr. H. Markarian Conference on Armenian Culture* (University of Pennsylvania Armenian Texts and Studies 6), ed. T. J. Samuelian and M. E. Stone, Chico, Calif. 1984, pp. 142–3.

[106] Venice 1980. As we have noted above, p. 85, according to Ebedjesus, Eusebius wrote ζητήματα on the Old Testament.

[107] I would like to take this opportunity to record my deep gratitude to Prof. Mahé. It is hoped that a full translation of the commentary in a Western language will soon appear. Yet it is unlikely that it will change our view of the basic character of Eusebius' exegesis of Genesis. For the total number of Greek fragments which

An obvious case in which Jerome appears to be dependent on the Antiochenes regards Gen. 31. In this chapter, we read that Jacob finally breaks off a long relationship with his uncle Laban. He explains his decision to his wives Leah and Rachel, and in verse 7 states his chief accusation against their father: וְהֶחֱלִף אֶת מַשְׂכֻּרְתִּי עֲשֶׂרֶת מֹנִים LXX: καὶ ἤλλαξεν [sc. Laban] τὸν μισθόν μου τῶν δέκα ἀμνῶν. Many Christian exegetes were at a loss as to what this means, both because of the ambiguous language of the Greek text, and because of the fact that there is no reference in the previous narrative to a salary of ten lambs or to a change of salary involving ten lambs in some way. According to one source, Laban had broken an original wage agreement and substituted a payment of ten lambs.[108] For his part, Origen turns to Aquila and Symmachus, noting that [in place of τῶν δέκα ἀμνῶν] the former renders δέκα ἀριθμούς, and the latter δεκάκις ἀριθμῷ. He says that according to a certain Hebrew, the reference is to Laban's constant (ten) attempts to change the terms of the agreement about which newborn sheep would belong to Jacob, the spotted or the striped. (There is mention of such attempts in the following verse.) Yet Origen, while relating this interpretation, none the less does not abandon the Greek text. He claims that even if an agreement about a payment of ten lambs has not been related previously, we must infer from Jacob's accusation that there was such an agreement.[109] Eusebius of Emesa and Diodore put forward the same

we have at our disposal is quite high, and these provide sufficient basis for a comparison with Jerome. On the one hand, we have some 90 *catena* fragments in which the attribution to Eusebius is uncontested in the MSS. These include the fragments edited by Devreesse in *Les anciens commentateurs*, pp. 57–82, and additional material edited by Petit in *CS*. On the other hand, there are an additional 20 fragments which have been identified by Lehmann, 'An Important Text', pp. 152–5, 157, on the basis of correspondences with the Armenian version. These fragments are found in the compilation of Procopius of Gaza and in *catena* fragments attributed to exegetes other than Eusebius or for which there are multiple attributions. From such a large number of fragments we are able to get a very clear idea of the character of Eusebius' exegesis. In addition, for many of the passages which survive only in Armenian we possess fragments of Diodore of Tarsus, whose comments often closely parallel those of Eusebius, and of other later Antiochene writers. Finally, it may be reiterated that our object is to point out certain basic differences between the approach of Jerome and that of Eusebius and the Antiochenes, on the basis of a large body of positive evidence.

[108] See the scholion cited by Field, i, p. 45 n. 1.

[109] *Sel. in Gen.* 31: 7 (*PG* 12. 125b–c). Cf. Petit, 'Le dossier', p. 91 (no. 1284). It is possible that the second part of this fragment originally constituted a separate comment on Gen. 31: 41, the verse in which Jacob repeats his accusation to Laban

explanation as Origen's Hebrew informant, but base it on the text of ὁ Σύρος and perhaps (in the case of Eusebius) ὁ Ἑβραῖος.[110] In addition, Diodore appeals explicitly to Gen. 31: 8 as corroboration. Jerome follows the same line of interpretation in *QHG* 31: 7–8, also alluding to Gen. 31: 8. Consequently, he seems to be following Eusebius and/or Diodore rather than Origen's Hebrew informant. However, Jerome has slightly 'Hebraized' his source. For he eliminates the reference to ὁ Σύρος, cites the Hebrew text alone, and indeed specifies the Hebrew word in question.[111] He also expresses his wonder as to why the LXX have translated the word as 'lamb', and in *QHG* 31: 41 refers to the translation as an error.[112]

Another notable example concerns the famous words of Gen. 1: 2: 'and the spirit of God [Greek, πνεῦμα θεοῦ] was moving [Greek, ἐπεφέρετο, Hebrew, מרחפת, Peshitta, מרחפא] over the face of the waters.' In the view of Eusebius, as preserved in the Armenian version of his commentary, the Greek translation ἐπεφέρετο does not adequately render the idea in the Hebrew word, which in addition to the idea of movement involves a notion of brooding over, or keeping warm, just as a bird broods over her young in a nest.[113] Such an activity would be particularly

himself. For a citation of this verse is introduced asyndetically in the middle of the fragment.

[110] Eusebius, in Devreesse, *Les anciens commentateurs*, pp. 77–8; Diodore, *C. Cois.* 246 (for the attribution problems of a third related fragment, see the comments of Petit, *C. Cois.*, pp. 229–30 n. a). The citation of 'the Hebrew' ascribed to Eusebius in codex 135 (numbering according to A. Rahlfs, *Verzeichnis der griechischen Handschriften des Alten Testaments* (*MSU* 2 = *NGWG.PH* 1914, Beiheft), Berlin 1914) as indicated by Wevers, p. 295 (second apparatus), does not appear in Devreesse, loc. cit., who takes full account of the same MS. The reliability of a reference to ὁ Ἑβραῖος in the Armenian (cf. Lehmann, 'The Syriac Translation', p. 77) is yet to be determined. On the other hand, the citation of Aquila ascribed to Eusebius in various MSS and the citation of 'the Hebrew' ascribed to him in codex 77 (Rahlfs), both noted by Wevers, loc. cit., have probably crept into the text transmitted in his name from the neighbouring fragment attributed to Origen which we have cited in the preceding note. Cf. Buytaert, *L'héritage*, pp. 116*–17*. It is no doubt for this reason that Devreesse excluded such citations from his edition of the text. (Concerning the meaning of the expressions ὁ Σύρος and ὁ Ἑβραῖος, see above, Ch. 1 n. 115, and below, pp. 150–1.)

[111] Jerome cites the singular in the form 'moni'. Although in the lexicons this word is usually given as מֹנֶ, the singular is not attested, so it is hardly surprising that Jerome gives the form that he does on the basis of the plural מֹנִים.

[112] Augustine, *Hept.* 1. 95, attempts to reconcile the text of the LXX/*VL* with the interpretation which Jerome gives in *QHG* on the basis of the Hebrew.

[113] Mahé's translation of the Armenian is quoted in full by J. R. Pouchet, *BLE* 87 (1986), p. 268 n. 101.

appropriate for the Holy Spirit, and Eusebius seems to favour the traditional interpretation according to which the πνεῦμα θεοῦ is to be identified with the Paraclete.[114] Nevertheless, he does allow that the phrase πνεῦμα θεοῦ could simply denote the wind, in which case the verb would indicate that the wind warms and caresses the waters not voluntarily, but 'par affinité de nature'. Diodore of Tarsus gives a similar interpretation, yet he emphasizes to a greater extent that the verb entails a life-giving power, and that the πνεῦμα θεοῦ gives life, as it were, to the waters.[115] It is this latter aspect of the view that was of most interest to Basil the Great. But unlike Eusebius and Diodore, he uses this interpretation of the verb, attributing it to 'a learned Syrian', only after concluding that πνεῦμα θεοῦ is best understood of the Holy Spirit. For his object is to refute those who would deny creative power to that being, in other words, the *Pneumatomachi*.[116] Thus it would appear that Basil is directly dependent on Diodore and not on Eusebius.[117] But this is not a necessary conclusion, since it may be that Diodore gives a more accurate account of the view of Eusebius than is preserved in the Armenian text, rather than a further elaboration of that view.[118] In any case, Basil also explicitly informs us that the interpretation of the verb was formulated not so much on the basis of the Hebrew as on the basis of the Syriac language and its proximity to Hebrew (whether a Syriac *text* was also used is not altogether clear). And that Eusebius relied on Syriac also seems evident from the Armenian version of the commentary.[119]

---

[114] That this is indeed the traditional interpretation is shown by K. Smoroński, *Bib* 6 (1925), pp. 275–9. Cf. M. Alexandre, *Le commencement du Livre, Genèse I-V: La version grecque de la Septante et sa réception* (Christianisme antique 3), Paris 1988, p. 85.

[115] *C. Cois.* 32. The idea that the πνεῦμα θεοῦ is a life-giving power is attested in early patristic sources. See Theophilus, *Autol.* 2. 13, and cf. Clement, *Ecl.* 7. 1; Alexandre, *Le commencement*, p. 84.

[116] See *Hex.* 2. 6. That Basil has the *Pneumatomachi* in view is noted by Pouchet, *BLE* 87 (1986), p. 266. Cf. S. Giet in his edition of the text (Paris 1968 = SC 26*bis*), p. 168 n. 1.

[117] The exact identity of Basil's Syrian informant has been a subject of debate since the late patristic period. It is now generally agreed that he was either Eusebius himself or Diodore (drawing on Eusebius). See Lehmann, *Augustinus* 26. 103–4 (1981), pp. 127*–39*; Pouchet, *BLE* 87 (1986), pp. 261–8.

[118] Petit, in her introduction to *C. Cois.*, p. cii n. 17, notes that the Armenian is often more of a paraphrase than an exact version. This has been confirmed to me by Mahé in a private communication.

[119] In addition to Mahé's translation (cited above, n. 113), see Lehmann's paraphrase of the passage in *Augustinus* 26. 103–4 (1981), p. 136*, and his remarks in 'The Syriac Translation', p. 73.

Nevertheless, this interpretation represents a penetrating attempt to approach the original text of the Bible. For Eusebius' suggestion is no doubt based on the parallel in Dtn. 32: 11, where the same verb in the Hebrew text (i.e. רחף; cf. the Peshitta) is used of an eagle hovering over its young. Such sophisticated use of a parallel passage is probably the reason why Jerome adopted the interpretation for himself in *QHG* 1: 2.[120] However, he has 'Hebraized' his source by omitting all reference to the Syriac and quoting the relevant Hebrew word in transliteration, 'marahaefeth'.[121] Moreover, in slight contrast to Eusebius and Diodore, he thinks that if the Hebrew verb is understood to mean 'incubare', one must conclude that the 'spirit of God' is the Holy Spirit. Like Basil, Jerome sees the passage as proof of the creative power and therefore of the divinity of the Holy Spirit.[122] The Latin Father is always anxious to point out that the 'Hebraica veritas' is in greater accord with orthodox doctrine than the LXX.

On the other hand, the explanation of the verb put forward by Eusebius and Diodore was not greeted warmly by later representatives of the Antiochene school. The later commentators, not unlike Jerome, regard the interpretation as a mainstay of the view that the words πνεῦμα θεοῦ denote the Holy Spirit. Since they object to this latter view, they also attempt to rebut the Eusebian–Diodoran understanding of the verb. The position of Theodore of Mopsuestia is known to us via later Syriac commentators. It is therefore difficult to reconstruct his arguments in an exact fashion,

[120] Since a Greek source is readily at hand, it is not necessary to conclude with Smoroński, *Bib* 6 (1925), p. 364, that Jerome is dependent on rabbinic sources such as *t. Hag.* 2. 6 (cf. the parallels in *y. Hag.* 2. 1 (77a–b); *b. Hag.* 15a; *Ber. R.* 2. 4). Nor need we conclude that Eusebius himself employed such sources, for the parallel verbal usage will have led commentators independently to Dtn. 32: 11.

[121] Eusebius for his part constantly refers to the verb in Greek translation. Indeed, an interesting point of contrast between Jerome's discussions of Hebrew philology and those of the Greeks is the fact that the latter normally cite words in translation rather than in transliteration. Sperber, *HUCA* 12–13 (1937–8), p. 109, notes that the vast majority of Greek and Latin transliterations of Hebrew which have survived from antiquity are to be found in the writings of Jerome.

[122] It is possible that Jerome is here dependent on Basil or some related Greek source yet to be identified. In support of his argument he cites Ps. 104(103): 30, which is also quoted in this same context by Ambrose, *Hex.* 1. 29. But Jerome may have become acquainted with this latter work only at a later date (cf. Paredi, 'S. Gerolamo', p. 191), and the citation of the same verse in Bar Hebraeus, *Scholia in Genesim* 1: 2, would also point to a Greek source. In any case, however, the verse had become standard in debates with subordinationists. See Athanasius, *Ep. Serap.* 3. 4–5; 4. 3; Ps.-Basil, *Eun.* 5 (*PG* 29. 713c).

but it would seem that he was not willing to sacrifice the authority
of the LXX and argue on the basis of the Syriac or the Hebrew.[123]
The motivation for such a position is not altogether clear, but one
may hazard a guess on the basis of his views as they can be
determined from other passages. On the one hand, he may have
thought that the Syriac text/language was not a better guide to
the Hebrew than the LXX, and on the other hand, to the extent
that the interpretation of Eusebius and Diodore was based on the
Hebrew text itself, he may have refused to accept the authority of
their statements concerning it.[124] In any case, this position of
Theodore became the influential one in Antiochene circles. Both
Theodoret and Gennadius are content to cite the LXX when
attempting to refute the view that the phrase πνεῦμα θεοῦ is used
of the Holy Spirit, despite the fact that they were probably well
aware of the interpretation of Eusebius and Diodore. Indeed, that
Theodoret takes direct aim at that interpretation seems clear from
the language he uses. For he contends that the text contains the
word ἐπεφέρετο and not ἐπέκειτο, and with this latter verb seems
to allude to the view of his predecessors (*Qu. in Gen.* 8). Gennadius
also points to the version of the LXX, and says that one would
not use the verb ἐπιφέρομαι even of a created living being, let alone
of the uncreated Holy Spirit. He apparently holds that the verb
is used only of inanimates, and notes that Moses employs the same
verb when describing the Ark of Noah floating on the water in
Gen. 7: 18 (*C. Cois.* 34). Yet in this instance, the Hebrew verb
underlying ἐπιφέρομαι is not רחף, but הלך. In other words,
Gennadius simply refuses to acknowledge the basis of the position
taken by Eusebius and Diodore.[125]

In short, we find that among later Antiochene exegetes, the
Hebrew text was not granted any sort of privileged position in
actual practice. Indeed, as we have seen in the final paragraphs of

---

[123] For a convenient juxtaposition of the later Syriac sources in which Theodore's view is reported (notably Isho bar Nun and Ishodad), see L. Van Rompay,
OLoP 8 (1977), pp. 231–3. That Theodore was aware of the basis of the interpretation put forward by Eusebius and Diodore is clear from his *Comm. in Ps.* 76: 11a
(ed. Devreesse, p. 512).

[124] For Theodore's negative view of the version of 'the Syrian', and his refusal
to consider the testimony of a contemporary individual, namely, Jerome, concerning the meaning of the Hebrew text, see above, pp. 39–40.

[125] It has been pointed out recently by Van Rompay, *StPatr* 19 (1989), p. 402,
that Gennadius was quite familiar with the work of Eusebius, Diodore, and
Theodore of Mopsuestia.

Chapter 1, Theodore of Mopsuestia advocated a return to reliance on the LXX on 'scientific grounds'. Yet responsibility for the development of such attitudes probably lies with Eusebius and Diodore themselves. For although on perhaps a theoretical level they did acknowledge the primacy of the original, the implications of such an acknowledgement are not clearly appreciated and implemented in their exegetical writings. Rather, Eusebius and Diodore developed a sort of mixed system, in which the various witnesses are given equal weight.[126] Indeed, (*a*) 'the Syrian' occupies a more prominent place in their interpretations than does the Hebrew original, a fact of which we have already seen some indication; (*b*) the Hebrew text, on the other hand, often takes the place of just another witness; and finally, (*c*) the LXX has not lost a central role.[127] Such a system may have appeared too 'anchorless' for the tastes of Theodore, and this perhaps led him to take the position that he did.

As for Jerome, he had serious reservations about all three of these aspects of the Eusebian–Diodoran system. That he regarded 'the Syrian' as irrelevant is clear from his 'Hebraizations' of the references to that version in the Antiochenes. In fact, it seems doubtful whether he ever even cites such a text.[128]

Jerome also had major objections to the manner in which the Antiochenes approached the Hebrew text. For it seems that a consequence of the assignment to the Hebrew text of a role subordinate or equal to the Syriac and the Greek texts was the fact that Eusebius and Diodore did not make a serious attempt to come to terms with the Hebrew language nor to develop a systematic procedure in dealing with the text. Rather, we find in their writings incidental references to the original, and a somewhat unstudied method in approaching it. This method was based on indirect knowledge and what Jerome might have called conjecture.[129] In

[126] Cf. the perceptive remarks of J.-P. Mahé, 'Traduction et exégèse: Réflexions sur l'exemple arménien', *Mélanges Antoine Guillaumont* (Cahiers d'orientalisme 20), Geneva 1988, p. 250.

[127] This point is acknowledged by Mahé, ibid.

[128] Cf. also the discussion of the relationship between ὁ Σύρος and *IH* in Field, i, pp. lxxix–lxxxii.

[129] Eusebius reveals his dependence on informants for Hebrew matters in the introduction to his *Commentarii in Octateuchum* preserved in Armenian. Indirect references to Hebrew via expressions such as φασί and λέγουσι are also a feature of the exegesis of Theodore of Mopsuestia. See Kihn, *Theodor*, p. 88.

fact, it is probably primarily this method that he has in mind when, in the preface to *QHG*, he makes the following statement: 'studii ergo nostri erit . . . eorum, qui de libris Hebraicis varia suspicantur, errores refellere'. That he indeed undertakes such a task in that work will be clear from the examples which we shall now consider.

In Gen. 22, the story of the sacrifice of Isaac is related. After Abraham is commanded at the last moment to spare his son, we read in verse 13 of the appearance of a substitute victim:

וישא אברהם את עיניו וירא והנה איל אחר נאחז בסבך בקרניו.

καὶ ἀναβλέψας Ἀβραὰμ τοῖς ὀφθαλμοῖς αὐτοῦ εἶδεν, καὶ ἰδοὺ κριὸς εἷς κατεχόμενος ἐν φυτῷ σαβὲκ τῶν κεράτων.

Eusebius of Emesa holds the common view that the entire episode of the *Aqedah* constitutes a 'type' of the crucifixion, and explains various features of this verse in accord with such a view. For example, he cites a variant of ὁ Σύρος and ὁ Ἑβραῖος, according to which κρεμάμενος is read instead of κατεχόμενος.[130] In this manner, the suspension of Christ from the cross is more clearly prefigured. He also points out that a ram and not a lamb is sacrificed, that is to say, the victim is mature and 'perfect', like Christ. He goes on to discuss the type of plant in which the ram was caught:

ὥσπερ δὲ φυτὸν σαβέκ, τουτέστιν ἀφέσεως, ἐκάλεσε τὸν ἅγιον σταυρόν, οὕτω καὶ ὁ Ἰεζεκιήλ, ἐν τῷ τέλει, ὕδωρ ἀφέσεως ἐκάλεσε τὸ ἐκτυποῦν τὸ ἅγιον βάπτισμα. δύο οὖν ἐστι τὰ ἄφεσιν ἁμαρτιῶν χαριζόμενα· πάθος διὰ Χριστὸν καὶ βάπτισμα. (*CS G* 189)

It will be clear from Eusebius' translation of σαβέκ by the Greek ἀφέσεως and his citation of the phrase ὕδωρ ἀφέσεως from Ezekiel 47: 3 that he regarded the term σαβέκ as a characterization of the plant in which the ram was caught, in the manner of a genitive of quality.[131] Such an idea may have been inspired by the analogy of the ξύλον τῆς ζωῆς of Gen. 2: 9 and similar cases. The translation

---

[130] This reading is found in various Antiochene and Syriac sources. See F. Nikolasch, 'Zur Ikonographie des Widders von Gen 22', *VigChr* 23 (1969), pp. 218–20. Concerning the question of ὁ Σύρος and ὁ Ἑβραῖος, see above, Ch. 1 n. 115, and below, pp. 150–1.

[131] Cf. Ephraem Graecus, *Abr. et Is.* 405–14 (ed. S. J. Mercati, Rome 1915 (= MBE 1), pp. 67–8); *Dial. Tim. et Aquil.*, ed. F. Conybeare, Oxford 1898 (= Anecdota Oxoniensia: Classical series, pt. 8), p. 85; and the Greek text of Severus of Antioch, *Homiliae cathedrales* 41 (*PO* 36, pp. 26–7), as it has been preserved in *CS G* 186.

of σαβέκ as ἄφεσις, on the other hand, seems to be derived from an interpretation based on the Aramaic root שֽׁבַק rather than the סְבַךְ of the Hebrew text.[132]

Jerome, however, attributes an additional interpretation of the word σαβέκ to Eusebius: 'ridiculam rem in hoc loco Emisenus Eusebius est locutus: "sabech" inquiens, "dicitur hircus, qui rectis cornibus et ad carpendas arboris frondes sublimis attollitur"' (*QHG* 22: 13). Such a suggestion does not appear in the extant *catena* fragment attributed to Eusebius. Indeed, for this reason, Buytaert thought that Jerome had misunderstood the comment of Eusebius. According to him, the Emesan was not concerned with the interpretation of the word סְבַךְ, but was either identifying the type of animal described by the word אַיִל, or was explaining how the animal came to be caught in the thicket, i.e. merely elaborating on the entire phrase נֶאֱחַז בַּסְּבַךְ. Jerome will have misunderstood the comment because he had it before him in the form of a marginal note, and did not perceive to which part of the text it pertained.[133]

Yet such a view cannot be accepted. For an additional fragment, which is attributed to Gennadius in some witnesses but is anonymous in others, allows us to maintain that Jerome understood Eusebius correctly. In this fragment we read as follows:

σαβὲκ ἑρμηνεύεται κυρίως τράγος ὀρθὸς ἐπαναβεβηκὼς φυτῷ· ἐνταῦθα δέ, ὀρθὸς τῶν κεράτων κατεχόμενος, ὡς εἶναι φανερὸν τύπον σταυροῦ. διὰ τοῦτο δὲ οὐχ ἑρμηνεύεται, ὅτι ἡ Ἑβραϊκὴ μία οὖσα λέξις, πολλὰ σημαίνει ἑρμηνευομένη.[134]

---

[132] See already the *Suda*, s.v. Cf. Schleusner, *Novus thesaurus*, iii, p. 19; Wutz, *Onomastica*, p. 657.

[133] See *L'héritage*, pp. 15–16, and cf. Devreesse, *Les anciens commentateurs*, p. 73 n. 1. Buytaert later changed his view, for in editing the *catena* fragment, he incorporates a retroversion of Jerome's Latin into the text. See p. 113*.

[134] *CS*, p. 183, no. 2, ll. 3–7, and *C. Cois.* 205, ll. 5–9. In some witnesses, which Petit follows in *CS*, these lines constitute the second section of a single fragment (ascribed to Gennadius or anonymous), the first part of which contains a brief summary of three different views of the word σαβέκ: (*a*) the view put forward by Eusebius of Emesa in *CS* G 189 cited above (known to Gennadius perhaps via the formulation of Diodore, *C. Cois.* 204, ll. 24–5); (*b*) the view expressed in the second part of the same fragment; and finally (*c*) the view of Diodore as stated in *C. Cois.* 204, l. 24, according to which σαβέκ is to be understood as the name of a plant. In another branch of the tradition, the two sections of the text are attested as separate units, of which the first is attributed to Gennadius and the second is without attribution. Petit follows this alternative tradition in *C. Cois.*, and prints the second unit under the heading 'Auctoris incerti'. It is this latter tradition that finds support on internal grounds. For the second part of the fragment does not constitute an elaboration of (*b*), but rather a distinct, parallel restatement. In

When we consider this fragment together with the testimony of Jerome, it will be clear that Eusebius put forward an additional interpretation of the word σαβέκ. According to this second interpretation, the word is understood to refer not to the plant but to the animal, and consequently the translation requires the nominative case.[135] This latter interpretation may have arisen from comparison with the version of 'the Syrian', which, according to the testimony of Diodore, did not include the words ἐν φυτῷ, but only σαβέκ.[136] In such a formulation, σαβέκ cannot be taken as a genitive of quality. Nevertheless, that it should be understood as a nominative is not excluded by the wording of the LXX. Indeed, in the fragment quoted above the rendering ὀρθός is cited together with the reading of the LXX, κατεχόμενος, rather than with that of 'the Syrian', κρεμάμενος.[137]

It would appear, therefore, that Eusebius put forward two interpretations of the word σαβέκ. He thought that it could refer either to the plant, in which case it was to be rendered as a genitive of quality, or to the animal, in which case it was to be understood as a nominative. However, it seems improbable that Eusebius gave preference to an interpretation of σαβέκ as ἄφεσις, as Petit has suggested.[138] For if the second sentence of the anonymous fragment which we have quoted also belongs to the Emesan, he was

addition, it is separated from (*b*) by (*c*). In short, the second part of the fragment must be attributed to an author earlier than Gennadius.

[135] Cf., for a parallel understanding, the exegetically looser uses of the root סבך in *CN* Gen. 22: 13 (margin) and *Wa. R.* 29. 10. Note also in this context Wutz, *Onomastica*, p. 696, l. 173 (variant readings).

[136] *C. Cois.* 204, ll. 23–4. According to the wording of this text, one would think that the reading of 'the Syrian' was σαβέκ, and not ἐν σαβέκ, as reported by Field, i, p. 38. The possibility that Eusebius cited this variant is raised by the text of Procopius, *Comm. in Gen.* 22: 13 (Greek text in *CS*, pp. 182–3), and by the Armenian version of Eusebius' commentary. However, the garbled form of these texts (the Armenian is accessible to me only in the retroversion of Buytaert, *L'héritage*, p. 113*) makes it difficult to arrive at a definite conclusion.

[137] Thus, if the formulation of the anonymous fragment goes back to Eusebius, it effectively refutes the view of Nikolasch, 'Zur Ikonographie', pp. 218–19 (cf. *Das Lamm als Christussymbol in den Schriften der Väter* (WBTh 3), Vienna 1963, p. 31), according to which Jerome misunderstood Eusebius, and the latter 'nicht unter dem Wort "Sabech" den Widder verstanden wissen wollte, sondern eine Erklärung für eine ihm vorliegende Textvariante bieten will, nach welcher der Widder vom Baum herunterhänge [i.e. the reading κρεμάμενος in 'the Syrian']'. Oddly, however, Nikolasch goes on to cite Eusebius not according to the transmitted text of the *catena*, but according to Buytaert's retroversion of Jerome's citation. This text would seem to contradict his assertion.

[138] See *CS*, p. 184 n. d.

apparently willing to accept the ambiguity of the text, and, in fact, to have regarded it as intentional.

For his part, Diodore of Tarsus mentions the view that σαβέκ means ἄφεσις, and attributes it to 'the Hebrews'.[139] In his own judgement, however, the word is simply the name of a plant.[140]

In *QHG* 22: 13, Jerome discusses some of these views advocated by the Antiochenes. As we have seen above, the idea that the word סבך could refer to the animal he regards as laughable. The reason for this is clearly the fact that such a view could not be reconciled with the original Hebrew text. Indeed, Jerome goes on to cite Aquila and Symmachus, whom he regards as the most accurate authorities concerning the meaning of the original. Aquila renders סבך with the Greek συχνεών, a term which he apparently coined and which Jerome translates as 'condensa et inter se implexa virgulta'.[141] Symmachus, on the other hand, uses the equivalent of the Latin 'rete', that is, 'net'. He is probably interpreting the Hebrew word on the basis of its apparent relation to the word שבכה, a common word in the Old Testament for latticework and other similar objects.[142] Now, it may be that Symmachus employed this term in a literal sense. For in some iconographic representations of the *Aqedah* the ram is pictured as tied to the plant or tree with an actual rope. F. Nikolasch has suggested that such a representation may have its origin in a certain rabbinic tradition, according to which the ram was created by God on the sixth day of creation, and was subsequently, at the appropriate time, brought by an angel to the site of the *Aqedah*. In the pictorial representations of the episode, the rope would represent a further development of this idea, signifying that the angel had secured

---

[139] *C. Cois.* 204, ll. 24–5. In Procopius we read, ὁ δὲ Ἑβραῖος . . . ἄφεσιν σημαίνει, and a similar comment is found in the Armenian version of Eusebius. See the passages cited above, n. 136.

[140] *C. Cois.* 204, l. 24. Clearly, for Diodore, the view that σαβέκ means ἄφεσις is distinct from the view that it is the name of a plant. The distinction is maintained by Gennadius, as we have seen in n. 134 above, and also seems to be reflected in various Byzantine lexicons. Compare the *Suda* with Hesychius and Zonaras, s.v. σαβέκ. On the other hand, the earlier exegetes may not have wanted to imply such a distinction. See esp. Ephraem Graecus, loc. cit. (n. 131 above) with Mercati's note on v. 405ss, p. 90, and cf. Amphilochius, *De Abraham*, ed. [Van Rompay and] C. Datema, Turnhout 1978 (= CChr.SG 3), pp. 298, 302.

[141] For the attestation of Aquila's reading in MSS of the Greek Bible, see Field, i, p. 38.

[142] Cf. Field, ibid. The Greek word employed by Symmachus was δίκτυον (a common equivalent for שבכה in the LXX).

the ram to the tree with a cord [or net?].[143] Whether Symmachus actually had such a tradition in mind need not concern us here, for Jerome clearly regards his use of 'rete' as metaphorical, since he paraphrases Symmachus' version with the words 'in modum retis inter se virgulta contexta' (*QHG* 22: 13). In short, in his view, both Aquila and Symmachus understand the סבך as a bush with dense branches.[144]

Jerome goes on, however, to consider the possibility that the word could be the name of a plant. His exact words are as follows:

Verum quibusdam in hoc dumtaxat loco melius videntur interpretati esse LXX et Theodotion, qui ipsum nomen sabech posuerunt, dicentes: 'in virgulto sabech cornibus suis'. etenim συχνεών sive rete, quod Aquila posuit et Symmachus, per sin literam scribi, hic vero samech literam positam: ex quo manifestum esse non interpretationem stirpium condensarum et in modum retis inter se virgulta contexta verbum sabech, sed nomen sonare virgulti, quod ita Hebraice dicitur. ego vero diligenter inquirens συχνεῶνα per samech literam scribi crebro repperi. (*QHG* 22: 13)

When Jerome says, 'etenim συχνεών . . . quod ita Hebraice dicitur', he is not giving his own view, as Nikolasch believes.[145] Rather, he is reporting the reasoning employed by those who claim that 'sabech' is the name of a plant. They argue that the word for 'dense net-work' is written with a *sin*, clearly having in mind the term שׂבכה, which appears in the Old Testament some sixteen times. In Gen. 22: 13, however, the relevant word is written with a *samech*, and accordingly should not be interpreted as if it were equivalent to שׂבכה, but must have a different meaning. Jerome, on the other hand (= 'ego vero'), has found this argument to be invalid. For his own research has revealed to him that 'dense network' can also be indicated by the word סבך, which is spelled with a *samech*. This word is much less common, appearing only five times when one takes into account different vocalizations.[146]

---

[143] See 'Zur Ikonographie', pp. 215–17.

[144] Nikolasch, ibid. pp. 213–15, calls attention to the fact that Tertullian and various Fathers after Jerome cite Gen. 22: 13 in a manner which may reflect the influence of Aquila or another non-LXX version. Yet it is not to be excluded that these passages are loose exegetical paraphrases of the LXX, and in any case they cannot be considered antecedents of Jerome's remarks, for they do not include any sort of discussion.

[145] 'Zur Ikonographie', p. 215 n. 82.

[146] When Jerome uses the phrases "συχνεών sive rete . . . per sin literam scribi", and "συχνεῶνα per samech literam scribi crebro repperi", he does not betray an

In other words, the versions of Aquila and Symmachus have been shown to be correct on the basis of an examination of the Hebrew text. The ideas put forward by the Antiochenes must be rejected.

On other occasions, although Jerome does not specifically mention Eusebius or Diodore, a comparison between the surviving exegesis of these writers and that of Jerome in *QHG* would lead one to believe that the Latin writer is critically responding to the method of the Antiochenes.

In Gen. 2: 8, the planting or creation of the Garden of Eden is described:

ויטע יהוה אלהים גן בעדן מקדם וישם שם את האדם אשר יצר:

καὶ ἐφύτευσεν κύριος ὁ θεὸς παράδεισον ἐν Ἐδὲμ κατὰ ἀνατολὰς καὶ ἔθετο ἐκεῖ τὸν ἄνθρωπον, ὃν ἔπλασεν.

In his comment on this verse, Eusebius of Emesa raises two issues. The first concerns the understanding of the phrase παράδεισος ἐν Ἐδέμ:

οἱ μέν φασιν Ἐδὲμ καλεῖσθαι τὸν τόπον ἐν ᾧ ἐφυτεύθη ὁ παράδεισος· οἱ δὲ Ἐδὲμ τὸν παράδεισόν φασι, τὸν δὲ ἑρμηνευτὴν καὶ τὴν ἑρμηνείαν θεῖναι καὶ τὸ ἑρμηνευόμενον τεθεικέναι.[147]

The first view reported by Eusebius, according to which God planted a garden in a place called 'Eden' corresponds to the simple meaning of the Greek text. Indeed, Eusebius provides no explanation for this view, and the text was generally understood in this sense.[148] On the other hand, he also mentions the view that the Garden (i.e. ὁ παράδεισος) and Eden are one and the same place and that the presence of the two words in the Greek text is due to the initiative of the translator.

The origin of this latter idea may ultimately depend on the etymology of the word 'Eden'. It was well known that this word

inadvertent citation of the wrong column of a Hebrew–Greek dictionary, as Burstein, 'La compétence', pp. 41–2, would have us believe. Such an idea is easily refuted by the fact that Jerome employs a Latin word as well in the phrase 'συχνεών sive rete'. That is, he quite naturally uses the versions of Aquila and Symmachus in saying, '[The word for] "dense net-work" . . . is written [sc. in Hebrew] with a *sin*'.

[147] Devreesse, *Les anciens commentateurs*, p. 59. Cf. Diodore, *C. Cois.* 86.

[148] See Origen, *Sel. in Gen.* 12: 8 (*PG* 12. 100a–b); Eusebius, *Onomast.* 80. 20–1; Ps.-Basil, *Parad.* 7 (*PG* 30. 68c–d); Ambrose, *Parad.* 3–4, 23.

could be translated as τρυφή. This rendering is found in the etymological lists, and it (or the Latin equivalent) is cited by Greek and
Latin exegetes in discussions of Gen. 2: 8.[149] Severian of Gabala,
however, goes beyond a simple rendering, and on the basis of the
presence of the same Greek word in the phrase παράδεισος τῆς
τρυφῆς, which appears in Gen. 3: 24 [and elsewhere, e.g. Gen.
2: 15 (v.l.); 3: 23; Joel 2: 3, as the normal Greek translation for
the Hebrew עדן גן], concludes that 'Eden' could be understood
as a common noun and interpreted in a concrete sense in Gen.
2: 8. He paraphrases the verse as follows: ἐφύτευσε παράδεισον ἐν
τρυφῇ, ἀντὶ τοῦ ἐν τόπῳ τρυφερῷ, ἐν τόπῳ καλῷ.[150] Hippolytus,
however, appears to go beyond this view. For he identifies the
τόπος τρυφῆς, called Eden, with the παράδεισος.[151] The logic of such
a position is easily at hand, for if 'Eden' can be rendered 'lovely
place', it will mean basically the same thing as παράδεισος.[152] One
could therefore conclude that only one place is designated by the
two terms. In this case, however, the formulation of the verse
appears redundant. It was this problem that probably led the
informants of Eusebius of Emesa to conclude that the presence of
two words was due to the translator.

Such an affirmation, however, can only be based on a failure to
consult the original text. And Eusebius' use of such inaccurate
hearsay evidence is probably the target of Jerome's remarks on
this verse. For he notes that underlying παράδεισος and Ἐδέμ are
different Hebrew words.[153]

On the other hand, it is interesting to note the commentary of
Theodore of Mopsuestia on this verse. For it would appear that

---

[149] *OGM* 180. 54; 186. 13; 190. 29–30; Wutz, *Onomastica*, pp. 703, 721; Philo,
All. 1. 45; Theophilus, *Autol.* 2. 24; Eusebius, *Onomast.* 80. 20–1; Gregory of
Nyssa, *Hom. opif.* 19 (*PG* 44. 196d); Ps.-Basil, *Parad.* 7 (*PG* 30. 68c–d); Ambrose,
Parad. 23; Augustine, *Gen. litt.* 8. 3. An alternative etymology, based no doubt
on a falsely assumed connection with the word אדמה, is found in Diodore, *C.
Cois.* 86, and Chrysostom, *Hom. in Ac. 9: 1* 2. 3 (*PG* 51. 129). Cf. also *OGM*
190. 29–30; 202. 74.

[150] *Creat.* 5. 5 (*PG* 56. 477). Cf. Procopius of Gaza, *Comm. in Gen.* 2: 8–9
(*PG* 87. 157d), and Jerome's translation of Gen. 2: 10 in *IH*.

[151] *Comm. in Dan.* 1. 17(18). See also the Greek text edited by M. Richard,
RHT 2 (1972), p. 6. Cf. *Recogn. Clem.* 1. 28. 3.

[152] Cf. the language used by Lactantius, *Inst.* 2. 12. 15: 'in paradiso id est in
horto fecundissimo et amoenissimo'.

[153] *QHG* 2: 8. The debate on the Hebrew text in *Ber. R.* 15. 2 is formulated
along different lines, and a position similar to that noted by Eusebius is not
advocated.

Theodore is also taking issue with the view mentioned by Eusebius (and Diodore; see above, n. 147), according to which the Garden and Eden are one and the same place. Yet he disputes this view not by citing the original, but by emphasizing the wording of the Greek text (the Garden is planted *in* Eden), and by pointing out the implications of the subsequent narrative. He shows that it was possible for Cain to live in Eden yet outside the Garden.[154]

In the two preceding examples, it is obvious that the remarks of Eusebius pertain to the Hebrew text. On other occasions, this is perhaps not so obvious. For although he refers to τὸ Ἑβραϊκόν and ὁ Ἑβραῖος, scholars have not always agreed on the meaning of these expressions. It has been thought by some that at least the phrase ὁ Ἑβραῖος may refer to a Greek version rather than to the Hebrew text itself.[155] To this question we shall return shortly. In considering the following examples it will be sufficient to point out that in the writings of Eusebius of Emesa the expression τὸ Ἑβραϊκόν seems to indicate the Hebrew text. This is hardly surprising, since in other sources as well it has this meaning, whether the reference is to the transliteration of the Hebrew in the 'second column' of Origen's *Hexapla*, or to the Hebrew text in a more general sense.[156] Nevertheless, it can be confirmed with regard to the usage of Eusebius of Emesa. For just as he employs the word φασί in introducing a statement concerning the Hebrew text with regard to Gen. 2: 8, as we have seen immediately above, so does he use this word in discussing τὸ Ἑβραϊκόν in the examples we shall now consider. And since he expressly acknowledges his need of informants concerning Hebrew matters in the introduction to the *Commentarii in Octateuchum* preserved in Armenian, we may assume that τὸ Ἑβραϊκόν denotes the Hebrew text and not a Greek version. For Eusebius would not require informants in consulting a Greek text.

In his treatment of Gen. 2: 8, the Emesan raises a second issue, namely, whether God created the Garden of Eden after creating man, as the context suggests [the creation of man is related in Gen. 1: 27 and 2: 7], or on the third day with the other trees [see Gen. 1: 11–13]. In order to elucidate the question, Eusebius cites

---

[154] The remarks of Theodore have been reconstructed by E. Sachau, *Theodori Mopsuesteni fragmenta Syriaca*, Leipzig 1869, pp. 19–20. Cf. Devreesse, *Essai*, p. 17 n. 2.

[155] See Field, i, pp. lxxv–lxxvii.   [156] See Field, i, pp. lxxi–lxxii, lxxiv.

the versional variants of the phrase which is represented by the words κατὰ ἀνατολάς in the LXX:

ὁ μὲν οὖν Σύρος οὕτως ἔχει γεγραμμένον· "καὶ ἐφύτευσεν ὁ θεὸς παράδεισον ἐν Ἐδὲμ ἐξ ἀρχῆς"· ἐξ ἀρχῆς δέ φασι μὴ ἐγκεῖσθαι τῷ Ἑβραϊκῷ. λέγουσιν οὖν πολλοὶ ὅτι μετὰ ταῦτα ἐφυτεύθη.¹⁵⁷

According to Eusebius, the absence of the expression ἐξ ἀρχῆς from the Hebrew text serves as a basis for the view that the Garden of Eden was planted after the creation of man. On the other hand, the presence of the phrase in 'the Syrian' would appear to constitute for him an argument in favour of the alternative opinion, namely, that the Garden of Eden was planted on the third day. For it is clear from his subsequent discussion that he understands the words ἐξ ἀρχῆς in this sense, and the same interpretation of the equivalent expression is found in Ephraem Syrus.¹⁵⁸ Eusebius no doubt takes ἀρχή in the sense of 'the six-day period of creation', i.e. ἡ ἑξαήμερος. In the remainder of his discussion, however, Eusebius goes on to mention other arguments adduced in support of the second view noted in the fragment, according to which the creation of paradise took place after the creation of man. One of these is based on the wording of Gen. 2: 9, where we read the words, καὶ ἐξανέτειλεν ὁ θεὸς ἔτι ἐκ τῆς γῆς πᾶν ξύλον ὡραῖον εἰς ὅρασιν καὶ καλὸν εἰς βρῶσιν. The presence of the word ἔτι in this verse is taken to indicate that the creation of the Garden, which is further described here, constitutes an event separate from and later than the creation of the other trees on the third day.

Theodore of Mopsuestia, in his discussion of this verse, again appears to be arguing against the view reported by his predecessor. He takes issue with the interpretation of Gen. 2: 9 given in Eusebius. According to Theodore, the trees of Eden were planted at the same time as the other trees [i.e. on the third day], and Gen. 2: 9 simply constitutes a reiteration of the earlier

---

¹⁵⁷ See Devreesse, *Les anciens commentateurs*, p. 59. The words ἐξ ἀρχῆς are written only once in the MSS, and Devreesse has corrected the text. Even if one does not accept the correction, Eusebius' report concerning the absence of the phrase ἐξ ἀρχῆς from the Hebrew remains. See the translation of de Montfaucon, *PG* 15. 171. That such an understanding of the text is correct can be confirmed from the similar remark which no doubt derives from Eusebius in Ishodad of Merv, *Comm. in Gen.* 2: 8.

¹⁵⁸ *Comm. in Gen.* 2. 5. The same interpretation, based on the Hebrew, is advocated in *Ber. R.* 15. 3, and goes back to early times. See *Jubilees* 2. 5–7; *II Enoch* ('long recension') 30. 1.

event.[159] As for the word ἔτι, as in Gen. 2: 19, it is simply added ἔκ τινος ἰδιώματος τῆς Ἑβραΐδος γλώσσης, i.e. it does not have real temporal force. In fact, however, a Hebrew equivalent of the word ἔτι is missing from both verse 19 and verse 9, and we may therefore assume that Theodore is following his well-known practice of appealing to the distinctive ἰδιώματα of the Hebrew language when explaining linguistic difficulties in the LXX.[160] It is hardly necessary to suppose that he has specifically in mind a different real or presumed Hebrew *Vorlage*.

For his part, Jerome again seems to be in concert with Theodore in arguing against the view explained in detail by Eusebius of Emesa, according to which Eden was created after man. By contrast, however, he takes up the first point raised by Eusebius, the alternative versions of the phrase which is rendered κατὰ ἀνατολάς by the LXX:

Quod sequitur, contra orientem, in Hebraeo meccedem scribitur, quod Aquila posuit, ἀπὸ ἀρχῆθεν, et nos ab exordio possumus dicere, Symmachus vero, ἐκ πρώτης, et Theodotion, ἐν πρώτοις, quod et ipsum non orientem, sed principium significat. ex quo manifestissime comprobatur quod prius quam caelum et terram Deus faceret, paradisum ante condiderat, sicut et legitur in Hebraeo: 'plantaverat autem Dominus Deus paradisum in Eden a principio'.[161]

It would appear that Jerome's intention is to stack up the evidence against the affirmation of Eusebius. For he cites not only the Hebrew word which the Emesan believes to be absent from the

---

[159] See his commentary as edited by Sachau, op. cit. (n. 154 above), pp. 20–1. It is clear that for Theodore, as well as for Eusebius, Gen. 2: 9 constitutes an elaboration of Gen. 2: 8. Cf. Procopius of Gaza, *Comm. in Gen.* 2: 8–9 (*PG* 87. 160c); Ishodad of Merv, *Comm. in Gen.* 2: 9; Augustine, *Doct. Chr.* 3. 52.

[160] See Schäublin, *Untersuchungen*, pp. 127–36, and below, pp. 158–9.

[161] *QHG* 2: 8. I follow Vallarsi in writing 'meccedem' rather than the variant 'mimizra' which de Lagarde adopts in his edition of *QHG* and discusses in his edition of the Greek Genesis (Leipzig 1868), pp. 23–4. Although de Lagarde's reading is *difficilior*, and he attempts to justify it by citing the testimony of Eusebius concerning the absence of the phrase ἐξ ἀρχῆς from the Hebrew, it is nevertheless indefensible. For it makes no sense within the context of Jerome's comment. Field, i, p. 13, seems to be of a similar opinion, since he cites the text according to Vallarsi and relegates the reading of de Lagarde to the status of variant. On the other hand, Field's own suggestion that perhaps both words should be incorporated into the text in the form 'meccedem non mimizra' is excellent. For it is typical of Jerome's practice to tell the reader what the Hebrew text would have to contain for it to have the meaning which others attribute to it. See *QHG* 1: 1; 32: 28–9; *Ep.* 20. 1.

text, but also each one of the *recentiores* as additional witnesses. He understands the versions to indicate that the Garden of Eden was created before the world itself. As M. Rahmer has noted, this interpretation of the verse is also found in rabbinic literature.[162] Moreover, Rahmer believes that this view underlies the versions of the *recentiores*.[163] This may be true, but it cannot be deduced from the simple Greek text of these versions, which need not necessarily be taken in this sense. For we have seen that according to the sources of Eusebius of Emesa, the presence of the equivalent expression ἐξ ἀρχῆς indicates that the Garden was planted on the third day. Accordingly, Jerome again is probably interpreting the *recentiores* in the light of rabbinic exegesis.[164] At the same time, he seems to be setting such an approach over against that of

---

[162] *Die hebräischen Traditionen*, p. 17. He cites *b. Pes.* 54a; *b. Ned.* 39b; *T. Ps.-J.* Gen. 2: 8. Cf. IV Esr. 3: 6. It would seem from most of these passages that the Rabbis had in mind the unworldly rather than the worldly Garden of Eden (for the distinction, see J. D. Eisenstein, *JE* 5 (1903), p. 38; 9 (1905), pp. 515–16). Nevertheless, Jerome need not have interpreted the 'pre-creation' in this sense, for he may have known the tradition from a source similar to *Ber. R.* 15. 3, where there is a reference to the pre-creation of the Garden of Eden, but the exact worldly or unworldly status of the Garden is not specified. For this reason, it is not necessary to assume that his use of the tradition implies an allegorical interpretation of the Eden narrative, as Martianay believes (see *PL* 23. 1632b–33c; cf. Ginzberg, 'Die Haggada' (*MGWJ* 43), pp. 120–1). Such an interpretation was vigorously opposed by many exegetes who rejected the extreme allegorism of Origen (see Alexandre, *Le commencement*, pp. 55–7). As R. R. Grimm has pointed out, Jerome himself was instrumental in promoting the anti-Origenist position, for he translated a letter of Epiphanius in which Origen's interpretation of the Garden of Eden narrative came under particular attack (*Ep.* 51 in the Hieronymian corpus). Accordingly, it is probable that Jerome's use of the tradition concerning the pre-creation reflects an extreme literalistic position. See *Paradisus coelestis, Paradisus terrestris* (Medium aevum: Philologische Studien 33), Munich 1977, pp. 72–3; cf. p. 43. Finally, it should be noted that the Jewish tradition employed here by Jerome is quite different from the one mentioned in Origen, *Sel. in Gen.* 2: 8 (*PG* 12. 100a–b). Origen cites the view that Eden was a place in which the Garden was planted, and consequently existed before it. Yet he does not connect this view with the words ἐξ ἀρχῆς or the equivalent. In fact, the view is perfectly reconcilable with the text of the LXX. It is therefore unclear to me what de Lange, *Origen*, p. 125, means when he says, 'Origen's informant, at any rate, stands outside the tradition represented by the LXX.'

[163] Loc. cit. (n. 162 *init.*). He cites Z. Frankel, *Vorstudien zu der Septuaginta*, Leipzig 1841, p. 182. Cf. Condamin, 'L'influence', pp. 7–8.

[164] See above, p. 122, and below, pp. 181–91. The view that Jerome is directly dependent on IV Esr. 3: 6, which might be inferred from the comments of M.-J. Lagrange, 'Saint Jérôme et la tradition juive dans la Genèse', *RB* 7 (1898), p. 564, is improbable in the light of Jerome's remarks concerning that book in *Vigil.* 6 (*PL* 23. 360a–b). Cf. also *Praef. in Esdr. et Neh.* 18–19. In addition, the passage from IV Esr. is not an explicit comment on Gen. 2: 8.

Eusebius, who was satisfied with hearsay evidence concerning the meaning of the original.

In Gen. 4: 26, we read of the birth of Enosh, the son of Seth:

וּלְשֵׁת גַּם הוּא יֻלַּד בֵּן וַיִּקְרָא אֶת שְׁמוֹ אֱנוֹשׁ אָז הוּחַל לִקְרֹא בְּשֵׁם יהוה:

LXX: καὶ τῷ Σὴθ ἐγένετο υἱός, ἐπωνόμασεν δὲ τὸ ὄνομα αὐτοῦ Ἐνώς· οὗτος ἤλπισεν ἐπικαλεῖσθαι τὸ ὄνομα κυρίου τοῦ θεοῦ.

Aquila (1): οὗτος ἤρξατο τοῦ καλεῖσθαι ἐν ὀνόματι κυρίου.

Aquila (2): τότε ἤρχθη τοῦ καλεῖν ἐν ὀνόματι

Symmachus: τότε ἀρχὴ ἐγένετο[165]

The second part of this verse has been interpreted in different ways by the translators, chiefly because of the problems caused by the word הוּחַל, a rare *hophal* form of the root חלל, 'to begin'. In the present passage it is probably to be understood as an impersonal passive, and a rendering of this sense seems to have been attempted by Aquila (2) and Symmachus. On the other hand, the different versions of the LXX and Aquila (1) may be due to the difficulty of the passive in this context, a different *Vorlage* (this will have been in all probability זֶה הֵחֵל, understood as זֶה הֵחֵל or זֶה הֵחֵל), or even the exegetical needs of the passage.[166] For present purposes, however, we shall be concerned not with the origins of these versions, but with their meaning in Greek and how they were interpreted by later Greek and Latin writers.

The second half of the verse in the version of the LXX is probably to be translated as follows: 'He (this one) hoped to invoke the name of the Lord God.' In other words, ἐπικαλεῖσθαι is to be understood as a middle and τὸ ὄνομα as the object of that verb. For this same phrase constitutes the standard rendering of the Hebrew קָרָא בְשֵׁם in the LXX.[167] And, in fact, in the early centuries of the common era, the expression was generally understood in this sense. In the *VL*, for example, the second part of the verse is rendered, 'hic speravit invocare nomen Domini Dei'.[168]

---

[165] The material in the edition of the Greek version of Genesis by A. E. Brooke and N. McLean (Cambridge 1906 = *The Old Testament in Greek*, i. 1), p. 10, and in Wevers, p. 101, constitutes an update of Field, i, p. 20. The attribution of two different versions to Aquila is not an uncommon phenomenon. Indeed, he may have produced a second edition or revision. See Jerome, *Comm. in Ezech.* 1 (3: 14b–15); Field, i, pp. xxiv–xxvii.

[166] For a discussion of the origin of the version of the LXX, see S. D. Fraade, *Enosh and His Generation* (SBLMS 30), Chico, Calif. 1984, pp. 5–11.

[167] See Fraade, *Enosh*, p. 10.   [168] See Fischer, p. 92.

Origen seems to have regarded ἐπικαλεῖσθαι as a middle, as did Eusebius and Gregory of Nazianzus.[169] On the other hand, the verb was understood as a passive by Julius Africanus. In his view, the verse indicates that Enosh hoped to be called by the name 'God'.[170] This understanding of the phrase probably originated as an attempt to solve an exegetical problem in Gen. 6: 2. According to the latter verse, the 'sons of God' (not previously mentioned in the narrative) took wives from among the 'daughters of men'. Needless to say, the idea of an actual sexual union between apparently semi-divine beings and earthly women caused a problem for interpreters.[171] However, if Gen. 4: 26 is taken to mean that Enosh 'hoped to be called by the name "God"', it would be reasonable to assume that the hope was realized in his own lifetime or in later generations, and that the phrase 'sons of God' simply denotes the descendants of Seth and Enosh. Although this connection between Gen. 4: 26 and 6: 2 is not explicitly mentioned in the transmitted fragments of Africanus, it is generally emphasized by later writers who adopt the passive understanding of ἐπικαλεῖσθαι.[172] That Africanus himself made the connection is probable, since he is apparently not only the first author to have suggested the rather unlikely interpretation of ἐπικαλεῖσθαι as a passive, but also the first to have understood the phrase 'sons of God' as indicating the descendants of Seth.[173]

---

[169] Origen, *Comm. in Rom.* 8. 3–5 (*PG* 14. 1165a–1166a). This text is preserved only in Latin, but from the discussion it can be determined that the sense of ἐπικαλέομαι in Gen. 4: 26 is regarded as equivalent to the sense of the same verb in Ps. 98: 6 (LXX) and Joel 2: 32 (LXX). Cf. also *Comm. in Rom.* 5. 1 (*PG* 14. 1011d–1012a). For Eusebius' understanding of the passage, see *PE* 7. 8. 2–10. That Gregory regarded the verb as a middle is clear from his use of the verse in *Or.* 43. 70; cf. *Or.* 14. 2; 28. 18.

[170] *Chronicon*, fr. 3, as edited by M. J. Routh, *Reliquiae sacrae*, ii, Oxford 1846, pp. 238–9. Fraade, *Enosh*, p. 88 n. 128, disputes the attribution of the fragment, but does not provide any argument for his view. Indeed, he seems unaware of the treatment of the issue in Routh, p. 362. His view is correctly ignored by W. Adler, *Time Immemorial* (DOS 26), Washington, DC 1989, p. 138 n. 33.

[171] See H. Lesêtre, *DB(V)* 2 (1912), col. 2256. Cf. Fraade, *Enosh*, p. 65.

[172] Eusebius of Emesa, in Devreesse, *Les anciens commentateurs*, p. 62; Chrysostom, *Exp. in Ps.* 49. 1 (*PG* 55. 241); Theodoret, *Qu. in Gen.* 47; *Haer.* 5. 7 (*PG* 83. 469b–c); Cyril of Alexandria, *Juln.* 9 (*PG* 76. 956b–d); *Resp.* 15 (ed. L. R. Wickham, Oxford 1983, p. 177); cf. *Glaph. Gen.* 2 (*PG* 69. 49d–52a, 53d). Many of these passages are discussed below. Didymus, *Comm. in Gen.* 4: 26, 6: 2, stands out as one who adopts the passive interpretation of ἐπικαλεῖσθαι without applying it to Gen. 6: 2.

[173] See *Chronicon*, fr. 7 (ed. Routh, p. 241); Fraade, *Enosh*, pp. 66–7. Cf. Adler, loc. cit. (n. 170 above).

Africanus seems to have interpreted the verb ἐπικαλεῖσθαι as a passive on the basis of the LXX text alone, and Didymus did the same (*Comm. in Gen.* 4: 26 (145. 4–8)). Nevertheless, this understanding of the verb can hardly have been obvious. The use of the middle ἐπικαλέομαι in the sense of 'invoke' is a common form of expression in the LXX, and was particularly widespread in late Greek generally.[174] Accordingly, it is not surprising that other Fathers exploit other text forms, especially the version(s) of Aquila, in putting forward interpretations similar to that of Africanus. For Aquila's use of the prepositional phrase ἐν ὀνόματι in place of τὸ ὄνομα in the LXX deprives the infinitive καλεῖσθαι or ἐπικαλεῖσθαι of an obvious object, and understanding that infinitive as a passive is greatly facilitated. For example, Chrysostom claims that Enosh came to be called 'God' because of his great virtue, and that this name was shared by his descendants. Speaking of the latter, he quotes Gen. 4: 26 in the following manner: ἤρξαντο ἐπικαλεῖσθαι τῷ ὀνόματι τοῦ θεοῦ (*Exp. in Ps.* 49. 1 (*PG* 55. 241)). In other words, while interpreting in a passive sense the infinitive which appears in the LXX, ἐπικαλεῖσθαι, he nevertheless cites the verse in a loose manner which belies the influence of Aquila (1).[175] Similarly, Theodoret, in *Qu. in Gen.* 47 (a discussion of the expression 'sons of God' in Gen. 6: 2), shows himself manifestly aware of the obvious connotation of the LXX version of Gen. 4: 26, and appeals explicitly to the version of Aquila, although he cites it in an apparently mixed form: τότε ἤρχθη τοῦ καλεῖσθαι τῷ [v.l. ἐν] ὀνόματι κυρίου. He understands these words to mean that Enosh was the first to be called 'God' because of his piety, adding that his descendants received the same appellation.[176]

---

[174] For the frequency of the usage in the LXX, see J. W. Tyrer, *JThS* 25 (1924), p. 140. For the usage in other late Greek sources, see W. Bauer and K. Aland, *Griechisch-deutsches Wörterbuch zu den Schriften des Neuen Testaments und der frühchristlichen Literatur*[6], Berlin 1988, s.v. ἐπικαλέω, 2b.

[175] Chrysostom's transformation of the prepositional phrase ἐν ὀνόματι into τῷ ὀνόματι is a natural Hellenization of Aquila's literalistic Greek as he understood it. There is perhaps a similar phenomenon in Theodoret, *Qu. in Gen.* 47, cited immediately below.

[176] In the new edition of N. Fernández Marcos and A. Sáenz-Badillos (Madrid 1979 = Textos y estudios 'Cardenal Cisneros' 17), Theodoret's citation of Aquila is given in a different form, namely, τότε ἤρχθη τοῦ καλεῖν ἐν ὀνόματι κυρίου. I have followed the edition of J. Sirmond and J. L. Schulze (*PG* 80. 148c–d; cf. the apparatus of Fernández Marcos). The citation as it is given in the new edition corresponds exactly to the second of Aquila's renderings preserved in the marginal scholia, and it is precisely for this reason that the reading of

Eusebius of Emesa also regards the infinitive as a passive, yet on the basis of hearsay evidence, finds support for such an interpretation in the Hebrew text itself: ἐν τῷ Ἑβραϊκῷ φασιν οὐχ οὕτως ἔχει [i.e. as the LXX], ἀλλ᾽, "οὗτος ἤλπισεν ἐπικαλεῖσθαι τῷ ὀνόματι κυρίου τοῦ θεοῦ", τουτέστιν υἱὸς θεοῦ λέγεσθαι καὶ θεός. οἱ γὰρ ἀπὸ τοῦ Σὴθ δίκαιοι γεγόνασιν.[177] Now, it is not to be excluded that the informants of Eusebius interpreted the Hebrew לִקְרֹא as if it were a *niphal* form which had undergone elision of the ה, namely, לִקָּרֵא. S. Fraade believes that such an interpretation may explain the rendering of the Samaritan Targum.[178] However, an independent assessment of the Hebrew seems unlikely here, since the citation is identical to the LXX with the exception of the fact that the dative τῷ ὀνόματι is substituted for the accusative τὸ ὄνομα. Indeed, we find that Chrysostom, *Hom. in Gen.* 22. 3, cites the verse in the exact same form, again while interpreting ἐπικαλεῖσθαι

Sirmond is to be preferred. For it is the *lectio difficilior*, which will have been amended according to the text of Aquila. Yet here we are interested in the correct reading of Theodoret, not that of Aquila. In fact, it is well known that the Fathers were wont to cite the texts in looser forms, and, as we have already seen, such loose citation in this specific instance is attested in Chrysostom, another Antiochene writer. In addition, although it is possible to reconcile the correct reading of Aquila (2) with the exegesis of Theodoret, so long as one understands 'Enosh' as the object of καλεῖν, a reading in which 'Enosh' is to be understood as the subject of a passive infinitive καλεῖσθαι would seem to bear more naturally the meaning ascribed to the verse by the interpreter. It should also be pointed out here that in *Haer.* 5. 7 (*PG* 83. 469b–c), Theodoret employs the reading of the LXX while advocating the passive interpretation of ἐπικαλεῖσθαι. In view of *Qu. in Gen.* 47, however, it would appear that his understanding of the LXX was determined by his use of Aquila.

[177] See Devreesse, *Les anciens commentateurs*, p. 62. The word φασίν is not found in the text of this fragment transmitted in the *catenae* and edited by Devreesse. I have added it from the version of the same fragment preserved in Procopius, *Comm. in Gen.* 4: 26. The correct reading of this latter text is to be found in A. Mai, *Classici auctores e Vaticanis codicibus editi*, vi, Rome 1834, p. 245. In *PG* 87. 261c the word is printed as φησίν, which is probably a misprint, since the text in *PG* 87. 21–365 is simply a reprint of Mai. The reading of Procopius is to be accepted here, for Eusebius uses the same word, φασί, when referring to τὸ Ἑβραϊκόν in his comment on Gen. 2: 8–9 (above, p. 142). Accordingly, as stated above, since Eusebius would not need informants in consulting a Greek text, the phrase τὸ Ἑβραϊκόν here denotes the Hebrew text. And even though the reading cited by Eusebius is found in the marginal scholia and attributed to ὁ Ἑβραῖος (see Field, Brooke and McLean, and Wevers, locc. citt. (n. 165 above)), this latter phrase should not in this instance be understood (as it is by Fraade, *Enosh*, pp. 63–4) to indicate a Greek version. For the reading in the scholia has no doubt been excerpted from Eusebius and the heading has been adjusted to the more standard form.

[178] *Enosh*, pp. 30–1.

as a passive.[179] The same is true of Cyril of Alexandria.[180] Yet, in the case of Chrysostom at least, the source of the dative is probably the translation of Aquila, since we have seen that elsewhere he is indebted to this version. It is therefore not to be excluded that Eusebius is dependent on the same source.

Yet whatever the source of Eusebius' view of the Hebrew, Jerome did not share that view. He does not comment on the problem specifically, but his views are clear from the way in which he cites the Hebrew text. He also makes use of the *recentiores*, but in a different manner. In *QHG* 4: 26, he renders the [Hebrew] text as follows: 'tunc initium fuit invocandi nomen Domini.' This formulation represents no doubt the rendering of Symmachus in a form more complete than we possess in the marginal scholia.[181] In *IH*, on the other hand, he translates as follows: 'iste coepit invocare nomen Domini.'[182] It will be clear that these words constitute an exact rendering of Aquila (1). It is therefore more logical to conclude that Jerome is dependent on that translator than that he has simply assimilated the Septuagint and the Hebrew text, as has been thought.[183] Yet what is noteworthy here is the manner in which he understood the Greek version. For the Antiochene Fathers thought it was possible to interpret the preposition ἐν in Aquila's version in a sort of instrumental sense (note the

---

[179] *PG* 53. 189. In this edition, the reading in the text is identical to that of the LXX. But the reading of Morel's edition (on which, see de Montfaucon, *PG* 47. ix–x) containing the dative, which is cited in the note, should be accepted here. It represents the non-standard text form. Cf. above, n. 176. Fraade, *Enosh*, pp. 72–3, is reluctant to admit that Chrysostom interprets ἐπικαλεῖσθαι as a passive here. But he fails to consider the relevance of *Hom. in Gen.* 21. 3 (*PG* 53. 179).

[180] *Glaph. Gen.* 1 (*PG* 69. 48a–c). In other passages, Cyril construes ἐπικαλεῖσθαι as a passive even when he cites the text according to the LXX. See *Glaph. Gen.* 2 (*PG* 69. 49d–52a); *Juln.* 9 (*PG* 76. 956b–d); *Resp.* 15 (ed. Wickham, p. 177). But perhaps, as in the case of Theodoret, he has understood the LXX in the light of Aquila or a related version. See above, n. 176.

[181] Cf. Fischer, p. 92.

[182] The same reading occurs in the Latin version of Origen, *Hom. in Jos.* 1. 1. But this reading probably represents an assimilation of the citation to the text of the Vulgate. For elsewhere Origen/Rufinus cites the verse according to the LXX. See *Comm. in Jo.* 20. 12; *Comm. in Rom.* 5. 1; 8. 3 (*PG* 14. 1011d, 1165a); *Comm. in Ep. ad Philemonem, apud* Pamphilum, *Apologia pro Origene* 6 (*PG* 17. 592c). Cf. also the manner in which other Latin forms of this verse containing the word 'coepit' are treated by Fischer, p. 92.

[183] Fraade, *Enosh*, p. 49, interprets Jerome's version in this sense. Cf. Alexandre, *Le commencement*, p. 376. However, both writers neglect to consider the updated evidence concerning Aquila provided by Brooke and McLean, and Wevers, locc. citt. (n. 165 above).

tendency to transform it into a simple dative), and consequently that the infinitive καλεῖσθαι in Aquila or ἐπικαλεῖσθαι in the LXX could be understood as a passive.[184] Yet, in all likelihood, Aquila is simply being extremely literal, employing καλέομαι as a middle, but using the preposition ἐν as a literal rendering of the complement as it is expressed in Hebrew. For Aquila almost automatically renders the Hebrew בְּ with the Greek ἐν.[185] Jerome clearly realized this, for he translates Aquila's infinitive with the active 'invocare'. This is probably because he was familiar with the idiosyncrasies of Aquila's translation technique, and because he interpreted the Greek in the light of the Hebrew infinitive as it was commonly understood (i.e. vocalized לִקְרֹא). Again, we see that Jerome regarded the *recentiores* as the supreme authorities concerning the meaning of the 'Hebraica veritas'. Yet they were to be interpreted very carefully, in the light of each other, their own usage, and the Hebrew text. The Antiochenes, on the other hand, took the liberty of applying the standards of normal Greek usage to Aquila's version. The contrast between the two kinds of approach is striking.

We also note a tendency in the fragments of Eusebius whereby what are clearly exegetical rather than literal renderings are cited as ὁ Ἑβραῖος. That is, we come across citations which cannot be reconciled with the Hebrew text as we know it, or more importantly, as Jerome and the *recentiores* knew it. Such citations are also found in other sources, and the question has sometimes arisen as to whether an exegete or an actual text or version is indicated.[186] With regard to Eusebius of Emesa, however, it appears fairly certain that when he employs the words ὁ Ἑβραῖος, he is referring to a text rather than to an exegete. This will be clear from the fact that the expression often takes the verb ἔχει,[187] is used of a numerical variation,[188] and generally is found in contexts where textual variants are in question.[189]

---

[184] They may have been influenced by passages such as Is. 41: 25 and Est. 2: 14, where unambiguous passive forms of καλέω are used with the dative.

[185] See K. Hyvärinen, *Die Übersetzung von Aquila* (CB.OT 10), Lund 1977, p. 48.

[186] See de Montfaucon, *PG* 15. 38c–40a, and cf. Field, i, p. lxxvii; Hanson, *Allegory*, pp. 174–5.

[187] See, e.g., Devreesse, *Les anciens commentateurs*, pp. 69, 75.

[188] See Devreesse, op. cit., p. 62.

[189] See *CS* G 209, cited immediately below, p. 154. Note by contrast Devreesse, op. cit., p. 58, where an exegetical tradition is introduced with the words, Ἑβραῖος δέ τίς φησιν.

There are a number of possibilities as to what the text in question could be. First of all, it may be that Eusebius is citing a sort of Greek targum which has been postulated on the basis of citations of this nature.[190] It is also possible that he is referring to a Jewish Aramaic targum. Finally, he may be citing the Hebrew text itself.[191] This latter use of the phrase ὁ Ἑβραῖος appears to be attested in other sources.[192] If we endorse this final alternative, however, we must conclude that Eusebius is exegetically interpreting the Hebrew text via a knowledge of Syriac, or that he grafts on to it interpretations which he knew from a Syriac (or Jewish Aramaic?) version. On the one hand, he refers to Syriac frequently in his discussions of translation preserved in the Armenian.[193] On the other hand, he often attributes the same or similar readings to ὁ Ἑβραῖος and ὁ Σύρος.[194] However, whatever the solution to this problem may be, one thing is clear: Jerome did not follow Eusebius and his Ἑβραῖος in *QHG*. The reason for this is readily available: Jerome believed that the key to understanding the original text of the Bible was the Hebrew language and the *recentiores*, not the Syriac language or more markedly exegetical versions/ 'targumim'.

In Gen. 15: 2–3, we read how Abraham expresses to God his sadness about the fact that he has no heir:

ויאמר אברם אדני יהוה מה תתן לי ואנכי הולך ערירי ובן משק ביתי
הוא דמשק אליעזר: (3) ויאמר אברם הן לי לא נתתה זרע והנה בן ביתי
יורש אתי:

λέγει δὲ Ἀβράμ Δέσποτα, τί μοι δώσεις; ἐγὼ δὲ ἀπολύομαι ἄτεκνος· ὁ δὲ υἱὸς Μάσεκ τῆς οἰκογενοῦς μου, οὗτος Δαμασκὸς Ἐλιέζερ. (3) καὶ εἶπεν Ἀβράμ Ἐπειδὴ ἐμοὶ οὐκ ἔδωκας σπέρμα, ὁ δὲ οἰκογενής μου κληρονομήσει με.

---

[190] See Field, i, p. lxxvii. Cf. R. Devreesse, *Introduction à l'étude des manuscrits grecs*, Paris 1954, p. 113 n. 6; N. Fernández Marcos, *Introducción a las versiones griegas de la Biblia* (Textos y estudios 'Cardenal Cisneros' 23), Madrid 1979, p. 145.

[191] Cf. Lehmann, 'The Syriac Translation', p. 74.

[192] See Field, i, pp. lxxiv–lxxv; Guinot, op. cit. (Ch. 1 n. 97), p. 44, 49 n. 1. As in the case of τὸ Ἑβραϊκόν, the reference may be given in transliteration, and in this circumstance would probably be derived from the 'second column' of Origen's *Hexapla* (see now Fernández Marcos, *Henoch* 9 (1987), pp. 41–2), or in translation. See esp. Theodoret, *Comm. in Is.* 3 (8: 21 = Guinot, op cit., p. 316), where the expression ὁ Ἑβραῖος is used to introduce both a transliteration and a translation obtained (apparently) from the versions of the *recentiores*.

[193] *Commentaire de l'Octateuque*, ed. Hovhanessian, pp. 1, 8, 218 (translations courtesy of Mahé). Cf. also the testimony of Basil mentioned above, p. 130.

[194] See Devreesse, *Les anciens commentateurs*, p. 65; *CS* G 64, G 189, G 209, E 11. The two versions are often coupled in other sources as well. See Field, i, p. lxxv.

Eusebius comments on these words as follows: ἡ Ἑβραία Δαμασκηνὸς λέγει, ὅθεν ἦν αὐτῷ ἡ μήτηρ.[195] However, in the Hebrew text we find the proper noun 'Damascus', not the gentilic adjective. Eusebius' description of what is in 'the Hebrew' in fact reflects the Peshitta and Targum Onkelos. The second part of Eusebius' comment may also be due to the influence of a Syriac or Aramaic version. The general appeal to the parentage of Eliezer may simply depend on the fact that the 'household-born' slave of verse 3 was naturally thought to indicate him. For if he was born in the household of Abraham, the gentilic 'Damascene' would have to be based on his ancestry rather than on his place of birth.[196] However, the specification of the place of origin of the mother of Eliezer is probably not based on the LXX, since, according to a literal understanding of verse 2 of that version, she too was an οἰκογενής. Eusebius, however, if a view cited by Gennadius may be attributed to him, seems to have thought that the term οἰκογενής, not only in verse 3 but also in verse 2, should refer to Eliezer and not to his mother.[197] Such a view may be based on Syriac and Aramaic versions, according to which the phrase בן משק ביתי, which underlies ὁ υἱὸς Μάσεκ τῆς οἰκογενοῦς μου, is rendered as 'one of my household', and refers to Eliezer, not his mother.[198] In this case, it is possible that she was originally a native of Damascus *de iure*, and not a (stateless) slave born in the household of Abraham. The fact, however, that the reference to the mother is maintained by Eusebius shows that his understanding of the verse was never-

---

[195] *CS* G 16. The fragment is ascribed to Diodore in some MSS, as are parallel texts (cf. *C. Cois.* 185), but the original comment probably goes back to Eusebius. See Petit, ad loc., and also Lehmann, 'An Important Text', p. 157, who has identified the text in the Armenian version. In this passage, the expression ἡ Ἑβραία is apparently regarded by Field, i, p. 32, as synonymous with ὁ Ἑβραῖος. In view of the parallel in Procopius, *Comm. in Gen.* 15: 2 (*PG* 87. 337b–c and *CS*, p. 19; cf. the *catenae* cited by Wevers, ad loc.), this assumption is probably correct. This is not because Procopius attributes the reading to ὁ Ἑβραῖος (he has no doubt simply standardized the form), but rather because he attributes the same reading to ὁ Σύρος. And, as stated, readings of ὁ Σύρος are often equivalent to and cited together with those of ὁ Ἑβραῖος in Eusebius. See the passages listed in the previous note.

[196] Cf. the remarks of C. Van den Eynde in his translation of the *Comm. in Gen.* of Ishodad of Merv (Louvain 1955 = CSCO 156), p. 161 n. 3. In this text we have a Syriac parallel to the comment of Eusebius. See also Bar Hebraeus, *Scholia in Genesim* 15: 2.

[197] *C. Cois.* 183, ll. 15–16 (ll. 13–18 seem to be a loose paraphrase of the view of Eusebius/Diodore).

[198] See the Peshitta, *CN*, and *T. Frag.*, ad loc.

theless anchored to the LXX. For she is mentioned only in that text,[199] and does not even appear in the surviving Aramaic and Syriac versions or the *recentiores*.[200] In other words, Eusebius seems to have grafted his readings of 'the Hebrew' (and 'the Syrian'?) on to the text of the LXX.

Jerome, on the other hand, in *QHG* 15: 2–3, understands the phrase בן משק ביתי to mean 'filius procuratoris mei vel villici', citing the versions of Aquila and Theodotion. That is, he regards the potential heir as the son of an unnamed male steward, not of a female household slave named Masek. Indeed, he expresses his disapproval of the LXX reading in *Sit.* 77. 7–9, and refers his readers to *QHG*. Moreover, he says in his paraphrase of the original that the man is called Damascus Eliezer. In other words, the word דמשק is to be understood as a proper name.[201] And, in fact, Jerome goes on to cite a tradition according to which Damascus was founded and named after Eliezer.[202]

In Gen. 24: 2–3, 9, we read of the oath which Abraham administers to his servant when entrusting him with the task of finding a

---

[199] Cf. Philo, *Her.* 61, who calls particular attention to the fact that the potential heir is identified by way of his mother rather than by way of his father.

[200] In *T. Ps.-J.* and *TO*, the phrase בן משק ביתי is rendered 'administrator of my household', or something to that effect. For the *recentiores*, see Wevers, ad loc. (p. 167), and immediately below.

[201] Cf. *Comm. in Is.* 7 (17: 1). The standard LXX text was of course also understood in this manner. See Philo, *Her.* 54, 61; Eusebius, *Onomast.* 76. 4–5. Gennadius, *C. Cois.* 183, after apparently describing loosely the view of Eusebius/ Diodore, goes on to suggest [a return to] a literal understanding of the words 'Damascus Eliezer' based on the LXX (ll. 18–20). Jerome, paraphrasing the Hebrew text in *QHG* 15: 2–3, will probably have confirmed the correctness of the LXX with regard to this detail on the basis of Aquila. The manner in which the latter translator rendered the relevant phrase may now be seen in *C. Cois.* 183*bis*, where a more complete excerpt from his translation of this verse has been re-edited.

[202] In *QHG* 10: 23, Jerome follows Josephus, *Ant.* 1. 145, in calling Uz the founder of Damascus. The origin of the tradition which he cites here (*QHG* 15: 2–3) is yet to be determined. Ginzberg, 'Die Haggada' (*MGWJ* 43), p. 497, thinks that Jerome is reporting a (lost) Jewish tradition. But if there is no Jewish parallel, it is more likely that he is dependent on a Greek or Latin source. See Justin, *Epitoma historiarum Philippicarum* 36. 2. 2, and Stephanus of Byzantium, *Ethnica*, s.v. Δαμασκός (for Jerome's knowledge of Justin, see *Comm. in Dan.* prol.). A Christian Greek source is also probably to be excluded, since in the anonymous Greek *catena* fragment where a similar view is mentioned (Nicephorus Hiero-monachus, *Catena in Octateuchum et libros Regnorum*, i, Leipzig 1772, col. 201Z), 'Damascus' is taken to refer to Abraham's female slave. For this view, cf. the comment attributed to Ephraem in the 'Catena Severi' printed in vol. i of the Syriac works of Ephraem edited by P. Benedictus (Rome 1737), p. 161.

wife for his son Isaac. He asks him to follow a strange procedure: 'Put your hand under my thigh [Hebrew, ירך, Greek, μηρός], and I will make you swear by the Lord.' Philo and Origen understand this verse to mean that the servant was required to swear by Abraham's reproductive organ, or power of generation.[203] In other Christian writers, including Jerome, we find a development of this idea, namely, the claim that the allusion is to the incarnation, since Christ was descended from the seed of Abraham.[204]

Syriac and Antiochene exegetes put forward a similar interpretation. They also think that the reference is to Abraham's penis, not so much as an organ of reproduction, but as the organ which bears the sign of the covenant, circumcision. We find this idea in Ephraem, *Comm. in Gen.* 21. 2 (cf. 41. 2), Theodoret, *Qu. in Gen.* 75, and Gennadius, *C. Cois.* 209. Eusebius of Emesa also advocates this interpretation. In addition, however, he finds a textual basis for it: ὁ Ἕλλην σεμνότερον ἑρμηνεύει· ὁ γὰρ Ἑβραῖος καὶ ὁ Σύρος αὐτὸ λέγει τοῦ ἀνδρὸς τὸ τεκνοποιὸν ὄργανον. κελεύει δὲ ἐκεῖ θεῖναι τὴν χεῖρα, ἵνα κατὰ τῆς περιτομῆς ὀμόσῃ τῆς τοῦ θεοῦ διαθήκης.[205] However, the surviving Syriac and Hebrew texts cannot be translated in this manner. On the other hand, Eusebius may have been influenced by a text similar to Targum Ps.-Jonathan ad Gen. 24: 2, (9), where the expression בגזירת מהולתי is used, although this corresponds more to Eusebius' interpretation of the literal meaning of ὁ Ἑβραῖος than to his description of it.[206]

Jerome, by contrast, in *QHG* 24: 9, mentions the same interpretation, but believes that it is based not on a text, but on a Hebrew *tradition*: 'tradunt Hebraei quod in sanctificatione eius, hoc est in circumcisione iuraverit.' In fact, the interpretation is attested in Jewish sources besides *T. Ps.-J.*[207] However, Jerome

---

[203] See Philo, *Quaest. in Gn.* 4. 86 (portions of the Greek text in Petit's edition of the Greek fragments of the *Quaestiones* (Paris 1978 = Les œuvres de Philon d'Alexandrie 33), pp. 172–3 (cf. *CS* G 208)); Origen, *Sel. in Ps.* 44: 4 (*PG* 12. 1429b), with the fragment edited by R. Cadiou, *Commentaires inédits des Psaumes*, Paris 1936, p. 78, and Jerome, *Ep.* 65. 10.

[204] Hippolytus, *De Cantico canticorum* 27. 8 (ed. G. Garitte, Louvain 1965 (= CSCO 264), p. 52); *CS* G 205 (anonymous and attributed variously to Didymus and Cyril); Isidore of Pelusium, *Epp.* 1. 43; Ambrose, *Abr.* 1. 83; Jerome, *Ep.* 65. 10; Augustine, *Hept.* 1. 62; *Civ.* 16. 33.

[205] *CS* G 209. Diodore, *C. Cois.* 208, cites the opinion of his master.

[206] Cf. Chrysostom, *Hom. in Gen.* 48. 2 (*PG* 54. 436), who claims that in the Hebrew (ἐν τῇ Ἑβραΐδι [sc. γλώττῃ]) we find the equivalent of the word ὀσφῦς. This seems in fact to reflect the Peshitta.

[207] See Rahmer, *Die hebräischen Traditionen*, p. 37, and Ginzberg, 'Die Haggada' (*MGWJ* 43), p. 532. In addition to *T. Ps.-J.*, they cite *Ber. R.* 59. 8 (on this

may be dependent on a Greek source here, for we find a close reflection of his comment in an anonymous *catena* fragment.[208] Nevertheless, he seems to have been unwilling to read such an interpretation into the text. Indeed, he retains the translation 'femur' in *IH*.

In short, Jerome seems to have been sceptical concerning readings attributed by Eusebius and Diodore to ὁ Ἑβραῖος.[209]

Thus, while it may be accepted that Jerome was influenced by Antiochene use of non-Septuagint texts, he did not share the Antiochene approach with regard to the evaluation and use of those texts. In particular, he had serious reservations about the manner in which the Hebrew text was interpreted by them.[210]

Finally, despite their citations of ὁ Σύρος and various 'Hebrew' readings, Eusebius and Diodore continue to rely heavily on the LXX. Some of Jerome's comments in *QHG* seem to constitute criticism of such reliance. In Gen. 47: 30, it is related that Joseph promised his father Jacob that he would return his body to Canaan for burial. According to the following verse, Jacob makes his son

passage see the note in the edition of Theodor and Albeck (above, n. 89), p. 636), and *Tan. B.* Chaye Sarah 6. Cf. also the allusions to the tradition in *T. Frag.* Gen. 24: 2 and *CN* Gen. 24: 9.

[208] *CS* G 207. In one branch of the tradition this fragment is connected to *CS* G 205 (above, n. 204), in which branch, however, the latter fragment is anonymous. Nevertheless, that the two belong together is supported by Jerome's comment in *QHG* 24: 9. For in addition to reporting the Jewish tradition, he also mentions the Christian interpretation, according to which the servant swore by the seed of Abraham, whence Christ was descended. And in this context he cites Mt. 1: 1, a text also cited in *CS* G 205.

[209] On Jerome and ὁ Ἑβραῖος, see also Field, i, pp. lxxvi–lxxvii.

[210] The preceding pages do not constitute a complete treatment of all the points of contact between the Antiochenes' use of 'Hebrew' material and *QHG*. Other passages which *might* reflect the dependence of Jerome on the Antiochenes (or Greek scholarship generally) include *QHG* 28: 19; 31: 46–7; 38: 29. Compare these passages with *C. Cois.* 235 and 237; Procopius, *Comm. in Gen.* 31: 47 (*PG* 87. 452b) and the scholion printed in Field, i, p. 47 n. 24; and *C. Cois.* 267. On the other hand, passages which may reflect the independence of Jerome or criticism of Antiochene readings or comments include *QHG* 2: 23; 6: 14; 24: 62–3; 36: 24. Compare these passages with *C. Cois.* 100; Procopius, *Comm. in Gen.* 6: 14–15 (*PG* 87. 273a) and the scholion cited by Wevers, ad Gen. 6: 14; Procopius, *Comm. in Gen.* 24: 63 (*PG* 87. 401b); and *C. Cois.* 258. Nor should this list be seen as comprehensive. Indeed, a new investigation of the relationship between 'Hebrew' readings cited in the entire Greek tradition and the Hebrew text as understood by Jerome remains to be done.

swear: εἶπεν δέ "Ομοσόν μοι. καὶ ὤμοσεν αὐτῷ. καὶ προσεκύνησεν Ἰσραὴλ ἐπὶ τὸ ἄκρον τῆς ῥάβδου αὐτοῦ. Eusebius appears to have understood from these words that Jacob performed an act of obeisance before the rod of Joseph, that is to say, he was paying homage to the symbol of Joseph's regal power. Such an act would border on idolatry, and Eusebius also mentions the view of 'others', who seem to have been sensitive to this problem. According to their view, the rod was not a sceptre which belonged to Joseph, but a cane which belonged to Jacob. When Joseph swore his oath, Jacob bowed his head, which quite naturally tilted towards his cane.[211] Later Antiochene exegetes appear to have had reservations about the interpretation of Eusebius, for they prefer the explanation of the 'others' or elaborations of it. Indeed Diodore, after noting the ambiguity of the sentence, mentions the possibility that Jacob was bowing down to God while leaning on [his?] rod (*C. Cois.* 291). This view is endorsed by Gennadius, who refuses to accept that an act of obeisance to the sceptre [of Joseph] is indicated, and cites the wording of the Greek text in support of his position: οὐδὲ γὰρ οὕτω γέγραπται, ὅτι προσεκύνησε τῷ ἄκρῳ τῆς ῥάβδου αὐτοῦ, ἀλλά, "προσεκύνησεν ἐπὶ τὸ ἄκρον τῆς ῥάβδου αὐτοῦ".[212]

Jerome prefers a simpler approach. He completely rejects the idea of Eusebius, eliminating the rod altogether by reference to the Hebrew:

Et in hoc loco quidam frustra simulant adorasse Jacob summitatem sceptri Joseph, quod videlicet honorans filium potestatem eius adoraverit, cum in Hebraeo multo aliter legatur: 'et adoravit' inquit, 'Israhel ad caput lectuli', quod scilicet, postquam iuraverit ei filius, securus de petitione, quam rogaverat, adorarit Deum contra caput lectuli sui. (*QHG* 47: 31)

Jerome arrives at an interpretation similar to that of the later Antiochenes but more efficaciously: he need not concern himself

---

[211] See Devreesse, *Les anciens commentateurs*, p. 79. Cf. Procopius, *Comm. in Gen.* 47: 31 (*PG* 87. 483–4c). The 'others' were apparently reading the last word of the verse as αὐτοῦ rather than αὐτοῦ, despite its position. Cf. Augustine, *Hept.* 1. 162.

[212] *C. Cois.* 289. He may be repeating in clearer form an argument employed by the 'others' cited by Eusebius. See Devreesse, loc. cit. Theodoret, *Qu. in Gen.* 111, while stating that the rod was Jacob's cane, was willing to allow that the father performed an act of προσκύνησις before his son. It is not clear whether Chrysostom, *Hom. in Gen.* 66. 2 (*PG* 54. 567–8), is expressing a view similar to that of Theodoret, or is following Eusebius of Emesa.

with the meaning of the rod. Augustine in fact, while refusing to abandon the LXX, notes that the Hebrew solution is said to be 'facillima' (*Hept.* 1. 162).

In claiming that in the Hebrew text we read the equivalent of the word 'bed', Jerome is following the *recentiores*, who render the Hebrew word מטה with κλίνη.[213] This Hebrew word, when vocalized differently, can also mean 'staff'. In *QHG* 48: 2, however, Jerome takes the LXX to task for translating the word as 'lectulus' in Gen. 48: 2, yet 'virga' in Gen. 47: 31. In other words, it was the context or *consequentia* of the text that served as his criterion in deciding which version(s) represented the 'Hebrew' in Gen. 47: 31.[214]

In the Greek text of Gen. 3: 24, we read that God expelled Adam from the Garden of Eden but established his abode near the Garden:

καὶ ἐξέβαλεν τὸν Ἀδὰμ καὶ κατῴκισεν αὐτὸν ἀπέναντι τοῦ παραδείσου τῆς τρυφῆς, καὶ ἔταξεν τὰ χερουβὶμ καὶ τὴν φλογίνην ρομφαίαν τὴν στρεφομένην φυλάσσειν τὴν ὁδὸν τοῦ ξύλου τῆς ζωῆς.

In the original Hebrew text, however, we find a slightly different formulation:

ויגרש את האדם וישכן מקדם לגן עדן את הכרבים ואת להט החרב המתהפכת לשמֹר את דרך עץ החיים:

According to Eusebius of Emesa, God placed Adam next to the Garden for a specific purpose, namely, that by constantly looking upon his former home Adam would remember his expulsion and forewarn his sons.[215] Chrysostom sees the placing of Adam's abode near the Garden as a sign of God's goodness. For his place of residence could serve as a reminder of his previous experience, and deter him from further sin (*Hom. in Gen.* 18. 3 (*PG* 53. 152)). For Theodore of Mopsuestia as well, that God allowed Adam to live near the Garden rather than banishing him to some remote place was an act of mercy, in that it afforded him a hope of

---

[213] See the second apparatus of Wevers, ad loc.; *C. Cois.* 290.

[214] For the criterion of *consequentia* in the interpretation of the Hebrew text, see *Ruf.* 1. 20, and below, p. 181.

[215] See Devreesse, *Les anciens commentateurs*, p. 62. The exact purport of the words of Eusebius is not altogether clear. See the manner in which his view is reflected in Procopius, *Comm. in Gen.* 3: 24 (*PG* 87. 228c), and in Ishodad of Merv, *Comm. in Gen.* 3: 23–4.

re-entering.[216] In the view of Jerome, however, none of these interpretations could be valid. Although he does not mention the various Greek interpretations, he points out that according to the Hebrew text, it was not Adam that God installed next to the Garden of Eden, but only the cherubim and the fiery sword.[217]

In their use of the LXX, Greek scholars from the time of Origen onwards placed heavy emphasis on close analysis of the linguistic features of that version. On the one hand, they applied to the Greek Bible the standard techniques of grammatical and rhetorical analysis employed in the exegesis of secular works of literature.[218] On the other hand, they were also aware that the Bible was a translation from the Hebrew and had to be seen as a literary work *sui generis*. Accordingly, they often point out linguistic and stylistic peculiarities which appear to be unique to the Bible. These peculiarities came to be ascribed to the συνήθεια τῆς γραφῆς and were identified as ἰδιώματα τῆς γραφῆς.[219]

In the fourth and early fifth centuries, the Antiochene Fathers, Eusebius of Emesa, Diodore of Tarsus, and above all Theodore of Mopsuestia, were the major exponents of this philologically oriented exegesis.[220] In particular, the treatment of the ἰδιώματα was refined by Diodore and Theodore. Many of these were identified in a more specific fashion as ἰδιώματα Ἑβραϊκά, i.e. 'Hebraisms'.[221] Theodore was especially articulate concerning this

---

[216] See Devreesse, op. cit., p. 176, and the (French translation of the) Syriac fragments published by R. M. Tonneau, *Muséon* 66 (1953), p. 62. Cf. also Didymus, *Comm. in Gen.* 3: 23–4 (112. 24–113. 5); 4: 16 (136. 7–11); Cyril of Jerusalem, *Catech.* 2. 7; Augustine, *Gen. Man.* 2. 34.

[217] *QHG* 3: 24. It would appear from *Cher.* 1, 11, that Philo had a Greek text which did not contain the pronoun αὐτόν and was thus a closer reflection of the Hebrew. While this text is also attested in various MSS of the LXX (see the apparatus of Wevers, ad loc.), it does not seem to have been used by later Greek exegetes.

[218] Origen's contributions in this regard have been best described by Neuschäfer, *Origenes*.

[219] See Neuschäfer, op. cit., pp. 143–5; G. J. M. Bartelink, *VigChr* 17 (1963), pp. 85, 93.

[220] The most important recent study of this aspect of Antiochene exegesis is Schäublin, *Untersuchungen*. However, he has not given adequate consideration to the influence of Eusebius of Emesa.

[221] With regard to Diodore, see the passages from the *Commentarii in Psalmos* (attributed to him by L. Mariès and others) cited by Mariès, *Études préliminaires à l'édition de Diodore de Tarse sur les Psaumes*, Paris 1933, pp. 106–8, and cf. the introduction to the edition of that text by J.-M. Olivier (Turnhout 1980 = CChr.SG 6), pp. xcvi–xcviii. With regard to Theodore, see Schäublin, *Untersuchungen*, pp. 127–36.

subject, and in the introduction to his *Comm. in Ps.*, he seems to have produced a sort of catalogue of ἰδιώματα.[222] The ἰδιώματα were also treated in a systematic form by Hadrian in his *Introductio in sacras scripturas*, a work which should probably be dated to the first half of the fifth century.[223] In the West, a similar method was employed by Augustine in his *Locutiones in Heptateuchum*.[224] However, as Devreesse and Schäublin have noted, in the case of Theodore, the identification of ἰδιώματα τῆς γραφῆς or ἰδιώματα Ἑβραϊκά was not based on a knowledge of Hebrew, but rather on a close analysis of the Greek of the LXX.[225] Indeed, that Theodore pursued this approach is not surprising, since we have already seen at the end of Chapter 1 that he regarded the LXX as superior to other versions because it represented the original in a most accurate fashion. In other words, for him the best practical way to arrive at the Hebrew was via a close study of the LXX.

These approaches were of course known to Jerome, and in particular the concept of 'consuetudo scripturarum' is not unimportant in his works.[226] However, while Jerome was indebted to his predecessors, he was also able to go beyond these methods as they were employed by the Greeks. Indeed, since it is the purpose of this study to identify the 'elementi geronimiani in Girolamo', it must be noted that Jerome's use of the Hebrew text often stands in contrast to the exploitation of Greek grammatical/rhetorical exegesis and the phenomenon of the ἰδιώματα or 'locutiones scripturarum'. Particularly valuable in this regard is *QHG*, for in this work we find Jerome employing 'solutiones Hebraicae' concerning problems which the Antiochenes solve by using grammatical/rhetorical solutions or by appealing to the ἰδιώματα or 'locutiones' of the Bible as they appear in Greek. This point should become clear from the following examples.

In Gen. 3: 1, we read a simple description of the serpent: ὁ δὲ ὄφις ἦν φρονιμώτατος [v.l. φρονιμώτερος] πάντων τῶν θηρίων τῶν ἐπὶ

---

[222] See Devreesse, *Essai*, p. 58.

[223] On this work, see the introduction of F. Goessling in his edition of the text (Berlin 1887), and Bardenhewer, *Geschichte*, iv, pp. 254–5.

[224] On this work, see W. Süss, *Studien zur lateinischen Bibel*, i. *Augustins Locutiones und das Problem der lateinischen Bibelsprache* (*Acta et commentationes universitatis Tartuensis (Dorpatensis)* B 29. 4), Tartu 1932.

[225] Devreesse, loc. cit. (n. 222 above); Schäublin, *Untersuchungen*, pp. 127, 136. Cf. also above, Ch. 2 n. 23.

[226] See Meershoek, *Le latin*, pp. 64–5, and the following section of the book. But cf. also Schäublin, *Untersuchungen*, pp. 127–8 n. 172.

τῆς γῆς (*VL*: 'serpens autem erat sapientior [v.l. prudentior, sapientissimus] omnium bestiarum quae erant super terram'). This characterization caused a problem for commentators, viz. how could a notoriously evil creature be regarded as 'wise' or 'prudent'? Such questions are typical of ζητήματα literature. At *Iliad* 3. 16, 27, 30, 37, Paris is described as θεοειδής. The exegetes ask διὰ τί δὲ θεοειδέα φησὶ τὸν πάσαις κακίαις χρώμενον;[227]

Yet, in the present case, the issue was not a purely literary one. According to the testimony of Irenaeus, *Haer.* 1. 30. 15, the description of the serpent in Gen. 3: 1 was exploited by some Ophite groups in their advocacy of the worship of that animal. And we know from legal texts that these sectaries were not without influence as late as the fifth and sixth centuries.[228] That Christian commentators were still concerned with refuting their doctrines in exegetical works is clear from Diodore's comment on Gen. 3: 7, where he argues vigorously against those heretics who would interpret the words, 'the eyes of both [sc. Adam and Eve] were opened', as favourable to the serpent.[229]

In approaching the description of the serpent as φρονιμώτατος, the Antiochenes rely on standard Greek grammatical techniques of exegesis. Diodore, for example, explains that the adjective refers not to τὸ συνετόν, but rather to τὸ πρὸς ἀπάτην ἐπιτήδειον ὄργανον (*C. Cois.* 103). As Schäublin has shown, this λύσις, which is attained via the attempt to change the object of reference of the adjective, is paralleled in pagan philological literature.[230] Indeed, in going on and justifying such an interpretation, Diodore cites a parallel, popular (as opposed to proper or grammatical), usage. That is, he appeals to τὸ ἔθος τῆς λέξεως, a concept often invoked by pagan λυτικοί.[231]

Theodoret, on the other hand, with a slightly different nuance, claims that the adjective φρόνιμος need not have positive connotations: πολλὰ τῶν ὀνομάτων ὁμωνύμως προφέρεται· καὶ γὰρ τὰ εἴδωλα

[227] Porphyry, *Ad Iliadem* Γ. 16–49. Cf. Theodoret, *Qu. in II Reg.* 28: τὸν Ἰωνάθαν [v.l. Ἰωναδὰβ] τοῦ Σαμαὰ τὸν υἱὸν τί δήποτε φρόνιμον ὠνόμασε, τοιαύταις χρησάμενον συμβουλίαις;
[228] See *Novellae Theodosii II* 3; *Codex Justinianus* 1. 5. 5, 19, 21. On the Ophites generally, see É. Amann, *DThC* 11. 1 (1931), cols. 1063–75.
[229] *C. Cois.* 109. See Petit's note, ad loc.; Schweizer, *ZNW* 40 (1941), p. 51 n. 109.
[230] *Untersuchungen*, pp. 60–1. Cf. also Theodoret, *Qu. in II Reg.* 28.
[231] See Carroll, *Aristotle's Poetics*, pp. 48–51, and below, p. 168.

τῶν ἐθνῶν θεοὺς ὠνομάκασι. . . . τοιγάρτοι κἀνταῦθα φρόνιμον τὸν ὄφιν ὡς πανοῦργον ὠνόμασεν· οὕτω γὰρ καὶ ὁ Ἀκύλας ἡρμήνευσεν· "καὶ ὁ ὄφις ἦν πανοῦργος ἀπὸ παντὸς ζῴου τῆς χώρας" (*Qu. in Gen.* 31). The solution to the problem lies in an appeal to the phenomenon of ὁμωνυμία, according to which different objects or concepts are indicated by the same word.[232] Consequently, φρόνιμος need not be used of one who is virtuous. In the present case, this is confirmed by reference to the version of Aquila. However, Theodoret employs the later translation not to arrive at an understanding of the original text, but as a guide to the context; that is, to confirm that the LXX employ the term φρόνιμος in a negative sense.[233]

We find related solutions in other Greek texts, specifically in some discussions of Proverbs 1: 2, where the term φρόνησις appears. In a comment attributed to Origen, the author takes as his point of departure the Stoic definition of φρόνησις, according to which the word is to be understood as ἐπιστήμη ἀγαθῶν καὶ κακῶν καὶ οὐθετέρων.[234] He proposes to check the usage of the word in Scripture, however, to determine πότερον πολύσημος ἡ λέξις, ἢ ἓν σημαίνει πρᾶγμα. He begins with Gen. 3: 1:

πρῶτον μὲν οὖν ἐν τῇ Γενέσει, κατὰ μὲν τοὺς Ἑβδομήκοντα, γέγραπται· "ὁ δὲ ὄφις ἦν φρονιμώτατος", κατὰ δὲ Ἀκύλαν, πανοῦργος, κατὰ δὲ Σύμμαχον, πανουργότατος· οὐκοῦν ὅσον ἐπὶ ταύτῃ τῇ λέξει τῶν Ἑβδομήκοντα λέγοι τις ἄν, ὅτι οὐκ ἔστιν ἀρετὴ ἡ φρόνησις· οὐδὲ γὰρ ὁ ὄφις εἶχεν ἀρετήν, πανουργίαν δέ, ἣν καὶ ψέγει τις κακεντρέχειάν τινα ὑπάρχουσαν. αὕτη φρόνησις νῦν νενόηται τοῖς Ἑβδομήκοντα, παρ' ἣν ὁ πανοῦργος φρόνιμος λέλεκται.[235]

In this passage, the author employs Gen. 3: 1 in order to show that the term φρόνησις has more than one meaning: it is πολύσημος, and need not denote a virtue in every case. Here again, the focus is on determining the meaning of the Greek word as it is employed by the LXX, and the version of Aquila is employed in order to illuminate that issue. Although the writer does not formally address the question of how the serpent can be called φρόνιμος in

---

[232] See Aristotle, *Categoriae* 1 (1ᵃ1–6); Dionysius Thrax, *Ars grammatica* 12 (ed. G. Uhlig, Leipzig 1883 (= Grammatici Graeci 1. 1), p. 36); Quintilian, *Institutio oratoria* 7. 9. 2; 8. 2. 13.

[233] Cf. now Simonetti, *Annali di storia dell'esegesi* 5 (1988), p. 46.

[234] See H. von Arnim, ed., *Stoicorum veterum fragmenta*, iii, Leipzig 1903, frs. 262, 265, 266, 598. The definition is attested in Christian literature. See Gregory Thaumaturgus, *Pan. Or.* 9, and the passage from Basil cited below, n. 236.

[235] *Fr. in Pr.* 1: 1 (1: 2) (*PG* 17. 149d–152a). Concerning the authenticity of this text, see *CPG*, i (1983), p. 155.

Gen. 3: 1, how he would answer that question is clear from the manner in which he interprets that verse in the present context. Basil the Great, however, in a discussion of Proverbs 1: 2 which may be related to the present passage, does indeed pose the question about the serpent, and answers that the word φρόνησις is διπλοῦν (that is, it has two meanings), and that in the case of the serpent it is used with a negative connotation.[236]

The terminology employed in the fragment attributed to Origen is equivalent to that used by Theodoret. For already Democritus employs both the words πολύσημος and ὁμωνυμία when referring to the same phenomenon.[237] It will be clear that the former term describes the words (i.e. φωναί, λέξεις), whereas the latter term (at least logically or originally) describes the phenomenon from the point of view of the objects indicated (i.e. πράγματα).[238] This issue of words with many meanings aroused considerable interest among scholars, and we find in both pagan and Christian literature actual surveys of the various meanings of different Greek words.[239] Indeed, Orus dedicated an entire book to the subject, which had the title Περὶ πολυσημάντων λέξεων.[240]

That this phenomenon was quite relevant in the interpretation of difficult texts is obvious. Origen, in some of his discussions preserved in the *Philocalia*, emphasizes how important it is for

---

[236] *Hom.* 12. 6 (*PG* 31. 397c–400a, cf. 1767c–68b). For the idea of a 'double' φρόνησις, cf. *Reg. Br.* 239 (*PG* 31. 1241c–d). The view that the term φρόνησις or φρόνιμος may have negative connotations in certain biblical passages is also expressed by various writers without detailed, technical explanations. See, e.g., Origen, *Fr. in Lc.* 200 (GCS 49, pp. 312–13); *Hom. in Jer.* 17. 3; Jerome, *Comm. in Jer.* 1. 85. 2–3; *Ruf.* 1. 24; 3. 7.

[237] *FVS*, ii (1952⁶), p. 148, fr. 26.

[238] Similarly, Aristotle, loc. cit. (n. 232 above), uses the adjective ὁμώνυμος of things which share a common designation. In other texts, however, the term is used of words, and therefore effectively has the same sense as πολύσημος. See (the transmitted text of) Dionysius Thrax, loc. cit. (n. 232); Quintilian, *Inst.* 8. 2. 13 (on this text, cf. H. Lausberg, *Handbuch der literarischen Rhetorik*³, Stuttgart 1990, pp. 513, 716). Both uses of the adjective are also found in patristic literature. See *PGL*, s.v. ὁμώνυμος, 2, 3.

[239] See Porphyry, *Ad Iliadem H.* 298; Θ. 1; *Scholia in Platonis Rempublicam* 521e (ed. G.(W.) C. Greene, Haverford, Pa. 1938 (= Philological Monographs Published by the American Philological Association 8), p. 248). For Christian texts, see Origen, *Comm. in Jo.* 1. 90–108; the passage from *Comm. in Rom.* cited in *Philoc.* 9. 1–2; Ps.-Hippolytus, *Fr. in Pr.* 32 (GCS 1. 2, p. 169); Eusebius, *E. th.* 2. 13 (cf. Jerome, *Ep.* 53. 4).

[240] On this work, see R. Reitzenstein, *Geschichte der griechischen Etymologika*, Leipzig 1897, pp. 335 ff.

readers of the Bible to have a knowledge of ὁμωνυμίαι.²⁴¹ Such a knowledge was of course particularly useful in dealing with apparently contradictory or offensive passages. For by invoking ὁμωνυμία the exegete could disallow meanings which might give rise to these and other types of προβλήματα. Already Aristotle gives the following advice to potential λυτικοί: δεῖ δὲ καὶ ὅταν ὄνομά τι ὑπεναντίωμά τι δοκῇ σημαίνειν, ἐπισκοπεῖν ποσαχῶς ἂν σημήνειε τοῦτο ἐν τῷ εἰρημένῳ (*Poetica* 25 (1461ᵃ31–3)). And, in fact, the appeal to ὁμωνυμία is well attested in the λύσεις found in the Homeric scholia.²⁴² In their attempts to solve the problem of the description of the serpent in Gen. 3: 1, Christian scholars have employed the same technique with reference to the Greek word φρόνιμος.

We find a related 'grammatical' solution to the problem in the work of Augustine. In explaining how the serpent could be called 'sapientissimus', he writes as follows: 'abusione quippe nominis ita sapientia dicitur in malo, quemadmodum in bono astutia, cum proprie magisque usitate in Latina dumtaxat lingua sapientes laudabiliter appellentur, astuti autem male cordati intellegantur' (*Gen. litt.* 11. 2; cf. *Serm.* 46. 28). In other words, Augustine believes that the word 'sapientissimus' should be translated not 'most wise', but 'most cunning', and justifies this interpretation through reference to the concept of *abusio*, that is, abuse of language. Elsewhere he explains the reverse phenomenon, and claims that in secular as well as in biblical literature words which in their proper sense denote vices are used 'by abuse of language' to indicate virtues: 'pleni sunt tamen libri eorum [sc. of the pagans], cum abusione istorum nominum, quae proprie vitia significant, etiam virtutes sic appellantur, cum vel cupiditas pro voluntate vel laetitia pro gaudio vel metus pro cautione vel misericordia pro clementia vel astutia pro prudentia vel audacia pro fiducia ponitur' (*Faust.* 22. 18).

What is the basis of this solution? From the philosophical perspective, the idea that the virtues and vices are related goes back to Aristotle, *Nicomachean Ethics* 2–5, where many 'moral' virtues and vices are characterized as the mean and extremes respectively

---

²⁴¹ See *Comm. in Gen.* 1: 16–18 (= *Philoc.* 14. 2); the passage from *Comm. in Rom.* cited in *Philoc.* 9. 3. Cf. Clement, *Ecl.* 32; Acacius, in Devreesse, *Les anciens commentateurs*, pp. 109–10.

²⁴² For a discussion of the passage from Aristotle, and examples of λύσεις based on ὁμωνυμία in the Homeric scholia, see Carroll, *Aristotle's Poetics*, pp. 51–5.

of the same essential quality or tendency. However, φρόνησις is not among the virtues listed, and Aristotle describes it in quite a different manner in *Nicomachean Ethics* 6, classifying it as an 'intellectual' virtue. On the other hand, in the transmitted text of *Eudemian Ethics* 2. 3 (1221ᵃ12), φρόνησις does appear as the mean between πανουργία and εὐήθεια. Philo also describes φρόνησις as the mean between πανουργία and μωρία.²⁴³ And, indeed, Origen applies this same distinction in solving the problem raised by the description of the serpent as φρόνιμος in Gen. 3: 1. However, he employs a text in which the adjective is given in the comparative rather than the superlative form, and emerges with the following solution: 'prudentia si in sua mensura sit, virtus est; si minus habeat, imprudentia; si plusquam oportet, malitia appellatur. inde puto quod et serpens in paradiso prudentior dictus sit caeteris bestiis, hoc est excedens mensuram prudentiae, et in partes malitiae prolapsus.'²⁴⁴ Thus Origen's solution is based on the same philosophical concept as that of Augustine. But he arrives at it by citing the use of the comparative form of the adjective, claiming essentially that it should be rendered 'excessively prudent'.

Augustine, on the other hand, appeals not to a comparative form, but to an 'abusive' use of the adjective. As Quintilian explains, the term *abusio* is the Latin word for what the Greeks call κατάχρησις (*Institutio oratoria* 8. 6. 34). In the strict sense, as defined by Tryphon,

κατάχρησίς ἐστι λέξις μετενηνεγμένη ἀπὸ τοῦ πρώτου κατονομασθέντος κυρίως τε καὶ ἐτύμως ἐφ᾽ ἕτερον ἀκατονόμαστον κατὰ τὸ οἰκεῖον, οἷον γόνυ καλάμου, καὶ ὀφθαλμὸς ἀμπέλου . . . κυρίως γὰρ ταῦτα ἐπὶ ἀνθρώπου λέγονται. . . . διαφέρει δὲ μεταφορὰ καὶ κατάχρησις, ὅτι ἡ μὲν μεταφορὰ ἀπὸ κατονομαζομένου ἐπὶ κατονομαζόμενον λέγεται, ἡ δὲ κατάχρησις ἀπὸ κατονομαζομένου ἐπὶ ἀκατονόμαστον, ὅθεν καὶ κατάχρησις λέγεται.²⁴⁵

According to this definition, however, the phenomenon noted by Augustine does not appear to qualify as κατάχρησις. The use of a term for a vice to indicate a virtue, or the reverse, does not

²⁴³ *Imm.* 164. Cf. R. Arnaldez in his edition of Philo, *Opif.* (Paris 1961 = Les œuvres de Philon d'Alexandrie 1), pp. 244–5 n. 4.

²⁴⁴ *Comm. in Rom.* 9. 2 (*PG* 14. 1210a–b). Cf. Jerome, *Comm. in Is.* 16 (57: 10).

²⁴⁵ *De tropis*, ed. L. Spengel, *Rhetores Graeci*, iii, Leipzig 1856, pp. 192–3. This text is that of the so-called 'Tryphon I'. For the definition of 'Tryphon II', see the edition published by M. West, *CQ* 15 (1965), p. 238. Cf. Ps.-Plutarch, *De vita et poesi Homeri* 2. 18, and the other texts noted by K. Barwick, *Probleme der stoischen Sprachlehre und Rhetorik* (*ASAW.PH* 49. 3), Berlin 1957, pp. 90–1.

constitute the 'transfer' of a word from its proper object to an object which in itself is nameless. Proper designations exist both for the vices and for the virtues. Indeed Aristotle, when referring to the interchange of terms denoting vices and virtues described by Augustine, uses the word μεταφορά, not κατάχρησις (*Eth. Nic.* 3. 6 (1115ᵃ14–16)).

Nevertheless, that the manner of expression specified by Augustine was termed κατάχρησις by some people is acknowledged by Quintilian: 'illa quoque quidam catachresis volunt esse, cum pro temeritate virtus aut pro luxuria liberalitas dicitur' (*Inst.* 8. 6. 36). And, in fact, K. Barwick has shown that while the definition of Tryphon goes back to Stoic theory, the later (i.e. post-Aristotelian) Peripatetics had a broader view of κατάχρησις and did not limit their use of the term to cases of 'necessary abuse'. One could apply it even when there already existed an appellation for that which was indicated by the 'abused' word, and thus *abusio* was another term for metaphor in the broad sense. We read the following definition in the *Rhetorica ad Herennium* 4. 45: 'abusio est, quae verbo simili et propinquo pro certo et proprio abutitur.'²⁴⁶ That the exchange of terms indicating vices and virtues as described by Augustine and Quintilian accords with this definition will be clear from the words of the former addressed to his antagonist Julian: 'sed videlicet homo eruditus eorum vitiorum veri similitudine falleris, quae finitima videntur et *propinqua* virtutibus, cum absint ab eis quam longe absunt a virtutibus vitia. nam sicut constantia est virtus, cui contraria est inconstantia: vitium est tamen ei quasi finitimum pertinacia, quae constantiam videtur imitari.'²⁴⁷ Accordingly, when Augustine explains the description of the serpent in Gen. 3: 1 as an 'abuse of language', he employs the term *abusio* in the broader, later Peripatetic sense.²⁴⁸

Origen as well might have regarded the usage cited by Augustine as a catachresis. For in his *Comm. in Jo.* 32. 179–80, he formulates

²⁴⁶ See Barwick, loc. cit. and pp. 95–7, for discussion and additional texts. See also the remarks of G. Calboli in his edition of the *Rhetorica ad C. Herennium* (Edizioni e saggi universitari di filologia classica 11), Bologna 1969, pp. 390–1.

²⁴⁷ *Jul.* 4. 20. It will be clear from this passage, *Faust.* 22. 18, and the foregoing discussion generally that P. Agaësse and A. Solignac, in their translation of *Gen. litt.* ([Paris] 1972 = BAug 49), p. 553, are incorrect in identifying the *translatio* to which Augustine appeals in *Gen. litt.* 11. 2 with antiphrasis as described in *Doct. Chr.* 3. 41.

²⁴⁸ In *Doct. Chr.* 3. 40, on the other hand, Augustine may be dependent on the Stoic view, according to which μεταφορά and κατάχρησις are to be distinguished.

the general principle that when one possesses a virtue in incomplete form, one may be described as having that virtue only by
catachresis.[249] In the same passage, however, Origen indicates that
in view of such catachreses the words denoting the virtues must
be regarded as homonymous, since they indicate the virtues in
their true forms and in their 'approximate' forms. Thus, he would
probably use the terms κατάχρησις and ὁμωνυμία when referring to
the same phenomenon. The relevance of this point in the present
discussion is that it raises the question of the relationship between
the solution of Theodoret, the author of the *catena* fragment,
and Basil, based on ὁμωνυμία, and that of Augustine, based on
κατάχρησις.[250] The two concepts are not identical. Rather,
κατάχρησις seems to have been regarded as one form of ὁμωνυμία.
Clement, for example, notes that ὁμώνυμα may be classified as ἀπὸ
τύχης (i.e. coincidental), ἀπὸ διανοίας (in turn classified as καθ'
ὁμοιότητα, κατὰ ἀναλογίαν, and κατ' ἐνέργειαν), and ἀπὸ τοῦ αὐτοῦ
καὶ πρὸς τὸ αὐτό.[251] Within this scheme, κατάχρησις would be
regarded as a form of ὁμωνυμία ἀπὸ διανοίας, as will be clear from
the definitions of that term cited above from the *De tropis* of
Tryphon and from the *Rhetorica ad Herennium*.[252] The implication

---

[249] Cf. the remarks of Harl, op. cit. (Ch. 1 n. 44), pp. 130–1 n. 2. It emerges
from some of the passages cited by her that the concept of κατάχρησις is often used
by Origen when he justifies the use of the same word(s) to indicate both a divine/
spiritual reality and a human/material reality when it is appropriate to only one.
Accordingly, he regards such catachreses as examples of 'necessary abuse',
resulting from the inadequacy or poverty of language. In this respect, his employ-
ment of the concept follows Stoic lines (cf. Neuschäfer, *Origenes*, pp. 222, 453 n.
603), and differs somewhat from the manner in which it is used by Augustine in
the passages cited (cf., however, the additional statement in *Jul*. 4. 20: 'nec istorum
vitiorum, quae finitima virtutibus diximus, possunt *omnium* facile nomina reper-
iri'). On the functional role of κατάχρησις in Origen generally, see now Neuschäfer,
pp. 221–3.

[250] Further on in the *catena* fragment concerning Prov. 1: 2 cited above, p. 161,
we do find the term καταχρηστικός used in the discussion of another passage
which is quoted in order to show that the word φρόνιμος need not have a
positive connotation, namely, Luke 16: 8a. This passage is given as follows: καὶ
ἐπαινέσας ὁ κύριος τὸν οἰκονόμον τῆς ἀδικίας, ὅτι φρονίμως ἐποίησε. However, the term
is used with reference to the word ἐπαινέσας, not φρονίμως (*PG* 17. 152b). Cf. the
fragment printed in *PG* 13. 20b.

[251] *Str*. 8. 24. 8–9. See Harl, *VigChr* 26 (1972), pp. 165–6 n. 14, who also
discusses the Aristotelian origin of the distinction.

[252] Cf. Harl, loc. cit. That Origen does express himself more explicitly concerning these distinctions than Harl allows (cf. also her remarks in op. cit. (Ch. 1
n. 44), pp. 129–30) is perhaps suggested by the passage from *Comm. in Rom*.
preserved in *Philoc*. 9. 3. In this passage, after noting that in Scripture the same
words may indicate different things (basically the manner in which he describes

of all of this is that both the solution of Augustine and that of Theodoret and Basil could be viewed as being based on ὁμωνυμία. However, they have been treated separately not because the phenomenon cited by Theodoret and Basil should be regarded as ὁμωνυμία ἀπὸ τύχης and that cited by Augustine as ὁμωνυμία ἀπὸ διανοίας and καθ' ὁμοιότητα, but rather because Theodoret and Basil appeal to the concept of ὁμωνυμία without further discussion or classification.[253]

All of these 'grammatical' or 'grammatical/philosophical' solutions, however, stand in sharp contrast to that of Jerome, which is grounded in the Hebrew text: 'pro sapiente in Hebraeo habet arom, quod Aquila et Theodotion πανοῦργον interpretati sunt, hoc est nequam et versipellem. magis itaque ex hoc verbo calliditas et versutia quam sapientia demonstratur' (*QHG* 3: 1). By means of this "λύσις Hebraica", Jerome dispenses with the Greek and Latin 'grammatical' solutions. He considers the Hebrew word itself, claiming that it carries no connotation of wisdom or virtue. The *recentiores* are employed not to confirm a solution based on a Greek philological concept, but as testimony to the meaning of the original. Indeed, no one understood this difference between the Greek and Latin solutions and that of Jerome better than Augustine himself. Although he does not mention Jerome by name, his allusion to him is clear from his remarks. For after putting forward his own solution, which, as we have said, is based on the appeal to *abusio*, he notes as follows: 'quid autem habeat Hebraea proprietas, utrum illic in malo non abusive, sed proprie possint dici et intelligi sapientes, viderint, qui eam probe noverunt' (*Gen. litt.* 11. 2).

ὁμώνυμοι φωναί in *Philoc.* 9. 1), Origen goes on to say that this may occur ὁτὲ μὲν παρὰ τὴν ὁμωνυμίαν, ὁτὲ δὲ παρὰ τὴν τροπολογίαν. In other words, he may have used the term ὁμωνυμία to indicate both the phenomenon taken as a whole and ὁμωνυμία ἀπὸ τύχης. In this case, his ὁμωνυμία παρὰ τὴν τροπολογίαν would roughly correspond to one or both of the other categories of ὁμωνυμία mentioned by Clement. If so, κατάχρησις would naturally fall within the domain of ὁμωνυμία παρὰ τὴν τροπολογίαν, since it is treated as a trope in the rhetorical treatises *De tropis*.

[253] In *Philoc.* 9. 3, the passage where Origen gives a rough listing of the various circumstances in which the same words may indicate different things (i.e. be homonymous, see preceding note), he also refers to a more inclusive, general category, namely, those passages where the context requires that a word have a sense different from that which it may have in another passage. In the explanations of Theodoret and the author of the *catena* fragment, which are based on an appeal to context, we have a reference to nothing more than this general circumstance of ὁμωνυμία.

In Gen. 19, the destruction of the cities of Sodom and Gomorrah is related. Lot, Abraham's nephew, is urged to leave by angels. Lot speaks to his sons-in-law, in order to relay the message to them:

ויצא לוט וידבר אל חתניו לקחי בנתיו ויאמר קומו צאו מן המקום הזה.

ἐξῆλθεν δὲ Λὼτ καὶ ἐλάλησεν πρὸς τοὺς γαμβροὺς αὐτοῦ τοὺς εἰληφότας τὰς θυγατέρας αὐτοῦ, καὶ εἶπεν Ἀνάστητε καὶ ἐξέλθατε ἐκ τοῦ τόπου τούτου. (Gen. 19: 14)

However, from Gen. 19: 8, it emerges that Lot's daughters are virgins, and the same is implied in Gen. 19: 30–5. How, then, can he have sons-in-law?

Already Josephus, paraphrasing this passage in *Antiquitates Judaicae* 1. 202, refers to the men as μνηστῆρες, suitors, and it may be that this passage inspired Christian exegetes. However, the latter were writing for a Bible-reading audience, whereas Josephus was not. Consequently, Christian commentators had the additional task of coming to terms with the biblical evidence itself. Eusebius of Emesa explains the use of the word γαμβρός as follows: δῆλον ὅτι τοὺς μνηστῆρας ἄνδρας καὶ γαμβροὺς καλεῖ, καθάπερ καὶ ἡ καινὴ ἄνδρα Μαρίας καλεῖ τὸν Ἰωσήφ [i.e. in Mt. 1: 16].[254] In other words, the solution is based on an appeal to an idiosyncratic usage of biblical Greek, according to which the term γαμβρός could mean more than 'son-in-law'. Already Aristotle had put forward solutions based on idiomatic usage (κατὰ τὸ ἔθος τῆς λέξεως).[255] In later times, such idiomatic usage was indicated by the term συνήθεια. This term was used to denote either everyday, popular usage, or the idiosyncratic usage of a particular author, for example Homer. Christian exegetes employed the word when referring to the peculiarities of the biblical idiom.[256] Although Eusebius does not employ this specific term here, it is clear that he is alluding to the phenomenon commonly indicated by it.

Chrysostom, on the other hand, deals with the problem of the participial construction by which the sons-in-law are further described, as well as with the word γαμβρός:

μὴ νομίσῃς ἐναντία εἶναι ταῦτα τοῖς πρότερον παρὰ τοῦ δικαίου ῥηθεῖσιν [i.e.

---

[254] *CS* G 100. Cf. Procopius, *Comm. in Gen.* 19: 14 (*PG* 87. 371–2b, Greek text in *CS*, p. 102).

[255] See Carroll, *Aristotle's Poetics*, pp. 48–51.

[256] See above, p. 158, and especially the remarks of Neuschäfer cited in n. 219.

the words of Lot in Gen. 19: 8].²⁵⁷ ἔθος γὰρ τοῦτο ἦν τοῖς παλαιοῖς πρὸ πολλοῦ τοῦ χρόνου τὰς μνηστείας ποιεῖσθαι, καὶ πολλάκις καὶ συνοικεῖν ταῖς μνηστευθείσαις, καὶ ἅμα τοῖς γονεῦσι διατρίβειν· ὃ καὶ νῦν ἐστι πολλαχοῦ γινόμενον. ἐπεὶ οὖν ἤδη τὰ τῆς μνηστείας ἐγεγόνει, διὰ τοῦτο καὶ γαμβροὺς αὐτοὺς ὀνομάζει καί φησι, "τοὺς εἰληφότας τὰς θυγατέρας αὐτοῦ"· τῇ γνώμῃ γὰρ καὶ τῇ συγκαταθέσει εἰληφότες ἦσαν. (*Hom. in Gen.* 43. 6 (*PG* 54. 403))

From the presence of the term ἔθος and the general tenor of the passage it is clear that Chrysostom is applying the type of solution which is characterized in the Homeric scholia as ἐκ τοῦ ἔθους or ἔθει. Such 'ethnographic' solutions involve an appeal to the different customs of peoples living in different places and different historical circumstances. Aristotle, for example, is said to have solved the problem of the ἀπρέπεια or unseemliness of Achilles' outrageous treatment of Hector's corpse by claiming that he was acting according to an old Thessalian custom.²⁵⁸ Ethnographic solutions were also used in Christian biblical exegesis.²⁵⁹

Jerome may also have been influenced by the paraphrase of Josephus. Yet if he was, in contrast to Eusebius of Emesa, he attempts to reconcile that interpretation not with the Greek but with the Hebrew text: 'Hebraea veritas exponenda est, in qua scribitur: "egressus est Lot et locutus est ad sponsos, qui accepturi erant filias eius". necdum ergo virgines filiae matrimonio fuerant copulatae' (*QHG* 19: 14–15). In the first place, Jerome renders the word חתן as 'sponsus'. This rendering may have been suggested by the Josephan paraphrase of this passage, but since Jerome claims that he is translating from the Hebrew it is more probable that he is relying on the Greek versions. While no attestation of the versions of the *recentiores* survives for this verse, in other passages both the LXX and the *recentoires* render the Hebrew חתן with νυμφίος as well as with γαμβρός. From this circumstance Jerome will have known that the Hebrew word could be interpreted in a wider sense than the Greek γαμβρός, and need not be understood as 'son-in-law'.²⁶⁰

---

²⁵⁷ The words ἐναντίον, ὑπεναντίον, ὑπεναντίωμα, etc., are technical terms of ζητήματα literature, and may be traced back to Aristotle. See Carroll, *Aristotle's Poetics*, pp. 21–3; Gudeman, Λύσεις, col. 2517.

²⁵⁸ For this Aristotelian solution, and on solutions ἐκ τοῦ ἔθους in general, see Carroll, *Aristotle's Poetics*, pp. 31–3.

²⁵⁹ See Schäublin, *Untersuchungen*, pp. 61–2; cf. pp. 148–9, and Neuschäfer, *Origenes*, pp. 164–5.

²⁶⁰ According to Liddell, Scott, and Stuart Jones, op. cit. (Ch. 1 n. 36), νυμφίος does not have the meaning 'betrothed', which is clearly what Jerome means by 'sponsus'. However, it would be closer to that meaning than γαμβρός. In addition,

With regard to his interpretation of the phrase לוקחי בנותיו,
Jerome is evidently aware that underneath the Greek perfect participle εἰληφότες lies the Hebrew present participle לוקחי, which is
actually timeless. Accordingly, he treats it as a future. Here again,
whether he is following the *recentiores* cannot be determined,
because of the lack of evidence. However, his interpretation of the
participle is paralleled in *Bereshit Rabba* 50. 9: 'He [sc. Lot] had
four daughters, two who were married, and two who were
betrothed, for it is not written לְקוּחֵי, but rather לוֹקְחֵי.' In this
passage, the interpreter understands the expressions חתניו and
לקְחֵי בנותיו as referring to two separate groups, and does not take
the participial phrase as attributive. The former term refers to the
sons-in-law and the latter phrase to the future sons-in-law. This
is the point behind the distinction between לְקוּחֵי and לוֹקְחֵי, and
a future sense is ascribed to the participle.[261]

However, Jerome is dependent on a source which had a form
different from that of *Ber. R.* 50. 9. In the same passage of *QHG*,
he also mentions the aggada according to which Lot had married
as well as unmarried daughters. Yet while in *Ber. R.* the aggada
is linked with the interpretation of לוֹקְחֵי as a future, Jerome sees
the aggada and the interpretation of the participle as two distinct
exegeses. Indeed, in his view the aggada owes its origin to the
interpretation of לוֹקְחֵי which is reflected in the LXX/*VL*. For
after citing the text according to the *VL*, namely, 'et locutus est
ad generos suos, qui acceperant filias eius', he writes as follows:

Quia postea duae filiae Lot virgines fuisse dicuntur, de quibus et ipse
dudum ad Sodomaeos dixerat: 'ecce duae filiae meae, quae non cogno-
verunt virum', et nunc scriptura commemorat eum habuisse generos, non
nulli arbitrantur illas, quae viros habuerant, in Sodomis remansisse, et
eas exisse cum patre, quae virgines fuerunt. (*QHG* 19: 14–15)

According to this version of the aggada, the existence of additional
married daughters is indeed deduced from Lot's words to his

the term 'sponsus' was often used to render νυμφίος. See, e.g., the Old Latin
version of Mt. 9: 15; 25: 1, 5, 6, 10; Mc. 2: 19, 20, as given in the edition of A.
Jülicher (= *Itala: Das Neue Testament in altlateinischer Überlieferung*, i². *Matthäus-
Evangelium*, Berlin 1972; ii². *Marcus-Evangelium* (1970)), and cf. the Vulgate
version of the same passages. This fact may have led Jerome to attribute a broader
sense to the Greek word.

[261] See the note in Theodor and Albeck's edition of *Ber. R.* (above, n. 89),
p. 525. Cf. Rashi, *Comm. in Pent.* ad Gen. 19: 14.

sons-in-law in Gen. 19: 14, but there is no mention of future sons-in-law in that verse, and consequently, no reference to betrothed daughters. That is to say, whereas, according to *Ber. R.* 50. 9, Lot is addressing both sons-in-law and future sons-in-law in Gen. 19: 14, according to Jerome's informants, he is addressing only sons-in-law. This is because the aggada is linked with the text as it appears in the LXX/*VL*, where although the word חתן is understood as 'son-in-law' as in *Ber. R.*, the phrase לוקחי בנותיו is interpreted as an attributive. Consequently, in the version of the aggada cited by Jerome, there is no mention of future sons-in-law or betrothed daughters at all, and the existence of virgin daughters is to be seen only in the explicit references in Gen. 19: 8, 30–5.[262]

Jerome, however, goes on to reject this aggada as lacking a basis in Scripture. He endorses the interpretation cited above, according to which the word חתן is to be rendered as 'sponsus', and the participle לוֹקְחִי is to be interpreted as future, but in an attributive sense. The reference is therefore only to the future sons-in-law of Lot's virgin daughters. In short, Jerome knew the aggada and the interpretation of the participle as two different solutions to the same problem. The aggadic solution, which is achieved through additional narrative (i.e. the supposition that Lot had married as well as unmarried daughters), obviates the need to connect the sons-in-law mentioned in Gen. 19: 14 with the daughters mentioned in Gen. 19: 8, 30–5. On the other hand, the interpretation of the participle as a future (together with the rendering of the word חתן as 'sponsus') allows such a connection. The problem of the contradiction in the biblical narrative is removed by either of the two solutions. In *Ber. R.*, on the other hand, there is an attempt to read into Gen. 19: 14 references both to the sons-in-law of the aggadic solution and to the future sons-in-law of the solution based on the interpretation of the participle. In other words, we have an attempt not only to explain a contradiction in the biblical text, but to reconcile the two solutions. This text

---

[262] The assumption that Jerome knows this tradition in a form different from that appearing in *Ber. R.* 50. 9 may be confirmed by the fact that he also mentions explicitly another detail absent from that passage, viz. that the married daughters remained in Sodom. This particular is found in other sources, e.g. *PRE* 25; *Ber. Rbti.* ad 19: 26 (ed. Albe(c)k, Jerusalem 1940, p. 82); *MHG Ber.* 19: 26 (ed. M. Margulies, Jerusalem 1947, p. 321). Cf. Theodor and Albeck, loc. cit. (n. 261 above).

therefore reflects a later stage in the history of the interpretation of the passage.[263] Indeed, that the solutions were originally distinct, in accord with the testimony of Jerome, may be confirmed by the fact that the interpretation of the participle as separate from the aggada probably underlies the paraphrase of Josephus.[264] In addition, the rendering of the text which Jerome sees as the occasion of the aggadic solution is not unique to the Greek tradition. The interpretation of the participle found in the LXX is also present in *T. Ps.-J.*, where the relevant phrase is rendered as follows: חתנויי דנסיבו ברתויי.[265] Consequently, Jerome's view of the origin of the aggada is equally valid in a Semitic setting.

In the present case, Jerome prefers the Hebrew philological solution to the aggadic solution. In this context, however, we are concerned not so much with the reasons for his preference or with the question of the exact source of this 'Hebrew' solution, as with the clear contrast between this solution and the Greek philological and ethnographic solutions put forward by the Antiochenes.

As noted above, similar 'grammatical' exegesis was also employed successfully by Latin Fathers, especially Augustine. An example of his approach as contrasted with that of Jerome regards Gen. 14. In this chapter, we read of the expedition of the 'kings of the North' against certain communities in the region of the Dead Sea. The kings sack the cities of Sodom and Gomorrah and carry away Lot, the nephew of Abraham. In verse 13, the news is reported to Abraham:

ויבא הפליט ויגד לאברם העברי והוא שכן באלני ממרא האמרי אחי
אשכל ואחי ענר והם בעלי ברית אברם.

παραγενόμενος δὲ τῶν ἀνασωθέντων τις ἀπήγγειλεν Ἀβρὰμ τῷ περάτῃ· αὐτὸς δὲ κατῴκει πρὸς τῇ δρυὶ τῇ Μαμβρῇ ὁ Ἀμορις [v.l. (τοῦ) Ἀμορραίου] τοῦ ἀδελφοῦ Ἐσχὼλ καὶ ἀδελφοῦ Αὐνάν, οἳ ἦσαν συνωμόται τοῦ Ἀβράμ.

---

[263] Both Rahmer, *Die hebräischen Traditionen*, p. 30, and Ginzberg, 'Die Haggada' (*MGWJ* 43), p. 501 (cf. *The Legends of the Jews*, i, Philadelphia 1909, p. 255, v (1925), p. 241 n. 177), regard *Ber. R.* 50. 9 as a parallel to Jerome's version of the aggada (already Vallarsi had suspected a rabbinic source, see *PL* 23. 1015c). Yet neither considers the actual differences between *Ber. R.* 50. 9 and *QHG* 19: 14, and the implications of these differences with regard to the historical development of the aggada.

[264] Cf. Ginzberg, 'Die Haggada', loc. cit., who also cites Ephraem, *Comm. in Gen.* 16. 11 (cf. 16. 5).

[265] In the other surviving Targumim, *TO* and *CN*, the structure of the Masoretic Text is retained.

Adveniens autem eorum qui evaserunt quidam nuntiavit Abram trans-
fluviali: ipse autem habitabat ad quercum Mambre Amoris fratris Excol
et fratris Aunan qui erant coniurati Abram.

In the Greek and Latin versions, the text is difficult to understand.
For it is not clear who is the subject of the verb 'habitabat'
(κατῴκει). It would seem to be Abram from the context, but then
the nominative 'Amoris' (ὁ Ἄμορις) is left without a verb. In
addition, on what noun is the genitive 'fratris' (ἀδελφοῦ) dependent? Augustine, *Locut. Hept.* 1. 47, suggests that we have both a
hyperbaton and an ellipse: the words 'ipse . . . Mambre' must be
taken as parenthetical and 'a certain Amoris' becomes the subject
of the verb 'nuntiavit'. In addition, we must understand the word
'filius' before 'fratris'. The African Father regards such an ellipse
as an ἰδίωμα τῆς γραφῆς: 'multae sunt tales locutiones scripturarum,
ubi filius tacetur et intellegitur.'

In *QHG* 14: 13, Jerome appears to be putting forward a textual
solution to the same problem. After giving the lemma and commenting on another matter regarding the verse, he continues as
follows:

Quod autem ait: 'apud quercum Mambre Amorris [correxi ex Amorraei]',
melius in Hebraeo legimus: 'apud quercum Mamre Amorraei fratris
Eschol et fratris (non Aunan ut LXX transtulerunt, sed) Aner', ut osten-
deret Mambre et Eschol et Aner Amorraeos atque germanos socios fuisse
Abrahae.

The correction, by which Jerome's text is assimilated to the
standard text of the *VL*, is based on a manuscript cited by D.
Vallarsi, in which the form 'Amorris' is read instead of
'Amorr(h)aei' in the main lemma, which also basically reflects
the *VL*.[266] This reading should be adopted in the main lemma
as well as in the passage quoted, for without it one does not see
the difference between the *VL* and the Hebrew text to which
Jerome is referring. It is clear from the last sentence that it does
not lie in the rival spellings of the name 'Mamre'. Jerome is
rather pointing out that one must understand הָאֱמֹרִי (i.e.
'Amoris') not as a proper name but as a gentilic noun characterizing 'Mamre'. For, in his view, 'Mamre' is to be regarded in this

---

[266] See *PL* 23. 1010c. The reading is neglected by Fischer, p. 166, in his account
of the Hieronymian evidence for this verse, because he relies on the edition of de
Lagarde.

context as a person, not a place.[267] This fact Jerome probably
deduces from Gen. 14: 24, where the three men are mentioned
together as Abraham's allies. Accordingly, he understands the
name as a genitive, dependent on 'quercus', and indicates this
by giving the word 'Amorraeus' in that case.[268] The phrases
'fratris Eschol' and 'fratris Aner', which constitute a problem
for Augustine, fall into place as appositives.

In rendering the Hebrew text as he does, Jerome is probably
following Symmachus, who renders הָאֱמֹרִי with τοῦ Ἀμορραίου, a
reading which also found its way (via Symmachus or not) into the
manuscript tradition of the LXX.[269] Here again, Jerome's
recentiores-based Hebrew philology obviates the need to appeal to
'grammatical' solutions and 'locutiones scripturarum' which might
be extracted from the Greek and Latin versions.

At the beginning of this chapter, it was pointed out that in *Ep.*
37. 3, Jerome indicates three sources on which interpretation of
the Hebrew text should be based: the commentaries of Origen,
the *recentiores*, and Jewish consultants [i.e. oral rabbinic sources].
In the composition of *QHG*, the works of Origen seem to have
been of little importance. Other sources which may be placed in
the same category as the works of Origen as far as the classification
of *Ep.* 37. 3 is concerned, namely, that of 'Greek exegetical
sources', play a larger role. These are the *Liber nominum* and
especially the works of the Antiochene Fathers, Eusebius of Emesa
and probably Diodore of Tarsus. However, while these sources
may have proved helpful, Jerome does not seem to have believed
that they could serve as the foundation for the interpretation of
the Hebrew text. Indeed, he appears to express this view explicitly
when he states in the prologue that one of his purposes will be to
refute the errors of those who have put forward 'conjectures'

---

[267] That 'Mamre' could be understood in both senses is noted by Eusebius,
Onomast. 124. 5–7. Cf. *Ber. R.* 41(42). 8.

[268] On the other hand, Cyril, *Ador.* 4 (*PG* 68. 353a), although he reads Ἀμορραίου,
and indeed further on in the same passage, paraphrasing Gen. 14: 24, understands
'Mamre' as the name of a person (353c, 356c–d), nevertheless (at least according
to the printed text) seems to regard 'Mamre' in Gen. 14: 13 as a dative, apparently
taking the word as a place-name (cf. the reading of the *Codex Alexandrinus* in
Gen. 13: 18).

[269] For the wide variety of readings attested in the Greek tradition, see the
edition of Wevers, ad loc. See also the citation of 'the Greek' in Ishodad of Merv,
Comm. in Gen. 14: 13.

concerning the Hebrew text. Such remarks are probably directed primarily towards the Antiochenes, since the word 'conjecture' is easily understood as a critic's characterization of their methods. The Antiochenes seem to have developed two major approaches in their attempt to move closer to the original Hebrew text. One might be termed the 'Aramaic' approach. It was based on a rather indirect knowledge of Hebrew (derived perhaps from the knowledge of Aramaic/Syriac), and on the use of 'targumic-like' texts such as 'the Syrian' and 'the Hebrew' (if the latter designation denotes a version rather than the original). This approach appears to have been developed primarily by Eusebius of Emesa. The second approach, which might be termed the 'Greek' approach, was based on close analysis of the linguistic features of the version of the LXX, and on the peculiarities of that version which were assumed to constitute 'Hebraisms'. This approach plays a major role in the writings of Theodore of Mopsuestia, and indeed may have been further developed by him in opposition to the 'Aramaic' approach of his predecessors. Nevertheless, the 'Greek' approach is present in the works of Eusebius and Diodore as well. Since these two approaches constitute the major advances of patristic biblical philology in the fourth and early fifth centuries, the approach of Jerome, which may be termed a *'recentiores*–rabbinic' approach, should by no means be taken for granted, as it often is. Indeed, we have seen that it stands in some contrast to the methods of the Antiochenes. Of this *'recentiores*–rabbinic' approach we have already given some indication. It remains to be considered in somewhat more detail, especially as regards the rabbinic component.

6

Jerome and his Jewish Sources

◆ ◆ ◆

It has long been recognized that rabbinic sources play a major role in *QHG*. As early as in 1861, Rahmer published his study of *QHG*, in which he collected parallels to Jerome's comments from the rabbinic corpus.[1] His study was supplemented by that of L. Ginzberg.[2] However, these works remain very much collections of parallels rather than attempts to understand the function of rabbinic sources in Jerome's philological system. Among patristic scholars it has also been acknowledged that in composing *QHG* Jerome had the intention of introducing the Latin world to rabbinic exegesis.[3] However, this objective has been seen as separate from the 'other' objective of the work, the defence of the Hebrew text.[4] F. Cavallera terms the work 'hybrid', and A. Penna regards the rabbinic material as merely ornamental.[5] Bardy puts forward a similar view, claiming that while Jerome is quite serious about the Hebrew text, he is collecting rabbinic traditions without accepting them for himself.[6] His motive would therefore be curiosity. Such views, in which Jerome's presentation of rabbinic material is seen as distinct from the defence of the Hebrew text, result in an indirect depreciation of the textual character of *QHG*.

The idea that Jerome is collecting rabbinic views for the sake of curiosity or ostentation is not altogether without support. For instance, in *QHG* 14: 18–19, he notes that he will inform his readers of the Jewish view, 'quia semel opusculum nostrum vel quaestionum Hebraicarum vel traditionum congregatio est'. Similar remarks may be found in some of his commentaries on the prophets.[7] And it may be said that Jerome's interest in Jewish

---

[1] *Die hebräischen Traditionen.*   [2] 'Die Haggada'.
[3] Cavallera, *Saint Jérôme*, i. 1, p. 146; Bardy, 'La littérature' (*RB* 41), pp. 357–8.
[4] For this latter objective, see above, p. 80.
[5] Cavallera, loc. cit. (n. 3 above), and cf. id., 'Les *Quaestiones*', p. 361, and Buytaert, *L'héritage*, p. 15 ('son ouvrage hybride'); Penna, *S. Gerolamo*, p. 155.
[6] Loc. cit. (n. 3 above).
[7] *Comm. in Zach.* 2 (10: 11–12); *Comm. in Nah.* 2: 1–2. Cf. *Ruf.* 1. 16, 22; 3. 11.

sources was not devoid of ethnographic and antiquarian considerations. He was a scholar of very broad interests and an heir to the tradition of Varro and Aulus Gellius. Accordingly, he was quite interested in Jewish lore for its own sake.

Nevertheless, his antiquarian interests do not constitute the fundamental reason for which he turned to contemporary Jewish scholarship. Rather, he believed that this material was an essential element in the study of the Bible. In the famous prologue of the third book of his *Comm. in Jer.*, he expresses his desire to be left alone, so as to be able to 'concentrate his efforts on the elucidation of Holy Scripture and give to Latin speakers the learning of the Hebrews and the Greeks'. Such statements reveal the centrality of the Jewish sources in Jerome's understanding of his own mission. However, he also believed that one had to use these sources critically. As he puts it in his *Comm. in Zach.* 2 (6: 9–15), 'semel proposui arcana eruditionis Hebraicae, et magistrorum synagogae reconditam disciplinam, eam dumtaxat, quae scripturis sanctis convenit, Latinis auribus prodere.' This of course implies that, according to Jerome, some of the Jewish material was 'appropriate to Holy Scripture', while some was not.[8] This may be confirmed by the fact that he claims to have approached the teachings of one of his Jewish tutors in the same critical manner as he approached the writings of Origen (*Ruf.* 1. 13). And with regard to the works of Origen, Apollinaris of Laodicea, and others of dubious orthodoxy, he says that he follows the advice of Paul as given in I Thess. 5: 21: 'omnia legentes, quae bona sunt, retinentes'.[9] Jerome no doubt saw it as his own responsibility to determine which Jewish exegesis was appropriate, and although the criteria he employed in making this judgement are complex, the basic rule

---

[8] Jay, *L'exégèse*, pp. 72, 146 n. 99, 194, translates the words, 'eam dumtaxat, quae scripturis sanctis convenit', by 'pour autant du moins qu'il touche aux saintes Écritures', and equivalent phrases. Such translations fail to convey that by employing the word 'convenit', Jerome is giving a positive evaluation of Jewish exegesis. This may be confirmed by the fact that he employs terms such as 'ineptus' (*Comm. in Agg.* 2: 16–18 (CChr.SL 76A, p. 740)), and 'noxius' (*Comm. in Ezech.* 11 (38: 1–23 = CChr.SL 75, p. 526)) in negative characterizations of Jewish interpretation. The corresponding Greek terms are ἀπρεπής and βλαβερός, and they represent the opposites of 'conveniens' (τὸ ἁρμόζον, τὸ πρέπον) in the language of literary criticism. Cf. Schäublin, *Untersuchungen*, p. 78 n. 44.

[9] *Ep.* 61. 1. Cf. *Ep.* 62. 2; 84. 7; and Origen's remarks concerning apocryphal books in *Comm. ser. in Mt.* 28 (23: 37–9 = GCS 38, p. 51), and concerning pagan wisdom in *Hom. in Ex.* 11. 6.

seems to have been that it was fitting 'cum non prophetia aliqua de Christo . . . sed historiae ex praecedentibus et consequentibus ordo texatur' (*Comm. in Zach.* 2 (8: 18–19)). Indeed, in the preface to the same *Comm. in Zach.*, he states his intention to employ the literal exegesis of the Hebrews as his foundation.

In view of this circumstance, it is highly probable that Jerome regards the rabbinic material which he puts forward in *QHG* as 'appropriate to Holy Scripture'. For the Book of Genesis, since it consists almost completely of narrative, would be, according to Jerome's statement in *Comm. in Zach.* 2 (8: 18–19), particularly suited to Jewish exegesis. And, in fact, it is clear from various indications that Jerome's intention is to treat his material from a primarily historical or literal perspective. First of all, throughout *QHG* he pays particular attention to the *ordo* and *consequentia* of the narrative.[10] In addition, he remarks on occasion that the deeper mysteries of given passages are not relevant to the present work. For example, with regard to certain aspects of the narrative of the 'covenant between the pieces', he notes, 'non pertinet ad praesens opusculum huius expositio sacramenti' (*QHG* 15: 10–11). He makes the exact same remark concerning the benedictions of the patriarchs (*QHG* 49: 19).

More important, however, is Jerome's own affirmation about *QHG*, *Sit.*, and *Nom. Hebr.* In the preface to the last work, he says that anyone who takes the time to study this trilogy will 'attribute little value to the belching and nausea of the Jews'. This statement is somewhat difficult to interpret. For in none of these works is Jerome's principal objective the refutation of Jewish interpretations of Scripture. They do not belong to the large class of *Adversus Judaeos* literature.[11] Nor is Jerome practising negative scholarship—that is, collecting samples of worthless Jewish exegesis and putting them on display for the Christian world to ridicule. Rather, as is obvious from the prefaces of all three compositions, he believes he is producing positive contributions to biblical scholarship. Indeed, in introducing the *Quaestiones*

[10] See 16: 7; 18: 10; 22: 3–4; 35: 21; note also 24: 59 with 35: 8; 26: 32–3; 35: 16; 47: 31 with 48: 2. On this issue in general, see P. Antin, 'Ordo dans S. Jérôme', in his *Recueil sur saint Jérôme* (CollLat 95), Brussels 1968, pp. 229–40.

[11] The view of B. Blumenkranz, *Die Judenpredigt Augustins* (BBGW 25), Basle 1946, pp. 45–6, according to which Jerome's trilogy may be compared to Cyprian's *Ad Quirinum*, cannot be substantiated on the basis of the material contained in the three works.

Hebraicae in the preface to *Nom. Hebr.*, he even apologizes for seeming to brag about the work. Accordingly, when Jerome claims that his works will reveal the worthlessness of Jewish exegesis, he means that in comparison with his own writings, Jewish interpretation will be found to have little value. Yet how can such a claim apply to *QHG*, if the latter work is largely based on Jewish sources? The statement must be understood within the context of Jerome's general view of Jewish exegesis. He probably means that he has adapted the Jewish material to fit a Christian context. This he will have achieved first of all by critically sifting this material, selecting that which is 'appropriate to Holy Scripture' and rejecting that which is not, and secondly, by interpreting and modifying his sources where necessary.

However, Jerome not only regarded the rabbinic material in *QHG* as 'appropriate to Holy Scripture'. He also employed it as an integral part of his philological apologetics. In other words, *QHG* is not a 'hybrid' composition, for the use of the rabbinic material is directly related to the defence of the Hebrew text. Those who have seen these two features of the work as separate have failed to appreciate its *Sitz im Leben*. Specifically, they have not sufficiently considered the implications of a defence of the Hebrew text undertaken by Jerome at this stage in his career.

It will be recalled that Jerome's 'conversion' to the Hebrew text was based on external grounds. That is to say, it was his experience with translation from Greek to Latin that led him to the view that the Hebrew original was to be preferred to the Greek translation. Yet, after his conversion, Jerome did not go on to play the role of the sober and judicious textual critic, evaluating each reading on its own merits. Rather, he gave his unconditional support to the Hebrew, and developed a sophisticated series of arguments by which to defend the Hebrew text on internal grounds. Some of these arguments are of a general nature, and are found in his prefaces to the volumes of *IH*. These we have considered in Chapter 2. However, in *QHG*, he attempts to substantiate his position with detailed philological reasoning, specifically, by presenting on a verse-by-verse basis internal arguments concerning a specific book.

In order to achieve this objective, he needed to put forward his own understanding of the Hebrew text. Yet this will have been a highly difficult task. The state of the consonantal Hebrew text in the time of Jerome was roughly the same as it is today, so we can appreciate the extent of the problems which he faced. The reader is constantly confronted with *hapax legomena*, textual corruptions, alternative vocalizations, and obscurities of every sort. Consequently, multiple interpretations of the same word or phrase are often possible. Jerome's profound awareness of this situation is clear from *Ruf.* 1. 20, where he tells Rufinus that he wishes he could communicate to him 'quanta silva sit apud Hebraeos ambiguorum nominum atque verborum'. The result of this awareness is the many discussions in his commentaries of possible renderings of Hebrew words and phrases. Indeed, he himself acknowledges his constant need 'disputare de verbis'.[12]

On what sources are these discussions based? Origen of course had also emphasized the need to pay attention to the ἀμφιβολίαι and ὁμωνυμίαι present in the text, but his concern was for the most part with the Greek text and Greek words.[13] On the other hand, Eusebius of Emesa shows an awareness of the problem as it relates to Hebrew.[14] However, this awareness did not produce the types of discussion concerning Hebrew words which we find in Jerome's commentaries. Indeed, we have seen in the previous chapter that Jerome had serious reservations about the manner in which the Antiochenes approached the Hebrew text. Accordingly, Jerome's linguistic discussions had to be based on the other types of sources mentioned in *Ep.* 37. 3, the *recentiores* on the one hand, and Jewish Hebrew teachers on the other.[15] In other words, he consulted these teachers in the first instance alongside the *recentiores* in order to be completely aware of the various possibilities of translation.[16]

---

[12] *Ruf.* 1. 20. See also *Comm. in Eccl.* 1: 14; cf. *Ep.* 36. 13–14.

[13] See *Comm. in Gen.* 1: 16–18 (= *Philoc.* 14. 2), and, for examples of such discussions, *Princ.* 2. 3. 6; *Comm. in Jo.* 20. 184–90.

[14] This is clear from a passage on pp. 217–18 of the *Commentaire de l'Octateuque* edited by Hovhanessian and translated by Mahé (see above, p. 127). Cf. also pp. 3–4. The comments of Hilary, *Psal.* 2. 2, may be *partially* based on these or similar passages from Eusebius. For evidence of Hilary's dependence on Eusebius regarding other matters, see P. Smulders, 'Eusèbe d'Émèse comme source du *De Trinitate* d'Hilaire de Poitiers', *Hilaire et son temps* (cited above, Ch. 5 n. 37), pp. 175–212. Cf. the remarks of Daniélou in the same volume, pp. 143, 147.

[15] For a recent survey of Jerome's statements concerning his Hebrew teachers, see Opelt, *Aug* 28 (1988), pp. 327–38.

[16] See, e.g., *QHG* 29: 34; 41: 43; *Comm. in Eccl.* 1: 14, where he notes that his Jewish sources are at variance with the *recentiores*, and *Ep.* 36. 13, where he states that the Jews explicitly agree with a certain rendering of Aquila.

Yet, when confronted with passages open to various renderings, on what basis could one select which meaning to follow? In Jerome's view, there could be no other criterion than the sense of the passage. As he puts it, 'unusquisque inter dubia quod sibi consequentius videtur, hoc transfert.'[17] And, in fact, that this was his own method may be confirmed by his *Praef. in Job (IH)* 22–3. Here he writes that he was not able to translate any passage before he fully understood it.[18]

In his attempt to judge the sense of any given passage, Jerome could have employed the *recentiores* and his own understanding alone. Indeed, as we have already seen in the preceding chapter, he seems to do this on various occasions. Nevertheless, the *recentiores* are only translations, and they do not always provide a satisfactory sense. And it must be remembered that Jerome was seeking not only a 'satisfactory' sense, but a sense which was preferable to that of the LXX. This will have been especially difficult, since it cannot be denied that in many passages the LXX represents a more readable text. Consequently, he was forced to employ the rabbinic material not only as an alternative to the *recentiores*, in learning additional possibilities of translation, but also in conjunction with the *recentiores*, in an attempt to appreciate the full meaning of their renderings in any given passage. Jerome simply needed to employ all available tools in order to reach his goal.

In fine, it was the great difficulty of the Hebrew text on the one hand, and Jerome's specific polemic needs on the other hand that rendered the rabbinic sources an essential component of his defence of the Hebrew text on internal grounds. Modern scholars who have attempted to separate use of the rabbinic material from

[17] *Ruf.* 1. 20. See also *Comm. in Jer.* 2. 82. 1 (9: 22). It is interesting to compare these observations with the similar remarks of I. Heinemann, *Darkhei ha-aggada*[3], Jerusalem 1970, p. 103.

[18] Cf. *Praef. in Is.* 15–16. It is important to stress two points which emerge from *Ruf.* 1. 20. First of all, Jerome was deeply cognizant of the fact that a major source of differences between the versions was the difficulty and ambiguity of the Hebrew text itself. Secondly, however, he also believed that it was the right and responsibility of all translators to reach a decision as to the meaning of the text on the basis of the context. It is therefore hard to accept the view of C. Estin, 'Les traductions du Psautier', *Le monde latin antique et la Bible* (Bible de tous les temps 2), ed. J. Fontaine and C. Pietri, Paris 1985, p. 85 (cf. *Les Psautiers*, pp. 116–17), according to which Jerome was unaware of a contradiction in the fact that he uses diverse translations to arrive at the 'Hebraica veritas', yet presents it as a unity.

the campaign in favour of the Hebrew text have failed to take these aspects of the *Sitz im Leben* of *QHG* into consideration. Rather, they seem to have cast Jerome in their own mould. For modern scholars have had the benefit of many centuries of non-rabbinic interpretation of the Hebrew text (including the innovation of pointing), and they have no need to defend the use of the original against translations. Accordingly, they hardly feel a need for rabbinic commentary.[19]

Jerome, on the other hand, saw the situation differently, and perhaps this may be confirmed from the manner in which he refers to Jewish sources in a discussion of Zach. 8: 19. Commenting on this verse, Jerome is concerned with the fasts of the fourth, fifth, seventh, and tenth months. He laments the fact that Christian commentators either fail to explain these fasts, or provide conflicting explanations of them. The solution is to turn to the Jews: 'cogimur igitur ad Hebraeos recurrere, et scientiae veritatem de fonte magis quam de rivulis quaerere' (*Comm. in Zach.* 2 (8: 18–19)). What is noteworthy in this passage is that in characterizing Jewish sources Jerome uses language similar to that which he employs in describing the Hebrew text. For, as we have seen in the first section of Chapter 2, he employs 'fons' in referring to the Hebrew text while he calls translations 'rivuli' or the equivalent. His use of the expression 'scientiae veritas' reminds us of course of the 'Hebraica veritas'. It may be, therefore, that in using the same language to describe both the Hebrew text and rabbinic exegesis, Jerome is alluding in this passage not only to the privileged position which he affords the latter, but also to the intimate connection between the two.[20]

It may be helpful to demonstrate by example the points we have made in the preceding pages. In Gen. 6: 3, we read God's threat concerning the generations living at the time of the flood:

---

[19] In addition to those mentioned in the first paragraph of this chapter, see also Lagrange, 'Saint Jérôme', and Condamin, 'L'influence'. These scholars, while implicitly acknowledging the influence of rabbinic sources on Jerome as regards the interpretation of the Hebrew text, nevertheless attempt to de-emphasize and minimize such influence, often on the grounds that in *IH* Jerome disregards rabbinic interpretations which he mentions in his commentaries. The reasons for this inconsistency are to be sought elsewhere, however, as has been noted above, pp. 69–70, 81, Ch. 5 n. 20.

[20] Compare Jay, *L'exégèse*, pp. 144–5, who argues that in the preface to book 5 of his *Comm. in Is.* Jerome uses the expression 'Hebraica veritas' to denote Jewish exegesis as well as the Hebrew text. See also his general remarks on pp. 45–6, and those of Vaccari, *Bib* 1 (1920), p. 471.

Then the Lord said, '‏לֹא יָדוֹן רוּחִי בָאָדָם לְעֹלָם‎ [LXX: οὐ μὴ καταμείνῃ τὸ πνεῦμά μου ἐν τοῖς ἀνθρώποις τούτοις εἰς τὸν αἰῶνα], for he is flesh, but his days shall be a hundred and twenty years.'

Commentators who employ the LXX as their base text understand this text in various ways. In Alexandrian writers, and those who were influenced by them, there is a tendency to stress the idea that (the spirit of) God becomes alienated, or removes (its)/his grace, from those who live their lives in a carnal fashion. One also finds in these writers the clearly expressed view, or the intimation, that such divine action is directed not only against the generation of the flood, but against all who show themselves unworthy.[21] Antiochene writers, on the other hand, interpret the verse in a more concrete fashion. According to Diodore of Tarsus, when God says that his spirit will not abide in these men εἰς τὸν αἰῶνα, he means simply that he will not allow that generation to live out the full term of their life.[22] Chrysostom interprets the passage in a similar sense (*Hom. in Gen.* 22. 4 (*PG* 53. 190)).

Symmachus, on the other hand, renders the key phrase as follows: οὐ κρινεῖ τὸ πνεῦμά μου τοὺς ἀνθρώπους αἰωνίως. We find a similar understanding in many rabbinic texts, in which ‏יָדוֹן‎ is interpreted as 'judge', ‏בָאָדָם‎ is understood as an object, and ‏לֹא‎ . . . ‏לְעֹלָם‎ is taken to indicate remote time in the future.[23] Nevertheless, this basic reading of the verse is explained in different ways. For example, God's words are interpreted by some to mean that he will never judge present or future generations of men in a similar manner—that is, he will never again cause such a deluge.[24] In *m. Sanhedrin* 10. 3, on the other hand, the words

[21] See Philo, *Quaest. in Gn.* 1. 90; *Gig.* 18–21; Origen, *Cels.* 7. 38; *Princ.* 1. 3. 7; Didymus, *Comm. in Gen.* 6: 3 (152–3); Ambrose, *Noe* 7 (drawing on Philo). It may be that this universal application of the verse was to some extent dependent on the absence of the word τούτοις from the text of Gen. 6: 3 as cited by Philo, Didymus, and Ambrose. On the other hand, this word is attested in all but a few MSS of the LXX, and in Origen, locc. citt. Note also the comment of the latter in *Princ.* 1. 3. 7.

[22] *C. Cois.* 137. Cf. Procopius, *Comm. in Gen.* 6: 3 (*PG* 87. 268d–269a). Diodore, for his part, emphasizes the presence of the word τούτοις.

[23] See J. P. Lewis, *A Study of the Interpretation of Noah and the Flood in Jewish and Christian Literature*, Leiden 1968, pp. 129–30. In *Lib. Ant.* 3. 2, ‏בָאָדָם‎ is not rendered as an object of 'judge', but rather as 'in hominibus istis'. The meaning of this rendering becomes clearer in *Lib. Ant.* 9. 8. On both passages, see the commentary of C. Perrot and P.-M. Bogaert (Paris 1976 = SC 230), pp. 86, 105.

[24] See the view of Judan b. Bathyra and the similar views cited immediately following his in *Ber. R.* 26. 6. Such an interpretation was probably inspired by Gen. 9: 11.

are taken to mean that in the world to come God will not 'judge'
those who perished in the flood. For the generation of the flood
will not rise for the final judgement and will have no share in the
world to come.[25] In *t. Sanhedrin* 13. 6, Gen. 7: 23 is cited as the
basis of this latter interpretation. In this verse we read as follows:
'He [sc. God] blotted out every living thing that was upon the
face of the ground, man and animals and creeping things and birds
of the air; they were blotted out from the earth.' It is said that
the phrase 'upon the face of the ground' refers to this world, and
'from the earth' to the world to come.[26] In the rabbinic literature,
other verses are also cited in support of the mishnaic interpretation
of Gen. 6: 3.[27] Yet whatever the origin of the interpretation, such
exclusion from the world to come is regarded by the Rabbis as
the gravest of punishments. Indeed, the generation of the flood
shares this fate with the greatest enemies of the rabbinic world
view, those who would deny the resurrection or the divine origin
of the law.[28]

In *QHG* 6: 3, after giving his *lemma* according to the LXX/*VL*,
Jerome writes as follows:

In Hebraeo scriptum est: 'non iudicabit spiritus meus homines istos in
sempiternum, quoniam caro sunt', hoc est, quia fragilis est in homine
condicio, non eos ad aeternos servabo cruciatus, sed hic illis restituam
quod merentur. ergo non severitatem, ut in nostris codicibus legitur, sed
clementiam Dei sonat, dum peccator hic pro suo scelere visitatur.

In translating the key phrase, Jerome appears to be following
Symmachus. In his explanation of it, however, he moves beyond
a literal rendering. For he not only renders ידון as 'judge', but
also understands לא . . . לעולם as indicating an absence of punishment of the generation of the flood in the world to come. This
hardly seems to be the self-evident meaning of the Greek of
Symmachus any more than it is the self-evident meaning of the
Hebrew, even when one interprets ידון as 'judge'. Accordingly, it
appears that Jerome has employed a rabbinic source in interpreting

---

[25] The view advocated by Judan b. Bathyra in *Ber. R.* 26. 6 and the mishnaic
view seem to be conflated in *CN*, *T. Frag.*, *T. Ps.-J.*, ad Gen. 6: 3.

[26] Cf. *y. San.* 10. 3 (29b); *b. San.* 108a. In the latter text, this use of Gen. 7: 23
is attributed to Akiba.

[27] See Lewis, loc. cit. (n. 23 above).

[28] See *m. San.* 10. 1. For a negative characterization of the appointed lot of the
generation of the flood, cf. *PRE* 34.

the later Greek version.[29] The exact identity of that source need not overconcern us.[30] What is significant, rather, is that unlike the Rabbis, Jerome sees God's treatment of the generation of the flood as an act of divine mercy. This is because they will suffer here on earth, but will be spared the fate of everlasting punishment. In the view of Jerome, therefore, whereas in the LXX we read of God's 'severitas', it is his mercy that is clearly manifest in the Hebrew text. He goes on to confirm that mercy is not out of place in the present context by citing Hos. 4: 14 and Ps. 89(88): 33–4, verses which indicate that despite his wrath, God does not cease to show his mercy to man. In short, in contrasting the sense of the Hebrew text with that of the LXX, Jerome employs a rabbinic tradition to reach his own interpretation of the verse, and supports that interpretation with an appeal to parallel passages.

Jerome then proceeds to comment on the remainder of the verse: 'porro ne videretur in eo esse crudelis, quod peccantibus locum poenitentiae non dedisset, adiecit: "sed erunt dies eorum CXX anni", hoc est, habebunt CXX annos ad agendam poenitentiam.' The interpretation of the 120 years as a period for penitence, rather than as the length of human life, is widespread in both Jewish and Christian sources.[31] It clearly owes its origin to the fact that many individuals who inhabited the earth after the time of the flood are recorded as having lived longer than 120 years. However, what interests us here is how Jerome employs that tradition. For his use of the word 'porro' implies that he sees

[29] Cf. the modern attempt of L. Prijs, *Jüdische Tradition in der Septuaginta*, Leiden 1948, pp. 74–5, to read the mishnaic view into the rendering of the LXX. He may be correct as to the original intention of the translators, but we have already seen that the text was not understood in this way in the Greek exegetical tradition.

[30] It seems logical to see an interpretation such as that advocated in *m. San.* 10. 3 as the source for Jerome's view. The suggestion of Ginzberg, 'Die Haggada' (*MGWJ* 43), p. 410, that Jerome's comment is paralleled by that of Simeon b. Eleazar as given in *ARN* ('version A') 32 seems both difficult to accept and unnecessary. It should also be pointed out that Jerome's view that the absence of divine action refers only to the generation of the flood and not to man in general is facilitated by his translation of the Hebrew, in which he includes the word 'isti'. There is no equivalent for this word in the Masoretic Text. Consequently, either Jerome has made an exegetical addition here, inspired both by the LXX and by the mishnaic understanding of the verse, or he (or a later copyist) has retained the pronoun inadvertently from the previous sentence (i.e. the lemma), in which the verse is cited according to the LXX.

[31] See Ginzberg, *The Legends*, v, p. 174 n. 19 (cf. 'Die Haggada' (*MGWJ* 43), pp. 410–11); Lewis, *A Study*, p. 130 with n. 8.

God's grant of a period for repentance as further evidence of his mercy towards man in this context. In other words, he adds an additional argument to his understanding of the first part of the verse.[32]

At the beginning of Gen. 38, we read that Judah took to wife the daughter of a certain Shua. In verse 5, it is related that she gave birth to her third son:

ותסף עוד ותלד בן ותקרא את שמו שלה והיה בכזיב בלדתה אתו:

καὶ προσθεῖσα ἔτι ἔτεκεν υἱόν, καὶ ἐκάλεσεν τὸ ὄνομα αὐτοῦ Σηλώμ. αὐτὴ δὲ ἦν ἐν Χασβί, ἡνίκα ἔτεκεν αὐτούς.

According to the LXX, the word כזיב is to be understood as a proper name. And indeed, in Eusebius, *Onomasticon* 172. 6–7, the place is listed and identified as a deserted site near Adullam in the territory of Eleutheropolis.

Jerome, although he faithfully translates the text of Eusebius in *Sit.* 173. 9–10, refers his readers to the *Quaestiones Hebraicae* for a fuller discussion. And in *QHG* 38: 5, we learn that he prefers to follow later Jewish exegetical tradition, as he often does in interpreting etymologically words treated as proper names by the LXX. After giving the *lemma* according to the received version, he writes as follows:

Verbum Hebraeum hic [i.e. in the LXX] pro loci vocabulo positum est, quod Aquila pro re transtulit dicens: 'et vocavit nomen eius Selom. et factum est ut mentiretur in partu, postquam genuit eum'. postquam enim genuit Selom, stetit partus eius. Chazbi [v.l. Cazib] ergo non nomen loci, sed mendacium dicitur.

It will be observed that the rendering of Aquila does not yield a readily intelligible meaning, and Jerome is forced to explain it.

---

[32] The layout of this passage in de Lagarde's edition, p. 12 (= CChr.SL 72, p. 9), is misleading. For a new paragraph begins with the word 'porro', as if to indicate that the second part of the verse constitutes a separate lemma in Jerome's commentary. On the other hand, the text is printed correctly in *PL* 23. 996c–97b, where no new paragraph is indicated.

In *Hom. in Gen.* 25. 2 (*PG* 53. 220–1), Chrysostom sees the fact that God shortens the period allowed for penitence from 120 to 100 years (a possible explanation of the chronological data provided in the narrative) as an act of mercy. For in this way God prevents the evil generation from being further entangled in sin, and perhaps diminishes the punishment awaiting them in the next world. Thus, although these general themes resemble those employed by Jerome, the actual configuration of ideas in this passage is quite unrelated to that in *QHG*.

Yet whence did Jerome derive his understanding of Aquila's version? On the one hand, he simply applied his own knowledge of biblical imagery. For he goes on to cite Hab. 3: 17 as a parallel, and notes that the phrase 'the work of the olive will lie' means 'the olive will produce no fruit'. In addition, he appears to have been influenced by Gen. 29: 35. For the phrase 'stetit partus eius', used with reference to Leah, is found in the Old Latin version of that verse.[33] Nevertheless, it is probable that he also consulted rabbinic sources with regard to this matter. This is because in *IH* he renders the metaphor *ad sensum* and translates the final phrase of the verse in the following manner: 'quo nato [sc. Sela] parere ultra cessavit.' It is hard to escape the fact that the verb 'cessavit' constitutes the exact equivalent of the word פסקת, which is employed in the same sense in a targumic rendering of this verse.[34] Accordingly, it seems that Jerome has combined the use of parallel passages with rabbinic sources in coming to endorse a *pro re* translation of Aquila against the interpretation of the LXX.

In Gen. 22, the story of the sacrifice of Isaac is narrated. According to ancient Jewish sources, the sacrifice took place at the very spot on which the temple of Jerusalem was later built. This is stated explicitly by Josephus, *Antiquitates Judaicae* 1. 226; 7. 333, and we find allusions to the same effect in *Jubilees* 18. 13 and in the Targumim.[35] Many Christian writers also accept the identification. They adapt it to their own needs, however, by adding that the same place was also the site of the crucifixion of Jesus. Exegetes who put forward such a view include Melito of Sardis, *CS* G 188, Eusebius of Emesa, *CS* G 163, G 177, and Diodore of Tarsus, *C. Cois.* 204.[36]

---

[33] See Fischer, p. 316. The corresponding phrase in the Hebrew text is תעמד מלדת.

[34] See now *CN* Gen. 38: 5, where we read: והוה דפסקת מן דילדת יתיה. Cf. *T. Frag.* ad loc.; *Ber. R.* 85. 4; Rashi, *Comm. in Pent.* ad Gen. 38: 5; Rahmer, *Die hebräischen Traditionen*, pp. 48–9 with n. 1; Stummer, *Einführung*, p. 108. For additional discussion of the targumic renderings, see C. Peters, *Muséon* 48 (1935), pp. 42–3.

[35] See the marginal reading in *CN* Gen. 22: 2. Cf. the renderings of the same verse in *TO* and *T. Ps.-J.*

[36] Diodore is dependent on Eusebius here. See the comments of Petit in *CS*, pp. 156–7 n. a, and in *C. Cois.*, p. 201 n. a. The material in Procopius, *Comm. in Gen.* 22: 2 (*PG* 87. 389–90a), and the marginal notes (in a *catena*) cited in *C. Cois.*, p. 201 n. f, clearly derive from these or similar Antiochene formulations. The tradition is also attested in Syriac sources. For these, see S. (P.) Brock, 'Genesis 22 in Syriac Tradition', *Mélanges Dominique Barthélemy* (OBO 38), Fribourg 1981, pp. 7–8, 25.

What is the basis for this idea? Eusebius of Emesa, whose
detailed discussion of the matter is preserved in *CS* G 163, provides three reasons for the legitimacy of the identification. The
first is theological: Isaac is a τύπος of Christ. The second is geographical: Abraham was living in the land of the Philistines at the
time of the incident. This area lies next to the territory of Jerusalem. The final reason is based on tradition: the identification is
reported by Josephus in the seventh book of his *Antiquitates*.

Such a line of reasoning stands in stark contrast to that of
Jerome, who searches out the philological basis for the tradition
in the Hebrew text. He deals with this question in his comment
on Gen. 22: 2. We read in the Greek text of this verse that God
commands Abraham to take his son Isaac, and go to the high
country (εἰς τὴν γῆν τὴν ὑψηλήν), and offer him there as a sacrifice
on a certain mountain. In *QHG* 22: 2, Jerome explains the Hebrew
text underlying the phrase, 'to the high country':

Ubi nunc dicitur, 'vade in terram excelsam', in Hebraeo habet moria,
quod Aquila transtulit, τὴν καταφανῆ, hoc est lucidam, Symmachus, τῆς
ὀπτασίας, hoc est visionis. aiunt ergo Hebraei hunc montem esse, in quo
postea templum conditum est in area Ornae Jebusaei, sicut et in Paralipo-
menis scriptum est: 'et coeperunt aedificare templum in mense secundo
in secunda die mensis in monte Moria' [II Par. 3: 1]. qui idcirco inlu-
minans interpretatur et lucens, quia ibi est dabir (hoc est oraculum Dei)
et lex et spiritus sanctus, qui docet homines veritatem et inspirat
prophetas.

It will be again clear from this passage that for Jerome the use of
Jewish sources is closely linked to the elucidation of the Hebrew
text. For, as he indicates through his use of the words 'aiunt ergo',
it is on vocabulary that the Jews base their identification of the
site of the sacrifice of Isaac with the site of the temple: the Hebrew
word employed to describe these places is the same, namely, *moria*.
On the other hand, those who employ the LXX as their base text,
such as Eusebius of Emesa, are forced, as we have seen, to
approach the matter in a different fashion. For the traditional
Greek version does not provide even a hint as to the basis for the
identification.

This is not the case with regard to the versions of the *recentiores*,
to which Jerome seems to refer in the final sentence of the passage
quoted in the previous paragraph. That the object here is an
explanation of the *pro re* renderings of Aquila and Symmachus

seems clear from the fact that Jerome cites them in the previous sentence, and also appears to be taking up Aquila's version 'lucidus' with the word 'lucens'. Yet he seems to interpret these translations in the light of rabbinic sources. In the extant rabbinic writings, a debate concerning the etymology of the name 'Moriah' is recorded. According to many Rabbis, the name is derived from the actual gift which proceeds forth into the world from that place. The debate concerns the identity of that gift. Various suggestions are put forward, among them הורייה (instruction), יראה (fear (of the divine)), אורה (light), תורה (law).[37] In some of the same sources, there immediately follows an account of a related debate concerning the words ארון and דביר. And the question is phrased in a similar way, namely, what issues forth from these things that provides them with their essential quality? In the discussion about the Devir, which is what concerns us here, answers to this question include 'revelation' (דיבר) and 'death' (דבר), i.e. punishment.[38]

Jerome, however, employs this material not in order to present alternative etymologies of 'Moriah' or 'Devir'.[39] Rather, he is interested in explaining why the translations of Aquila and Symmachus are valid. For he points out that 'Moriah' may be translated as 'bright' or 'illuminating' precisely because it is the seat of the Devir (that is, the oracle of revelation), law, and instruction.[40] In other words, for Jerome, versions such as this are accurate because they imply the full range of meanings which permeate the word 'Moriah'.[41] The rendering of the LXX, on the other hand, does not successfully serve this purpose.

We learn from the preceding examples that Jerome employed rabbinic sources not only as alternatives to the *recentiores* in deter-

---

[37] See *Ber. R.* 55. 7; *y. Ber.* 4. 5(6) (8c); *b. Taan.* 16a; *Shir. R.* 4. 11 (ed. S. Dunsky, Jerusalem 1980[2], p. 110); *Pes. R.* 40 (ed. Friedmann, p. 169b); *Tan. B.* Va-Yera 45.

[38] *Ber. R.*, *y. Ber.*, *Shir. R.*, locc. citt. The discussion about דביר is also found in *M. Teh.* 30. 1.

[39] For Jerome's awareness of the various possible meanings of the root דבר which result from different pronunciations (i.e. vocalizations), see *Comm. in Is.* 4 (9: 8–13); *Comm. in Abac.* 2 (3: 5).

[40] The presence of the word 'docet' in Jerome's comment shows that the suggestion of Rahmer, *Die hebräischen Traditionen*, pp. 34–5, to correct הורייה to אורה in *Ber. R.*, is unnecessary.

[41] The discussions of *QHG* 22: 2 in Rahmer, *Die hebräischen Traditionen*, pp. 34–5, and Ginzberg, 'Die Haggada' (*MGWJ* 43), p. 529 (cf. *The Legends*, v, p. 253 n. 253), fail to do justice to Jerome's use of the rabbinic material.

mining the translation of a given passage, but also in conjunction
with the *recentiores* in order to justify the translation of a given
passage. This point requires special emphasis. For in the older
works on *IH* one finds a tendency to pose the question of whether
Jerome is dependent on the *recentiores* or other Jewish sources,
and not of how he employs the two together.[42] This is of course
quite natural, because in dealing with the translation, scholars are
limited to those cases in which the influence of rabbinic sources
is visible in the text, and in these circumstances the use of these
sources is necessarily parallel to that of the *recentiores*. Accordingly, in studies concerning *IH* the borrowings from the Rabbis
and from the *recentiores* are usually discussed under separate rub-
rics.[43] For their part, those who have studied rabbinic influence
in Jerome's commentaries have generally been more interested in
collecting passages where such influence is visible than in understanding the function of rabbinic sources in Jerome's philological
system.[44]

More recently, on the other hand, it has been claimed by C.
Estin that Jerome's knowledge of rabbinic exegesis was very superficial, and that he employed the *recentiores* 'comme des photo-
graphies privées de leurs légendes'.[45] While it may be that Jerome
was not aware of the subtleties of the exegetical principles underlying the versions of Aquila and Symmachus, it will be abundantly
clear from the examples which we have discussed that he
attempted to understand and interpret the later translations with
the help of the rabbinic exegesis of his own day. It is true that
Origen seems to have made some steps in this direction.[46] Never-

---

[42] See Gordon, *JBL* 49 (1930), p. 415; Stummer, *JPOS* 8 (1928), p. 37.

[43] See, e.g., Stummer, *Einführung*, pp. 102–10. Elsewhere, the great scholar of
the Latin Bible does observe that Jerome may have been influenced by more than
one source in rendering a given passage. See, e.g., *ZAW* 58 (1940–1), p. 256. But
he does not seem to have pursued this point in detail with reference to rabbinic
sources and the *recentiores*.

[44] See esp. Rahmer, *Die hebräischen Traditionen*, and Ginzberg, 'Die Haggada'.

[45] 'Les traductions', p. 82. Cf. J. Gribomont, 'La terminologie exégétique de
S. Jérôme', *La terminologia esegetica nell'antichità* (Quaderni di *Vetera Christianorum* 20), Bari 1987, pp. 133–4. It is odd that Estin, who says she is not competent
to deal with the question of rabbinic influence on Jerome (*Les Psautiers*, p. 34),
should make the claim that he had a superficial knowledge of rabbinic exegesis.
For evidence against such a claim, see my article in *JThS* 41 (1990), pp. 62–5.

[46] See *Sel. in Gen.* 31: 7 (*PG* 12. 125b–c), discussed above, pp. 128–9 with
n. 109. Cf. also (J.-)D. Barthélemy, 'Est-ce Hoshaya Rabba qui censura le *Commentaire allégorique?*', *Philon d'Alexandrie*, Paris 1967, pp. 72–3 (for the text in
question, see now *C. Cois.* 160, and Petit, 'Le dossier', pp. 76–7, 78–9).

theless, the Greek Fathers for the most part pay infinitely less attention to the Jewish background of 'the Three' than does Jerome. Indeed, it is this effort on his part, in addition to the mere quantity of his observations on these versions, that establishes him as the leading exegete of the *recentiores* in antiquity. For the Rabbis, in their turn, rarely even mention readings from these texts.[47] Consequently, it may be said that the works of the Latin Father represent the most important extant link between the *recentiores* and Jewish exegesis.

The fact that in *QHG* Jerome often employs his rabbinic sources in concert with the *recentiores* in the manner described shows that he does not cite such sources for the sake of curiosity or in order to show off, but rather as an integral part of his philological system. That is to say, *QHG* is not a 'hybrid' composition, but a work in which Jerome has one twofold objective, viz. to justify a return to the Hebrew text, and to put forward his own system for interpreting that text. The system which he advocates may rightfully be termed a '*recentiores*–rabbinic' philology, and must be seen against the background of the Antiochene systems discussed in the previous chapter in order to be fully appreciated.

---

[47] There are roughly a dozen extant citations of Aquila in the rabbinic corpus. For these, see S. Krauss, 'Akylas, der Proselyt', *Festschrift zum achtzigsten Geburtstage Moritz Steinschneider's*, Leipzig 1896, pp. 151–5; J. Reider, *Prolegomena to a Greek–Hebrew and Hebrew–Greek Index to Aquila*, Philadelphia 1916, pp. 151–5.

Summary and Conclusion

♦ ♦ ♦

Among early Christian scholars, the importance of the Hebrew text was first recognized by Origen. Nevertheless, Origen's approach remained fundamentally 'LXX-centred'. Indeed, this is implied by the manner in which the lines of debate concerning his textual position were drawn by Jerome and Rufinus. Recent views, according to which Origen went beyond a 'LXX-centred' approach, and attempted to arrive at the original Hebrew text of the Bible, or advocated a two-text 'dualisme biblique', as was put forward by Augustine in the later part of his career, cannot be accepted.

Origen's appreciation of the relevance of the Hebrew text, however, led to important developments in the period following his death. On the one hand, it brought about attempts to strengthen the position of the version of the LXX as an independent entity *vis-à-vis* the original. In Hilary of Poitiers, we find the view that the Greek version contains not only the text, but the correct interpretation of the text as based on the oral tradition. This is a brilliant response to the rabbinic claim that the Jewish Torah is superior because it includes the oral in addition to the written tradition. According to Hilary, it is rather the Greek version that is the depository of both written and oral tradition. From a different angle, Epiphanius and Augustine promoted the idea that the version of the LXX represents a special dispensation for gentile Christians. In other words, it constitutes a more advanced stage of revelation than the Hebrew text. In both cases, the implication is that the Hebrew text has become in a sense superfluous.

On the other hand, Origen's achievement also led to a greater awareness of the importance of the Hebrew original, especially in the area of Antioch. In particular, Eusebius of Emesa made significant use of the Hebrew text in his exegetical works. However, by no means did he abandon the LXX, and he also extensively employed the version of 'the Syrian'. This mixed approach may have 'backfired' to a certain extent, since it seems to have led to a more 'scientific' yet closer reliance on the version of the LXX on the part of Theodore of Mopsuestia, an exegete of enormous influence. Consequently, at least as far as Greek scholarship is concerned, the potential implications of the *Hexapla* were not fully realized.

This was not the case in the Latin world. Jerome, as an heir to a highly sophisticated bilingual culture, appears to have had a clearer cognizance than Greek scholars of the gap which could separate version from original. Accordingly, he advocated the 'centrality' as well as the 'priority' of the Hebrew text. Yet if it is Latin bilingualism that explains such a position, why was it not until more than a hundred years after the death of Origen that a representative of Latin culture endorsed this view? The answer to this question may lie in historical circumstances. That is to say, perhaps it was necessary for the literary as well as the text-critical problems created by reliance on a translation rather than on an original to come to the surface. Such problems did come to the surface in a manner more concrete than ever before during the reign of Julian. For Julian's school edict forced Christians to reflect more deeply on the lack of literary quality in the Greek Bible. The response of Apollinaris was to rewrite the Bible in an acceptable Greek style and in Greek literary genres. The Latin response was to propose a return to the original Hebrew text.

Such a proposition, however, went against three hundred years of tradition. Accordingly, Jerome proceeded with caution. He gradually formulated a three-tier approach by which to advance the cause of the Hebrew original. His bottom-line position was the support of the 'Hebraized' Hexaplaric recension, which he himself published in Latin form. His middle-line position was the promotion of his own translation *iuxta Hebraeos*, but only as an auxiliary version, to be used as an exegetical aid to better understand the LXX or as a tool in disputations with the Jews. His top-line position was the propagation of *IH* as a rival version to that of the LXX, to be used by both Greeks and Latins as a means to understanding the original, and by Latins as a text with some form of official role.

At about the time when Jerome began issuing volumes of the new translation, he published his *Quaestiones Hebraicae in Genesim*. This text is not an experimental work, undertaken by a man gradually moving away from the Hexaplaric LXX in the direction

of the 'Hebraica veritas'. Nor is it merely an attempt to demonstrate the 'utility of the Hebrew text', which had in fact already
been recognized by most Greek scholars. Rather, Jerome goes
beyond this objective, and puts forward and justifies the system
by which he interprets the Hebrew text. That is, he defends the
philological foundations of *IH*. Jerome's system may be termed a
'recentiores–rabbinic' philology. However, this system can only be
appreciated when seen in the light of the other major systems of
the time. These are the 'Aramaic/Syriac approach', which may be
associated with Eusebius of Emesa, and the 'Greek approach',
present in the works of Eusebius and Diodore of Tarsus, but
more fully developed by Theodore of Mopsuestia. If Jerome's
'recentiores–rabbinic' philology is understood against the background of these other systems, it is possible to see what he meant
by describing *QHG* as an 'opus novum', and to acknowledge that
by and large he was justified in making such a claim.

The *'recentiores*–rabbinic' philology was just what that description implies. In other words, the rabbinic sources were to be used
in close association with the *recentiores*. The 'looser' use of aggadic
material, present in some early Syriac exegesis, is less characteristic of the work of Jerome. Nor is *IH* a Latin version of the
Palestinian Targum. Jerome was a philological rigorist, and he
advocated a more literal approach based on the versions of Aquila
and Symmachus. He sought, however, to understand these versions with the help of contemporary Jewish interpretation. Nevertheless, the result was not a 'Bible des rabbins', as Barthélemy,
playing the role of a modern day Rufinus, describes *IH*.[1] For the
philological system underlying the version was forged together by
the translator himself, and this system was more a Latin than a
Jewish or a Christian achievement.

[1] *ThZ* 21 (1965), p. 370.

Select Bibliography

◆ ◆ ◆

The primary purpose of this bibliography is to serve as a guide to the secondary works cited in the footnotes. However, an effort has also been made to include some works which seem to have more than passing relevance for the subject of the book as a whole.

A more comprehensive bibliography of work on Jerome has been compiled by P. Antin and may be found at the beginning of the first volume of Jerome's works published in the series Corpus Christianorum, Series Latina, vol. 72. References to earlier bibliographies are included. Antin's listings, published in 1959, may be supplemented by more recent bibliographies in J. Gribomont, 'Girolamo'; P. Nautin, 'Hieronymus'; H. Hagendahl and J. H. Waszink, 'Hieronymus'; J. R. Baskin, 'Rabbinic–Patristic Exegetical Contacts'. Full citation of all four of these articles is given below.

ALEXANDRE, M., *Le commencement du Livre, Genèse i–v: La version grecque de la Septante et sa réception* (Christianisme antique 3), Paris 1988.

ALLENBACH, J., *et al.*, *Biblia patristica*, i-iii, *Supplément: Philon d'Alexandrie*, iv–v, Paris 1975–80, 1982, 1987–91.

ALTANER, B., and STUIBER, A., *Patrologie*[8], Freiburg (im Breisgau) 1978.

BACHER, W., *Die exegetische Terminologie der jüdischen Traditionsliteratur*, i. *Die bibelexegetische Terminologie der Tannaiten* (= *Die älteste Terminologie der jüdischen Schriftauslegung*), Leipzig 1899.

BARDENHEWER, O., *Geschichte der altkirchlichen Literatur*, i–iii[2], iv[1–2], v, Freiburg im Breisgau 1913–32.

BARDY, G., 'La littérature patristique des *Quaestiones et responsiones* sur l'Écriture sainte', *RB* 41 (1932), pp. 210–36, 341–69, 515–37; 42 (1933), pp. 14–30, 211–29, 328–52.

—— 'Saint Jérôme et ses maîtres hébreux', *RBen* 46 (1934), pp. 145–64.

—— *La question des langues dans l'Église ancienne*, i, Paris 1948.

BARNES, T. D., *Constantine and Eusebius*, Cambridge, Mass. 1981.

BARTHÉLEMY, (J.-)D., 'La place de la Septante dans l'Église', *Aux grands carrefours de la révélation et de l'exégèse de l'Ancien Testament* (1967 = RechBib 8), pp. 13–28.

—— 'Eusèbe, la Septante et "les autres"', *La Bible et les Pères*, Paris 1971, pp. 51–65.

BARTHÉLEMY, (J.-)D., 'Origène et le texte de l'Ancien Testament', *Epektasis* (*FS* J. Daniélou), [Paris] 1972, pp. 247–61.

[The preceding three studies are available in the author's collected essays, *Études d'histoire du texte de l'Ancien Testament* (OBO 21), Fribourg 1978.]

BASKIN, J. R., 'Rabbinic–Patristic Exegetical Contacts in Late Antiquity: A Bibliographical Reappraisal', *Approaches to Ancient Judaism*, v (Brown Judaic Studies 32), ed. W.S. Green, Atlanta 1985, pp. 53–80.

BENOIT, P., 'L'inspiration des Septante d'après les Pères', *L'homme devant Dieu*, i (*FS* H. de Lubac = Theol(P) 56), Paris 1963, pp. 169–87.

BRAVERMAN, J., *Jerome's 'Commentary on Daniel'* (CBQ.MS 7), Washington, DC 1978.

BROCHET, J., *Saint Jérôme et ses ennemis*, Paris 1905.

BURSTEIN, E., 'La compétence en hébreu de saint Jérôme' (Diss.), Poitiers 1971.

BUTTERWECK, A., *Jakobs Ringkampf am Jabbok* (Judentum und Umwelt 3), Frankfurt am Main 1981.

BUYTAERT, É. M., *L'héritage littéraire d'Eusèbe d'Émèse* (BMus 24), Louvain 1949.

CARROLL, M., *Aristotle's Poetics, c. XXV, in the Light of the Homeric Scholia*, Baltimore 1895.

CAVALLERA, F., *Saint Jérôme: Sa vie et son œuvre*, i. 1–2 (SSL 1–2), Louvain 1922.

——'Les *Quaestiones Hebraicae in Genesim* de saint Jérôme et les *Quaestiones in Genesim* de saint Augustin', *Miscellanea agostiniana*, ii, Rome 1931, pp. 359–72.

CLAUS, F., 'La datation de l'*Apologia prophetae David* et l'*Apologia David altera*', *Ambrosius Episcopus*, ii (SPMed 7), ed. G. Lazzati, Milan 1976, pp. 168–93.

CONDAMIN, A., 'L'influence de la tradition juive dans la version de saint Jérôme', *RSR* 5 (1914), pp. 1–21.

COTTINEAU, L. H., 'Chronologie des versions bibliques de S. Jérôme', *Miscellanea geronimiana*, Rome 1920, pp. 43–68.

COURCELLE, P., *Les lettres grecques en Occident de Macrobe à Cassiodore²* (BEFAR 159), Paris 1948.

DECONINCK, J., *Essai sur la chaîne de l'Octateuque* (BEHE.H 195), Paris 1912.

DE LABRIOLLE, P., *La réaction païenne¹⁰*, Paris 1950 (1948).

DE LANGE, N. R. M., *Origen and the Jews* (UCOP 25), Cambridge 1976.

DEVREESSE, R., *Essai sur Théodore de Mopsueste* (StT 141), Città del Vaticano 1948.

——*Les anciens commentateurs grecs de l'Octateuque et des Rois* (StT 201), Città del Vaticano 1959.

DORIVAL, G., HARL, M., and MUNNICH, O., *La Bible grecque des Septante*, Paris 1988.

DÖRRIE, H., and DÖRRIES, H., 'Erotapokriseis', *RAC* 6. 43 (1964), cols. 342–70.

DREYER, O., 'Lyseis', *KP* 3. 16–17 (1968–9), cols. 832–3.

DUVAL, Y.-M. (ed.), *Jérôme entre l'Occident et l'Orient*, Paris 1988.

ELLIOT, C. J., 'Hebrew Learning among the Fathers', *DCB* 2 (1880), pp. 851–72.

ESTIN, C., *Les Psautiers de Jérôme à la lumière des traductions juives antérieures* (CBLa 15), Rome 1984.

——'Les traductions du Psautier', *Le monde latin antique et la Bible* (Bible de tous les temps 2), ed. J. Fontaine and C. Pietri, Paris 1985, pp. 67–88.

FRAADE, S. D., *Enosh and His Generation* (SBLMS 30), Chico, Calif. 1984.

GEORGII, H., *Die antike Äneiskritik aus den Scholien und anderen Quellen*, Stuttgart 1891.

GINZBERG, L., 'Die Haggada bei den Kirchenvätern und in der apokryphischen Litteratur', *MGWJ* 42 (1898), pp. 537–50; 43 (1899), pp. 17–22, 61–75, 117–25, 149–59, 217–31, 293–303, 409–16, 461–70, 485–504, 529–47.

——*The Legends of the Jews*, 7 vols., Philadelphia 1909–38.

GRIBOMONT, J., 'Girolamo', *Patrologia*, iii, ed. A. di Berardino, [Turin] 1978, pp. 203–33.

GRÜTZMACHER, G., *Hieronymus: Eine biographische Studie zur alten Kirchengeschichte*, 3 vols. (SGTK 6. 3, 10[. 1], 10. 2), Leipzig (then Berlin) 1901–08.

GUDEMAN, A., Λύσεις, *PRE* i. 13. 2 (1927), cols. 2511–29.

HAGENDAHL, H., and WASZINK, J. H., 'Hieronymus', *RAC* 15. 113 (1989), cols. 117–39.

HANSON, R. P. C., *Allegory and Event*, London 1959.

HARDUF, D. M., *Dictionary and Key to the Exegesis of Biblical Proper Names in the Talmud and Midrash* (in Hebrew), Tel Aviv 1960.

HAYWARD, R., 'Saint Jerome and the Aramaic Targumim', *JSSt* 32 (1987), pp. 105–23.

HEINRICI, G., 'Scholien', *RE*[3] 17 (1906), pp. 732–41.

——'Zur patristischen Aporienliteratur', *ASGW.PH* 27 (1909), pp. 841–60.

HYMAN, A., and HYMAN, A. B., *Torah hakethuba vehamessurah*[2], 3 vols., Tel Aviv 1979; *Sepher hahashlamoth*, Jerusalem [1985].

JAY, P., *L'exégèse de saint Jérôme d'après son 'Commentaire sur Isaïe'*, Paris 1985.

JELLICOE, S., *The Septuagint and Modern Study*, Oxford 1968.

JORDAN, H., *Geschichte der altchristlichen Literatur*, Leipzig 1911.

KAHLE, P., *The Cairo Geniza²*, Oxford 1959.

KARPP, H., '"Prophet" oder "Dolmetscher"', *Festschrift für Günther Dehn*, Neukirchen Kreis Moers 1957, pp. 103–17.

KASHER, M. M., *Torah shelemah*, i– , Jerusalem 1926/7– .

KEDAR-KOPFSTEIN, B., 'The Vulgate as a Translation' (Diss.), [Jerusalem] 1968.

——[Kedar], 'The Latin Translations', *Mikra* (Compendia rerum Judaicarum ad Novum Testamentum ii. 1), ed. M. J. Mulder, Assen and Maastricht 1988, pp. 299–338.

KELLY, J. N. D., *Jerome: His Life, Writings, and Controversies*, London 1975.

KIHN, H., *Theodor von Mopsuestia und Junilius Africanus als Exegeten*, Freiburg im Breisgau 1880.

KRAMER, B., and KRAMER, J., 'Les éléments linguistiques hébreux chez Didyme l'Aveugle', *ΑΛΕΞΑΝΔΡΙΝΑ* (*FS* C. Mondésert), Paris 1987, pp. 313–23.

KRAUSS, S., 'The Jews in the Works of the Church Fathers', *JQR* 5 (1893), pp. 122–57; 6 (1894), pp. 82–99, 225–61.

LAGRANGE, M.-J., 'Saint Jérôme et la tradition juive dans la Genèse', *RB* 7 (1898), pp. 563–6.

LEHMANN, H. J., 'An Important Text Preserved in MS Ven. Mekh. No. 873, Dated A.D. 1299', *Medieval Armenian Culture: Proceedings of the Third Dr. H. Markarian Conference on Armenian Culture:* (University of Pennsylvania Armenian Texts and Studies 6), ed. T. J. Samuelian and M. E. Stone, Chico, Calif. 1984, pp. 142–60.

——'The Syriac Translation of the Old Testament—as Evidenced around the Middle of the Fourth Century (in Eusebius of Emesa)', *Scandinavian Journal of the Old Testament* 1987. 1, pp. 66–86.

——'Evidence of the Syriac Bible Translation in Greek Fathers of the 4th and 5th Centuries', *StPatr* 19 (1989), pp. 366–71.

LEWIS, J. P., *A Study of the Interpretation of Noah and the Flood in Jewish and Christian Literature*, Leiden 1968.

MARTI, B., *Übersetzer der Augustin-Zeit* (Studia et testimonia antiqua 14), Munich 1974.

MEERSHOEK, G. Q. A., *Le latin biblique d'après saint Jérôme* (LCP 20), Nijmegen 1966.

MÜLLER, K., 'Die rabbinischen Nachrichten über die Anfänge der Septuaginta', *Wort, Lied und Gottesspruch*, [i] (*FS* J. Ziegler, [i] = fzb 1), Würzburg 1972, pp. 73–93.

NEUSCHÄFER, B., *Origenes als Philologe* (SBA 18. 1–2), Basle 1987.

NAUTIN, P., *Origène*, i. *Sa vie et son œuvre* (Christianisme antique 1), Paris 1977.

——'L'activité littéraire de Jérôme de 387 à 392', *RThPh* 115 (1983), pp. 247–59.

——'Hieronymus', *TRE* 15. 1–2 (1986), pp. 304–15.

Nikolasch, F., 'Zur Ikonographie des Widders von Gen 22', *VigChr* 23 (1969), pp. 197–223.

Paredi, A., 'S. Gerolamo e s. Ambrogio', *Mélanges Eugène Tisserant*, v (StT 235), Città del Vaticano 1964, pp. 183–98.

Pavan, M., 'I Cristiani e il mondo ebraico nell'età di Teodosio il Grande', *AFLF(P)* 3 (1965–6), pp. 367–530.

Penna, A., *S. Gerolamo*, Turin 1949.

——*Principi e carattere dell'esegesi di San Gerolamo* (SPIB 102), Rome 1950.

Petit, F., 'Le dossier origénien de la chaîne de Moscou sur la Genèse', *Muséon* 92 (1979), pp. 71–104.

Quasten, J., *Patrology*, 3 vols., Utrecht [1950]-60.

Rahmer, M., *Die hebräischen Traditionen in den Werken des Hieronymus*, i. *Die 'Quaestiones in Genesin'*, Breslau 1861.

Rüting, W., *Untersuchungen über Augustins Quaestiones und Locutiones in Heptateuchum* (FChLDG 13. 3–4), Paderborn 1916.

Schade, L., *Die Inspirationslehre des heiligen Hieronymus* (BSt(F) 15. 4–5), Freiburg im Breisgau 1910.

Schäublin, Chr., *Untersuchungen zu Methode und Herkunft der antiochenischen Exegese* (Theoph 23), Cologne 1974.

Schleusner, J. F., *Novus thesaurus philologico-criticus sive lexicon in LXX et reliquos interpretes Graecos ac scriptores apocryphos Veteris Testamenti*[2], 3 vols., London 1829.

Schwarz, W., *Principles and Problems of Biblical Translation*, Cambridge 1955.

Sgherri, G., 'Sulla valutazione origeniana dei LXX', *Bib* 58 (1977), pp. 1–28.

Skehan, P. W., 'St. Jerome and the Canon of the Holy Scriptures', *A Monument to Saint Jerome*, ed. F. X. Murphy, New York 1952, pp. 257–87.

Sparks, H. F. D., 'Jerome as Biblical Scholar', *CHB*, i (1970), pp. 510–41.

Stummer, F., *Einführung in die lateinische Bibel*, Paderborn 1928.

Sutcliffe, E. F., 'Jerome', *CHB*, ii (1969), pp. 80–101.

Swete, H. B., *An Introduction to the Old Testament in Greek*[2], Cambridge 1914.

Thomas, E., *Scoliastes de Virgile: Essai sur Servius et son Commentaire sur Virgile*, Paris 1880.

Wallace-Hadrill, D. S., *Eusebius of Caesarea*, London 1960.

Wendland, P., 'Zur ältesten Geschichte der Bibel in der Kirche', *ZNW* 1 (1900), pp. 267–90.

Wutz, F. X., *Onomastica sacra: Untersuchungen zum Liber interpretationis nominum Hebraicorum des hl. Hieronymus* (TU 41. 1–2), Leipzig 1914–15.

Zöckler, O., *Hieronymus: Sein Leben und Wirken aus seinen Schriften dargestellt*, Gotha 1865.

Addendum

◆ ◆ ◆

RECENTLY, the article of R. Hayward, 'Some Observations on St Jerome's *Hebrew Questions on Genesis* and the Rabbinic Tradition', *Proceedings of the Irish Biblical Association* 13 (1990), pp. 58–76, came into my hands. I completely disagree with his assertion (and that of his informant) that 'slow, deliberate, and careful study of *Heb. Quest.* reveals no obvious discernible over-arching plan or theme' (p. 59). Indeed, the argument of the present work is that exactly the opposite is the case. I also believe that the reason for such an assessment is the failure to consider the work in its proper context, namely, the Greek (and Latin) biblical philology of the 'golden age', or the period from Origen to Cyril and Theodoret. Hayward places too narrow a focus on the rabbinic and targumic background of *QHG*. The difference between his 'Semitic' approach and the 'Graeco-Latin' approach employed in the present work is clearly visible in the contrasting solutions to the problem of the interpretation of *QHG* 14: 13. See Hayward, p. 65, and above, pp. 172–4.

With reference to another problem raised by Hayward, that is, Jerome's view of rabbinic exegesis, I would refer to my article, 'The Evaluation of the Narrative Aggada in Greek and Latin Patristic Literature', to appear in *JThS* 45 (1994).

Index of Sources

◆ ◆ ◆

Numbers in parentheses indicate footnotes.

I. BIBLE

HEBREW, GREEK, AND LATIN BIBLE
This list includes references to the Hebrew text and all Greek and Latin versions. However, separate listings for Aquila, Symmachus, Theodotion, *recentiores*, 'the Hebrew' (ὁ Ἑβραῖος, etc.), and 'the Syrian', are also provided in the Index of Subjects.

II. INTERTESTAMENTAL LITERATURE

III. GREEK, LATIN, AND SYRIAC AUTHORS AND WORKS

IV. RABBINIC AND MEDIEVAL JEWISH LITERATURE

Index of Subjects

◆ ◆ ◆

Numbers in parentheses indicate footnotes.